The Life and Thought of Isaiah Bowman

The Life and Thought

of

Isaiah Bowman

by

Geoffrey J. Martin

1980

ARCHON BOOKS

© Geoffrey J. Martin 1980

First published 1980 as an Archon Book,
an imprint of The Shoe String Press, Inc.,
Hamden, Connecticut 06514

Library of Congress Cataloging in Publication Data

Martin, Geoffrey J
    The life and thought of Isaiah Bowman.

    Bibliography: p.
    Includes index.
    1. Bowman Isaiah, 1878-1950.   2. Geographers—
United States—Biography.   I.   Title.
G69.B75M37   917.3 [B]   80-14650
ISBN 0-208-01844-1

Contents

List of Illustrations

Foreword

A college administrator widely known for his wisdom once defined a university as "a community of scholars made as useful as possible." This book is about one scholar—a geographer—who made himself extraordinarily useful over a wide range of functions, both within and outside the learned institutions with which he was affiliated.

I think of the functions of a scholar as fourfold: the pursuit of learning—in a word, research; the transmittal of learning to others—both by teaching and by publication; the promotion of these functions by others, which is the ultimate purpose of administration in learned institutions; and the application of learning to the problems of humanity beyond the field of learning. Most scholars make contributions in several of these ways; many have been highly successful in two or three. The outstanding scholar-teacher turned successful administrator is by no means as unusual as popular thinking often assumes. Extraordinary in the case of Isaiah Bowman is that he faced widely different challenges and had outstanding success in all of these forms of service.

Becoming director of the American Geographical Society in 1915 brought an end to Bowman's formal teaching at Yale University and limited the time available to him for his own research, though he

vii

continued to participate in the pursuit and transmittal of learning. As is true of all but a very few scholars, most of his research had to be carried on in the study, using observations of others, but to this work he brought the experience of earlier years of field study, especially in South America in 1907, 1911, and 1913. And when opportunity offered, as in the program he developed for studies of pioneer settlement, he returned to direct observations and interviews in the field. His continuing concern for the transmittal of knowledge in geography was evident in the large number of reviews and short articles which somehow he found time to write and publish, in the numerous addresses he gave, and in the personal correspondence with a wide number of scholars who like myself came to look to him for counsel.

For nearly two decades Bowman's major role was that of planning, stimulating and guiding the work of the major institution of geographic research and publication in the United States. Through this activity he came to occupy a leading position in organizations concerned with research in many fields, both of the natural and social sciences. Offices which he held included that of president of the International Geographical Union (1931–1934), chairman of the National Research Council (1933), vice chairman and director of the Science Advisory Board (1933), and president of the American Association for the Advancement of Science (1943). He maintained his concern for geography as a specialization which could and should contribute to the general advancement of knowledge. In his view, this purpose could best be served not by debate over the definition or scope of geography but by demonstrating to nongeographers what geography had to offer, especially in the study of problems of human organization of the land. Thus, in his *Geography in Relation to the Social Sciences,* he drew upon the substantive work of a large number of students to demonstrate the effective use of geographic, particularly cartographic, techniques in the study of historical and social problems of land use.

With the shift from direction of an institution specializing in geography to the presidency of The Johns Hopkins University in 1935, Bowman was called on to promote the conditions and activities necessary for teaching and scholarship over the full sweep of the fields of learning.

It is particularly in the area of service outside the world of learning—in matters of public affairs, especially international relations—that Isaiah Bowman's career was most unusual, and in which his name may well be most known to history. Here one can see his understanding of the ideal and the practical not as in opposition or mutual exclusion, but rather as calling for some reasonable linkage.

Bowman's career demonstrates, I think, the mutual interrelation of these diverse functions of a scholar serving as usefully as possible. Working with scholars in other fields and serving the government on international problems brought new information and new ideas. For Bowman, this called for evaluation, writing, and necessarily, publication. It is said that Bowman once observed that the slogan "publish or perish" should not be taken as an institutional commandment, but as a blunt statement of reality: whatever thoughts you may have, whatever you may teach, if not put in print, will almost surely die with you or soon after. Likewise it was characteristic of Bowman's sense of the practical within learning, that—as he once wrote me—though he was aware in his work in political geography of the lack of development of principles and training in that field and in himself in particular, experience had brought him into close contact with the problems and many of the basic facts. His mind was teeming with ideas; thus, he felt challenged to organize all this as best he could in print. The result, *The New World,* whatever its merits or demerits as a work of scholarship, was for decades uniquely valuable to students all over the world. Others, he concluded, must work on the principles; he had done what he could.

It is a large task that Geoffrey Martin has undertaken. We know of the high success in the many-sided career of this geographer and public servant. We have been told by those who worked closely with him of his "personality of versatility, intellectual vigor, industry, and disciplined forcefulness, joined to clear high purpose and great charm." Now revealed for the first time are those qualities which produced that result.

This is the third in an unprecedented triad of works—Mark Jefferson, Ellsworth Huntington, and now Isaiah Bowman—which Geoffrey Martin has written for the purpose of revealing U.S. geography in the making in the first half of the twentieth century. Geographers are the particular beneficiaries of such studies in their recent history.

Richard Hartshorne
August, 1979

Preface

Isaiah Bowman grew up in an age in American academic life when it was not possible to specialize in geography on the university level. Instead, would-be students of earth lore were obliged to study geology or physiography. At Harvard, William Morris Davis offered his own inimitable brand of physiography to students. By a combination of initiative, sacrifice, ability, and chance, Bowman was one of that group of young intellectuals who studied with Davis between 1890 and 1912, and who later helped to form much of what came to be recognized as geography in the United States. Davis introduced "man" into his physiographic intellectual construct, suggested biological response to environment, then left the subject for his disciples to develop. They extended that construct to include the life response ... which Davis called ontography. This was the origin of something very vital in native American academic geography.

Bowman belonged to a generation in geography (one is tempted to write "the last generation") when the individual felt at ease to wander intellectually, and read and write widely. His legacy of thirteen books and more than two hundred articles have enriched geographical science. His contributions to regional geography, the "science" of settlement, and political geography, once so very well known in the

United States and internationally, are today seldom read. Recent studies, recurring proclamations of "the new geography," and the operation of J. K. Wright's "law of the disparagement of the past," place Bowman's writings with that body of achievement sometimes referred to as "the history of geography." Even less well known today is his work with the United States Geological Survey, the Inquiry and the Paris Peace Conference, the International Geographical Union, the "M" project, the Stettinius Mission and the Dumbarton Oaks Conference (both of which led to the San Francisco United Nations Conference), and his role as director of the American Geographical Society and as president of The Johns Hopkins University. This host of activities did much to bring the geographer and the geographical point of view into the councils of power.

The intellectual history of a discipline, whose record is only partly available in the archives and which remains largely unwritten, requires construction. Particularly significant is the quest for origins of thought. An active geographer's life is of interest to all geographers: therein lie lessons of history for each individual. A geography can only be understood in the context of its occurrence, and the writings of an individual can only be appreciated in a setting of disciplinal evolution. Tracing the genesis of an individual's ideas in correspondence, notes, and so forth suggests the gestation period required for the completion of a given work, and reveals the influences which play upon the geographer's mind. That is geography in the making. The recent history of geography is, in part, revealed, and an understanding of the way in which the current paradigm has been formed is more nearly possible. A subject is very much what its creative scholars make it, and intellectual genesis, or more frequently rebirth, is sought and confirmed in inspiration. It is in this way that discipline is fashioned from subject.

In 1960 I began to plan to unravel something of the evolution in American geographical thinking in the first half of the twentieth century. My program was to concentrate on the life and thought of Mark Jefferson, Ellsworth Huntington, and Isaiah Bowman. *Mark Jefferson: Geographer* was published in 1968; *Ellsworth Huntington: His Life and Thought* was published in 1973. *The Life and Thought of Isaiah Bowman* is the last in a triad of works which seek to reveal a geographical heritage. The work is not primarily biography as others have proclaimed it, but may be thought of as a contribution to the intellectual history of the geographic discipline necessitating the study of persons and institutions, recording fact, reason, and motive, for what previously we may have thought happened. For it is all too possible to develop an *idée fixe* relative to the thought of individuals— and opinion of a geographer's worth—quite at variance with the reality.

Jefferson, Huntington, and Bowman were selected as representing the ontography which Davis urged as a departure from his physiography. These three students of Davis were prolific: between them they had published 62 books, parts of 33 other books, 575 articles, and 69 papers presented before the membership of the Association of American Geographers. The word *ontography* was apparently minted by Davis in 1902, though it was preceded by *ontogeny* (the history or science of the development of the individual being) and *ontology* (the science or study of being). The word *ontography* did not last as long as the theme. Perhaps the term *biome* would have endured longer than the Graeco-Davisian *ontography*. Davis urged the study of organic response to a physical environment and thus facilitated disciplinary evolution. The movement he inspired constituted a departure from his own physiography. The structure around which professional competitive discussion began to flow created what was perhaps the first paradigm in American geography.

In the 1920s Davis remained authoritative (and to some extent authoritarian) in the established physiographic orthodoxy, but an eclecticism had characterized the ontographic departure. The physiography of Davis and some of his disciples, and the ontography of others of his disciples, are still essential components of geography today, despite more sophisticated apparatus, measurement, and technique.

Bowman early supposed that his life's work would later be studied, and to this end he retained correspondence, memoranda, notebooks, photographs, and papers written and revised. He was approached on the subject of writing his autobiography but he did not find it difficult to decline. In responding to such a suggestion from Robert D. Williamson in 1944, Bowman replied:

Your pleasant letter finds me not wholly unprepared.... The trouble is that I am an actionist and I always think of the writer of an autobiography as a fellow who moves around in slippered ease, mumbling to himself about things that have passed and that no

one cares about any longer except a few students of history.....
However I have plenty of material.....[1]

Yet in writing a memorandum concerning a review of the memoirs of
Benes, he wrote in February 1949, "See this review in writing my
autobiography."[2] Upon retirement in January 1949 he did embark
upon a book dealing largely with his experiences in the field of foreign
policy, but it was never completed. Nor was a further series of six
books, planned since the early 1930s, nor a summation of his
philosophy.

Few geographers have the opportunity to influence governmental
decisions. Bowman, aware of that circumstance, redoubled his efforts
to save archival material for the record. He had the more significant of
his papers locked in a vault at The Johns Hopkins University, and in his
will ordered that this collection not be opened until twenty-five years
after his death. Other material of a prized or confidential nature he
placed in the vaults of the American Geographical Society. He
recognized the significance of the papers which he had collected from
the Inquiry, the Paris Peace Conference, the Dumbarton Oaks
Conference, the Stettinius Mission, and the San Francisco United
Nations Conference. They are extensive, and among the most vital of
the collections on these subjects.

My study of the life and thought of Isaiah Bowman borrows
essentials from these collections, though I have not attempted to
chronicle matters in detail which are more properly the province of
political scientist or diplomatic historian. By "essentials" I mean the
thoughts, feelings, ideas, and suggestions which he committed to paper
in informal memoranda or published works, or which otherwise helped
influence and shape the world in which he lived. No attempt is made
here to rewrite the history of the Inquiry and the Paris Peace
Conference, of Bowman's directorship of the American Geographical
Society, or of American governmental operations during 1940-45. In
these cases I have sought only to introduce information obtained from
sources hitherto little known or quite unknown, which hopefully adds
to our understanding of the way in which geography and geographers
can serve humanity.

GJM

Acknowledgments

Individuals too numerous to identify have helped me with this undertaking. Yet especial mention must be made of: The Johns Hopkins University librarians John H. Berthel and David H. Stam; Johns Hopkins archival staff members Kathryn Jacob (née Allamong, now with the U.S. Senate Historical Office), Caroline Smith, and Mary C. Beecheno; James Glenn and Ralph Ehrenberg for assistance with the papers of the Association of American Geographers; and the staff of the American Geographical Society, Harvard and Yale University archival holdings, the National Archives, the Royal Geographical Society, and the University of Chicago. Lise Perpillou of the Geographical Society of Paris, Robert P. Beckinsale (Oxford University, retired), and Gary S. Dunbar (University of California at Los Angeles) have each helped in notable manner. I also owe my sincere thanks to Richard Hartshorne, who knew Bowman personally, and who has written the Foreword.

To members of the Bowman family I am much indebted: Robert G. Bowman has provided frequent access to his privately maintained Isaiah Bowman deposit and shown me all possible courtesy; Walter P. Bowman gave abundantly of his time in recollection and analysis of his father's life and thought; Olive Bowman Gerwig provided her thoughts and archival material. Each of Isaiah Bowman's children has read the manuscript, improved, and approved it.

And finally to Jeanne Ferris of Archon Books, my sincere thanks for editorial assistance with the manuscript.

Chapter One

From Rural Michigan
to the Harvard Yard

The earliest record of the Bowman family from which Isaiah was descended appears in the Swiss archives in 1269, with the spelling Buman or Buwman.[1] Early in the eighteenth century Wendel Baumann (1681-1735), a coppersmith, and his wife Anne, both Bernese Swiss living near Thun, made the arduous journey to Germantown, Philadelphia, arriving in 1707. There they formed part of the Mennonite community, living a rigorous life close to nature on a tract of 530 acres on the Pequea Creek. Two generations later the Reverend Joseph Bowman (1766-1849) and his wife Maria Baer led the Bowman family into Waterloo, Canada.[2] There the Bowmans flourished.

Twenty minutes after midnight following Christmas Day, 1878, a son was born to Samuel and Emily (Shantz) Bowman in the Canadian town of Berlin, later renamed Kitchener, Ontario. Emily's sister Esther, present to help with the delivery of the child, had been reading the Book of Isaiah, and suggested that name for her nephew. Emily agreed provided that no one within the family would call him Ike. Isaiah was the third of eight children and the first of two sons.

It was a particularly harsh winter in Berlin. Samuel Bowman was away from home seeking a larger tract of fertile ground to settle in

1

eastern Michigan. Just outside Brown City some sixty miles north of Detroit he found a log cabin on 140 acres of land. With a knowing eye, he walked the land before purchasing it. Then he returned to Berlin and hurried the family for departure. Spring ploughing and sowing would take place in April. At the age of eight weeks, Isaiah was pulled in a horse-drawn sleigh to that log cabin near Brown City where he was to grow up knowing something of the pioneer stage of settlement firsthand. Isaiah later wrote:

> Both my grandparents were well-to-do people in Canada but they had large families and their estates were necessarily divided rather finely. My father was caught in the hard times of Cleveland's second administration.... Only a country school education was available. Judging by present-day standards, it was very poor schooling. But it had one great quality: discipline. I use the word in the good sense, meaning discipline of the mind. Teachers were not trying to find easy ways out of difficulties.[3]

It was this sense of discipline that was to equip him so well for the struggle ahead. Home life was simple, austere, and God-fearing. Samuel Bowman demanded physical toil and obedience from his sons. The family did not know extravagance, but some books had been passed down from Isaiah's paternal grandfather, who had been a teacher:

> Our own collection of books in my home could not be called a library. The earliest book that my father bought, which I can remember, was Captain Cook's Voyages. I was about ten years old, or less, and found it so thrilling that I always read the degrees, minutes and seconds of latitude which he recorded as if they were exciting words, as indeed they were to me. The next book was Stanley's *Darkest Africa*....[4]

The young Isaiah delighted in capturing quail eggs in the long grass and taking long walks on his own. He had two older sisters at school who would return home and tell him what they had learned. "Their talk greatly excited me, especially what they said about the settlement of America and the Indian battles, massacres, and ways of life."[5] At age five he began his formal education in a nearby country school.

When I was seven years old I was taken out of school for a year
because I "read too much" according to the doctor. But this only
resulted in my reading more.... My father and mother tried to
keep me out-of-doors and away from books, but I remember I had
a discarded history book of my sister's under the front steps and
that coverless, dog-eared volume drew out all my attachment. It
ranks with a *Life of Alexander of Macedon* lent me a few years
after this by Mrs. McRae, a neighbor of ours who brought it to our
house one day for me especially. The only trouble with the
volume was that the first fifteen or twenty pages were missing. I
have gone through life never knowing how the story started. If
anyone were to put a "Life of Alexander" on my desk today I
could not possibly be as interested in it as I would be in
recovering that incomplete book of my boyhood, getting the title
of it, and finding out what was in those first missing pages![6]

Bowman's earliest religious teaching was at a Baptist Sunday school,
not doctrinal "but a Bible-reading school with simple and perhaps
naive commentary by unscholarly interpreters. When I grew to young
manhood I attended services in many different churches in search of
something I came to identify as origins, causes, or verifiable things."[7]

Apart from his schooling with its rigorous emphasis on fundamentals,
the young Bowman shared in the work of his father's farm. At the age
of ten he was able to manage a horse-drawn plough, milk the cows, help
with barn raising, clean out the stables, and plant the fields. He
gathered beechnuts in the woods and in winter there were sleds,
sleighing parties, and neighbourhood gatherings where apples would
be passed around before guests went home.[8] It was a demanding life; of
his upbringing Bowman later wrote:

Among the books of Middle Western life that I have read, Hamlin
Garland's *Son of the Middle Border* most nearly describes the
conditions in our neighborhood, though the scene of his life was
farther west.... There were so many things to be curious about in
those days when each family was isolated for so long a part of the
time. I recall my mother's great interest in nature and the day she
stopped to pick up a piece of porphyry and a piece of granite.
Looking closely at the rocks, which were a part of the glacial drift
that covers the Great Lakes region, she said, "I have always been

curious to know how rocks like these were made and how they came to be here. Perhaps some day when you grow up you will be a student and will learn what happened." Her interest was keen and wide. The first map I ever drew I brought home to show her the "A" which the teacher had marked upon it and I have carried through life a vivid picture of her face that day as she beamed on me and said, "I think you are going to be like me when you grow up—you are going to like geography best !"[9]

When he was seventeen Bowman passed a teachers' examination in Sinclair County, Michigan, and began to teach in a country school. During the next four years he taught in three different school districts "in ascending order of importance as to size, salary, and appreciation of parents for the worth of education."[10] During these years he was able to study as well as to teach, and he acquired a sense of social organization and community life that remained with him throughout his career.

He finished four years of teaching in a deeply discouraged mood. He had given his father all the money left over from his small income ($19.50 a month in 1896-97 and $35 a month in 1899-1900). At the age when most boys were graduating from college, young Bowman had not taken the customary preparatory school subjects, though he had attempted to further his education by enrolling for summer school at Port Huron and Saginaw.

> One day my mother came out into the yard where I was chopping wood and the look of concern on her face was so marked that I asked her what the trouble was. She answered me by saying, "Son I am worried about you. What are you going to make of your life?" I replied that I did not know, because I was nearly twenty-two years old and without any means for continuing my education. She asked me what it was I wanted to do, and I told her that I wanted to go to college but that such a plan was out of the question. Her comment was, "If I were a young man of your age and had your strength and interest in intellectual work *I would go to college!*"[11]

That exchange encouraged Bowman to enroll in the summer of 1899 at the Ferris Institute, a college preparatory school in Big Rapids, in the southwest corner of Michigan. After one more year of teaching, Bowman returned to Big Rapids in the autumn of 1900 where he began a course that continued until the end of the summer of 1901. When he arrived in Big Rapids he had seven dollars in his pocket, but he was prepared to work to earn his way. He tended seed beds in a local nursery, and provided and planted seeds for members of the community. He was paid to offer military drill to a class of physical culture students at the Institute when the instructor learned that Bowman had organized one hundred young men of his school district and of two adjoining districts into a private military company in the autumn of 1898, when the Spanish War began. He received some financial help from home when his mother came into a small inheritance, but it was the assistance of Charles Carlisle that was most important to Bowman while at Ferris:

> He was the first person who greeted me when I entered the school feeling very insignificant and overawed in the new surroundings. He remained a poor bachelor all of his life. . . . When he died, his bank books showed that for a period of fifty years he gave something each month to poor students. He might be without a proper suit of clothes, but he always had money to help others. No one ever knew the extent of his benefactions.[12]

Carlisle was a dwarfed man who taught English and elocution, and often led prayer sessions. He invited Bowman to stay with him without charge in return for chores undertaken. The arrangement worked well, and Carlisle tutored Bowman in various social graces. At the Ferris Institute Bowman discovered that four years of teaching had not been lost time. He had learned how to study and was hungry for knowledge. During a twelve-month period at Ferris Bowman took eighteen subjects, including Latin and German, history, political economy, rhetoric, dynamic geology, structural and systematic botany, physics, zoology, chemistry, solid and plane geometry, algebra, and physical geography. His average grade in these eighteen subjects was 96%, which remained the highest percentage achieved by any student when Bowman died fifty years later. Bowman studied under Harlan Harland Barrows who had graduated from the Michigan State Normal School in 1898. Barrows had studied geography under Charles T. McFarlane at the Normal School, and arranged for his teacher to lecture in Big

Rapids. Bowman listened to McFarlane and was impressed. He decided to resume his studies under McFarlane's guidance at the Normal School in Ypsilanti. Later Bowman wrote:

> the teachers of the Institute ... were an extraordinary group ...
> they, as well as President Ferris, opened great windows upon vast
> possibilities of self-improvement—a kind of transcendentalism
> that was in favor then. All preached it consciously and
> earnestly.[13]

Meanwhile he visited the Federal District Court of Port Huron, Michigan, and applied for naturalization. He became a citizen on 31 March 1900. That spring he cast his first vote at a country polling booth, voting Republican:

> In a school district in Michigan in which I taught in the late
> nineties one would not have been engaged to teach if he were not
> a Republican. . . . To be a Democrat was to be a French-Canadian,
> or a ne'er-do-well, or a crank. It was afterward and elsewhere that
> I learned that even respectable people could be Democrats![14]

At the age of twenty-two Bowman arrived in Ypsilanti and commenced a distinguished undergraduate career. Initially he was disappointed to learn that McFarlane had left the Normal College to take a post at the Brockport Normal School in New York, but he was soon favorably impressed by McFarlane's successor, Mark Jefferson. Bowman's roommate, John Munson, who later became president of the college, commented that Bowman said of Jefferson, "I believe this new man is going to be all right. He seems to know his onions."[15] Later Bowman described Mark Jefferson as

> a Boston University man who had spent six years in the
> Argentine and returned to take an M.A. at Harvard under Davis.
> He was a travelled and cultivated man, one of the first type
> common enough in New England but at that time rather rare in
> the Middle West. He had a great influence upon me because of
> the breadth of his culture.[16]

Jefferson encouraged Bowman, had him attend as many of the

classes in geography as possible, invited the young man to his house for occasional meals and discussion, introduced him to local rivers that meandered, then trudged along their banks with him. That work led to Bowman's first two publications, "Deflection of the Mississippi"[17] and "A Typical Case of Stream-Capture in Michigan."[18] At the end of one year Jefferson proposed to Bowman that he study under William Morris Davis at Harvard for one year, then return to Ypsilanti and teach in Jefferson's department for a year. The savings from his year of teaching would enable Bowman to return to Harvard for a final year and graduation. By June 1902 Bowman had taken fourteen courses, including "Teachers' Geography," "Field Geography," "Map Study," "Physiography of the Lands," "Glacial Geology," and "Mineralogy." He had made a remarkable showing at the Normal College and was now anxious to begin study at Harvard University.

After spending the summer helping his father on the farm at Brown City, Bowman journeyed to Cambridge and introduced himself to Professor Davis. Bowman had probably not traveled in the United States outside of Michigan before. He entered Harvard as a junior in the Lawrence Scientific School in the autumn of 1902, and enrolled in "Research Physiography," "Physiography of the U.S.," "Paleontology," "General Geology," "Astronomy," and "Mechanical Drawing." His intellectual fortitude was initially tested by Jackson, the paleontologist. Thirty years later Bowman wrote of his experience:

> I yet remember the day when "Old Jackson," as we called the paleontologist at Harvard, gave us twenty-eight genera in a single fifty-minute period and expected us to have the physiology and fossil appearance of each one of these genera in the next lab period. Years later I told him what I thought of him. He quit teaching after a while, and I think the twenty-eight had something to do with it.[19]

He attended lectures on geology by the poet-scientist Shaler, who so impressed him that later he occasionally gave a lecture entitled "Nathaniel Southgate Shaler." The poetic eloquence of Shaler, his largeness of manner, "a teaching by example" as Bowman later wrote prompted Bowman frequently to attend Shaler's lectures even when he was not enrolled in the course.[20] Bowman possessed an incurable romantic streak perhaps most easily recognized by his appreciation of good poetry, and his own composition of many pieces of verse throughout a lifetime. He also dedicated himself to the writing of good prose. At Harvard he attended "lectures by James, Royce, Kittredge, Baker, Copeland, Briggs, and others ... regularly but took no examination and received no credit."[21]

And of course he came to know W. M. Davis, who introduced him to science, and who showed him the meaning of dedication and accomplishment. At the height of his powers, Davis was guiding American geology through a stage of physiography, and in the process of searching for a discipline of geography presented a spectacle to the young and impressionable Bowman which he was never to forget. During Bowman's first semester in Cambridge the Harvard Geological Club was formed. It met every Friday evening in the house of one of the professors, and Bowman became a member. Of course the first meeting of the Club was held at the Davis's home on Francis Street. And it was there that the formation of an American geographical association was first proposed. That proposal bore fruit in the 1904 formation of the Association of American Geographers.

When Davis asked Bowman whether he had an interest in any special physiographic problem, Bowman

> told him about reading G. K. Gilbert's paper on rotational deflection of rivers in relation to assymetrical valleys. "Good," he said, "why not measure the cutting of the river banks in a real case, the Mississippi River?" The overprinted sheets of the river, produced by the Mississippi River Commission, showed river channel changes during a thirteen year interval. In doing this, Professor Davis placed not only the river but also the globe in my hands, an act which gave a sense of importance to the work; it was a real job whose outcome would interest mature men. Later on it led to still more exciting field discoveries.[22]

Davis set him to work on "Geographical Features of Extinct Glacial Lakes." Bowman enjoyed the work, finding it "encouragingly difficult. When I complete the paper I'm working on I think I shall be able to recognize a glacial lake in the dark."[23] On the advice of Davis he visited the remains of such a lake at Hillsboro, New Hampshire, with a newfound class friend, James Walter Goldthwait. Other lifelong friends from Davis's class included Henri Baulig, William M. Gregory,

Ellsworth Huntington, and Walter S. Tower. Bowman also began a long-standing association with Vilhjalmur Stefansson, whom he met in Jaggar's class.

Walter Goldthwait invited Bowman to his home in Lynn for Thanksgiving dinner, after which the two undergraduates walked along the seashore watching a heavy surf. Bowman was thrilled by the ocean and intoxicated by the tang of salt air. It was on this occasion, too, that Bowman was introduced to Walter's sister, Cora Olive Goldthwait. Cora had graduated from Radcliffe College with the class of 1898 and since that time had travelled, taught, and played the cello with a band in New England. She was a woman of charm and social grace. In 1909 she and Bowman were married.

That Thanksgiving visit to the Goldthwait home had created in Bowman an excitement for the ocean. He had read M. F. Maury's *The Physical Geography of the Sea*, and in a short time he was working on a tide model

> which promises to be something pretty good if all plans succeed. A half dozen shore forms illustrate different rates of tidal-wave advance, the stimulus being given to the water by means of a plunger run by clockwork. The very present problem is to get two stimuli having the same relation in strength and time as the tides of sun and moon. I like it because it gives a chance for originality and because it's a problem.[24]

For the second semester Bowman was appointed one of six assistants by Professor Woodworth in "Geology 5," which he found to be "great fun—three of us have a section of about 50 men, twice a week. They're all Freshmen ... Professor Davis is very much pleased over my opportunity to 'practice.' "[25]

In the summer of 1903 Professor Davis had intended to take three or four students from his course "Research Physiography," including Bowman, to Montana. Bowman had been anticipating the Montana work with pleasure, but was forced to change plans when Davis instead joined his former teacher Raphael Pumpelly in an expedition to the Trans-Caspian region. However, when Arthur C. Veatch of the United States Geological Survey wrote to Professor Woodworth requesting an assistant for the summer to help make a study of the geology and underground water resources of Long Island, Woodworth recommended

Bowman. The faculty were prepared to give the young student full credit for his courses provided the Administrative Board approved. Bowman presented his request to Nathaniel S. Shaler, Chairman of that Board, who replied, "You go—go to that larger school of earth science—the Survey, and good luck to you."[26] Receiving $60 a month and all expenses, Bowman enjoyed his new life.

> One day I'm in New York, another at Jamaica, and perhaps the next away out in the country or along the seashore—getting a brown skin, hard muscles, lots of fresh air. I like the work. It's practical. I'm meeting men of all types and learning to handle them, which is worth a great deal. Then I see every now and then, and talk with a man in some other division of the Survey. There are mighty few fossils among them.[27]

Bowman was given the task of studying the water resources available to New York City:

> A knowledge of the geological structure of the Island was basic to a proper interpretation. . . . The chances of finding fossils in key beds were about 100 to 1. . . . One day, near the town of Roslyn, I was idly running through my fingers the drilling slush last brought up by the bucket when I felt a grain of sand in the midst of the usual sticky clay. . . . It was obviously just a grain of sand. It meant nothing. I was walking toward a pail of water where I could wash my hands and leave the job and was on the point of tossing away the grain of sand when it occurred to me that it had no business to be where it was. It came from a depth of 250 feet from ocean-floor deposits laid down far from land. My fancy began playing with it, speculation followed speculation. Only after this enjoyment had ceased did it occur to me to ask, what if it were not a grain of sand? In a moment my pocket lens showed that it was in fact a striated shell! Here was the first invertebrate fossil of the season from this horizon, and the last as it proved to be.[28]

The specimen was sent by express the next day to W. H. Dall of the National Museum at Washington. Bowman had found *Terebratula filosa,* base of the Matawan, and member of a marine series of the Cretaceous. The discovery was Bowman's first triumph for training and field experience. That same field work on Long Island found mention in his first publication, "Deflection of the Mississippi."[29] Some of Bowman's findings of that summer were incorporated in *Underground Water Resources of Long Island.*[30]

Bowman learned much from his work with the Survey, and commented, "It is a pleasure to feel that you are helping in a humble way to make a subject and not take the other fellow's word for it all the time."[31] Early in July M. L. Fuller, Chief of the Division of Hydrology, proposed to Bowman that he stay with the Survey at $75 a month. If he were to pass a civil service examination the following spring a permanent appointment would be available at $1,000 with $100 annual increments. Bowman was intrigued, but Jefferson encouraged him to remain with his original plan of teaching for one year, then returning to Harvard to complete his undergraduate studies.

From September 1903 until August 1904 Bowman taught at the Michigan State Normal College. He worked with Mark Jefferson and learned a great deal about geography and pedagogy. Bowman's work was good, and when in the summer of 1904 Jefferson visited the Jostedalsbrae ice cap in Norway he left all the summer school geography to Bowman. That summer Bowman reports taking "65 students on the Huron Excursion; 60 on the trip to Rawsonville; 180 on the Put-In-Bay excursion; 35 to Port Huron." All in all Bowman could declare "the summer work was a great success ... I believe the class got a great deal out of it (the Teacher's Course)."[32] Bowman gave two extra talks on "The Teaching of Geography" and "Geographical Material," which attracted 200 and 250 students respectively. At that time,

> Mill's *International Geography* had appeared, a large book with chapters by individual and distinguished geographers throughout the world. This book became one of my choicest possessions. The reading of each chapter was an exciting experience. It revealed to me the breadth and depth of geographical knowledge in a vast world of ideas and action. It made the deepest impression upon my mind of any professional book that I have ever read.[33]

By August Bowman was working once again for the U.S. Geological Survey with a party led by Leverett working on the water resources of Michigan. Bowman saved most of his pay of three dollars a day in preparation for his final undergraduate year at Harvard; that, in conjunction with a scholarship for $150, relieved Bowman of the financial concerns that had been with him since his collegiate career had begun. On 26 August 1904 Bowman was awarded a certificate, "a Specializing Diploma," by the Michigan State Board of Education, which licensed him to teach in the public schools of Michigan. It was a privilege which he would never exercise.

Late in September Bowman returned to Cambridge. He took three courses in geology, one in anthropology and one in French. In Jaggar's "Advanced Geology Field Work" he had François E. Matthes for a partner, and they labored together

> on Saturdays, starting early in the morning and working until dark. He is a delightful companion and I keep him talking about his western experiences all the way out to the field and back. He has a field map of the Canyon here—it's a great piece of work [by Matthes] and represents an outlay of $7,000 so he's pretty careful of it.[34]

Bowman's work was proceeding well and in October 1904 he wrote, "I had a sharp tug westward a few weeks ago in the form of an instructorship in geology at the Northwestern University but I thought I'd better be here a year longer."[35] By 30 November he had "been offered the assistantship in physiography in the Yale University summer school. Three afternoons a week and $150—was offered the same place here but they pay $50 less."[36] Bowman was to accept the Yale offer, and stay with that institution for eleven years.

In the autumn of 1904 Davis arranged for Albrecht Penck to speak at Harvard. Bowman was thrilled:

> One of my ambitions has been to see and hear Penck—the real *Penck!* I can scarcely wait to see him. I suppose you know of the monograph he's getting out, in sections, on the glacial features in the Alps? I'm reading Ratzel on "Die Erde und das Leben" and find him even more interesting here than in "Anthropogeographie." Those old German boys make me realize that not all the geography is west of the Atlantic.[37]

Upon Penck's arrival Bowman was designated his assistant:

> Through Professor Davis' kindness I am having the great
> opportunity of becoming thoroughly acquainted with Penck. He
> finds the English phrase somewhat elusive and on his having
> expressed a desire for someone who knew German and could help
> him in writing out his lectures Davis spoke of me. I meet him for
> two hours each day. . . . His arrangement of the lectures is rather
> novel and very effective. He is going to get out a new edition of
> the 'Morphologie'—and will follow the same order as that of
> these lectures. The first chapter will deal with landslides! The
> torrent as the epitome of the river comes next. So effective is this
> order and this point of view that Davis frankly says that in any
> new books he may get out he's going to crib the idea and start his
> chapter on Rivers and Valleys with the landslide and torrent.[38]

When the Harvard Geology Department gave a dinner at the
Colonial Club for Albrecht Penck and Sir John Murray, Davis asked
Bowman to accompany him. Davis's approval was demonstrated even
more clearly when he asked Bowman to assist in Geology 6 during the
spring term. Jefferson suggested to Bowman that he return to the
Ypsilanti Normal College and take a permanent position, but Bowman
politely declined the invitation and suggested F. W. Emerson or
Ellsworth Huntington for the post. Bowman toyed with the notion of a
position at Harvard. He admired Davis profoundly and valued working
with him. Yet Bowman could not forget his poverty as an
undergraduate. He had little money, never attended a Harvard Union
meeting, and did not share in social events in quite the same way as did
his peers. He was aware of missing the fun of being a student.[39] He later
wrote:

> I was extremely poor and conscious of my poverty. During my
> senior year at Harvard I had a single suit of clothes the entire year
> and I declined all social invitations, even those from my own class
> (I have never attended a class meeting) because I was painfully
> conscious of the fact that I was ill dressed and conspicuously so.
> But it never occurred to me to be bitter about it or to want to

upset society because my father had eight children and was unable to help me. I had to earn every dollar of my education. This is the literal fact, for I returned to my parents, with interest, the sums which I had to borrow from them.[40]

Even so he considered the possibility of graduate study at Harvard where he had been offered two $250 scholarships. But on 15 February 1905 Bowman took the civil service examination in hydrology. He finished at the head of the list, and was given an appointment on the U.S. Geological Survey. His full-time employment with the Survey began in June 1905 on Long Island. That summer he taught at Yale, intending to return to Survey work, but when a position on the Yale faculty was offered to him for the following year he accepted. He did not severe his relationship with the Survey.

In fact he was employed by the U.S. Geological Survey intermittently until 1913, and in different field seasons worked with Arthur C. Veatch, François E. Matthes, Frank Leverett, Nevin M. Fenneman, and Henry C. Cowles. Following his field studies of Long Island underground water resources in 1903, he spent much of his time the following summer with the Indiana State Geological Survey dealing with the pollution by oil wastes of the water supply of a small Indiana city. That work resulted in coauthorship with geologist Robert L. Sackett of "The Disposal of Strawboard and Oil-Well Wastes."[41] In subsequent years he spent time in Illinois, Texas, Oklahoma, Alabama, Michigan, and New York. Two books resulted from this work: *Water Resources of the East St. Louis District* (in which Bowman was assisted by Chester Albert Reeds, then a Yale University graduate student in geology) and *Well-Drilling Methods*. The latter was a comprehensive treatise on the subject in the United States, and long remained a classic in its field. Perhaps the first book written on well-drilling, it was referred to as late as 1973.[42] This work in geology helped create a very strong foundation for Bowman's later studies of human geography. It also meant that he would be able to associate intelligently with geologists while teaching geography at Yale in the years 1905–15.

To Bowman, Harvard had meant above all else William Morris Davis. On the occasion of Davis's seventy-fifth birthday Bowman wrote him:

There will always be the recollection of my first year at Cambridge and of the help you gave me there. The second year that I returned to Cambridge I was honored to become your assistant, though I could not for the life of me tell in what I "assisted" you—unless it was to consume the delicious breakfasts that you offered me on the mornings of your lectures. Only a person who was a regular attendant at Randall Hall could appreciate what that kindness meant!

It is always difficult to write or to speak praise of a man for whom one has an extraordinary regard, but I think if ever praise or appreciation should be spoken for you it is now and not later. Like all of your other serious students, I have always felt that there was something quite unique in the quality of your mind. It would be presumptuous of us, or at least myself, to say that I had learned to think but if I have it is owing to your instruction and criticism more than to the help of any other one person. In a very real sense we have all regarded ourselves as continuously at school to you.[43]

Chapter Two

The Yale Years

Bowman arrived in New Haven early in the summer of 1905 and was greeted by Herbert E. Gregory, another onetime student of William Morris Davis. Head of the Yale Geology Department, Gregory was a geologist by affiliation but a geographer at heart. He alone had been teaching classes which were geographic in a large and forceful geology department. As early as 1898, Yale anthropologist William G. Sumner had encouraged him to offer a course entitled "Environmental Influences on Man." Only four years later this course, with title changed to "Physical and Commercial Geography," became the foundation of an emerging substantial geographic course offering. Albert G. Keller, Sumner's disciple, encouraged and assisted Gregory with this work; the geologists tolerated but did not participate in this development.

Gregory's attempt to add geography to the Geology Department was bold, for geology was strongly entrenched at Yale. Benjamin Silliman had been appointed to the Yale faculty in 1802 and offered geology, "which was the cause of great wonder in academic circles."[1] The first doctorate in geology in the United States was granted at Yale in 1867 to William North Rice for a dissertation entitled "The Darwinian Theory of the Origin of Species." Since that time, Yale had been one of the leading American academic and doctoral granting institutions in the subject.[2]

Before 1903 no university department of geography offering a specialization in geography existed in the United States. In that year Rollin D. Salisbury founded one at Chicago.[3] In 1904 William Morris Davis founded the Association of American Geographers. These were critical accomplishments. University and college presidents were being shown that geography was serious business. Nonphysiographic courses began to emerge gradually though sporadically in the universities.[4] Richard Elwood Dodge began to offer such work at Columbia University Teachers College in 1897. Then followed other universities: California (1901), Pennsylvania (1901), Wisconsin (1908), Minnesota (1908), Nebraska (1909), Michigan (1915), Missouri (1917). These were among the beginnings that established geography in the United States.

When Herbert Gregory was added to the faculty at Yale in 1898 he brought with him a devotion to Davisian physiography. Soon this physiography began to penetrate the Yale geology department, and offered the possibility of the study of life responses. Geographic study, research, and teaching ensued.

Bowman's arrival in New Haven that summer of 1905 and his attachment to the Yale geology department supplemented the geographic enterprise which Gregory had commenced and which was shortly to become widely known and respected. Bowman was unaware at that time of his place in this academic development. He later wrote:

> I went to Yale for the simple reason that I was offered a job there and I wanted to teach so as to earn a living while working for a doctor's degree.... Yale was friendly in a warm and personal sense but again this may have been due to the fact that I was a faculty member and was very kindly treated. I always thought that I was especially well treated because I had come from Harvard and had been a student of Davis.[5]

Bowman was a valuable addition to the geographical center which Gregory was attempting to develop. To that end he had acquired Angelo Heilprin and Leonard M. Tarr in 1903, and Avard Bishop in 1904. After Bowman came Ellsworth Huntington in 1907, and George

T. Surface and Theodore H. Boggs the following year. And in the summer of 1907 he had Mark Jefferson take Bowman's classes while the latter was in South America. He sought other geographers:

> It is planned to increase the number of specialists on the regional geography of the world so that Yale may have men for Europe, Polynesia and Africa. . . . To keep the department up to date, it demands that those who are engaged in teaching should have at least one year out of every three for exploration.
>
> When these plans are completed, Yale will have men in all parts of the world engaged in exploration.[6]

Between 1907 and 1911 Gregory had invited into his department five men, other than himself who at one time or another were to hold the presidency of the Association of American Geographers (Heilprin, 1907; Jefferson, 1916; Gregory, 1920; Huntington, 1923; Marius Campbell, 1927; and Bowman, 1931).

It was in this milieu that Bowman learned the meaning of first-class geographical work. Here he associated with first-rate minds, undertook research leading to many publications, conducted field work, and lectured to students—many of whom themselves later became men of consequence. Perhaps especially important was the attitude of the geologists Barrell, Lull, Pirsson, and Schuchert, who encouraged the geographers with warm friendship and shared social occasions, and who provided the medium of the Yale Geology Club for geographical presentations. Credit also belongs to Herbert Gregory for retaining harmony when the geographic point of view was evolving within the geology department. And from the Michigan State Normal College, Bowman's friend Mark Jefferson sent maps, articles, and books to help and encourage his former student. From Harvard William Morris Davis sent Bowman this advice:

> You have an extraordinarily good chance, and I expect to see you make fine use of it. The chief thing I wish to emphasize is that you should develop geography proper, physiography and ontography properly combined, and not simply physiography (as I have done too much). New Haven always impressed me as a delightful place to live; just the proper size for a city; neither too large nor too

small. . . . Of course you must work hard, work like fury on your
regular work, but you must not neglect either healthful exercise
or social relations.

One of the things that I lost several years on, was not rising to a
real appreciation of my chances, waiting too long before putting
my oar in various matters. . . . Don't imagine that I write to
everyone this way; but your chance is so fine that I want to see
you make the most of it; and some of the things that I have
suggested above are not found out by young men until they are
half way to being old.[7]

Initially Bowman's appointment at Yale was for the summer of 1905
only. He gave a regional course on South America and some lectures in
physiography. That South America course may have been the first
regional geography class offered in an American university. It may also
have been the first geography course given in a North American
university concerning South America. In July Bowman's Yale
appointment was extended to 15 December and he was accorded the
rank of instructor. During the autumn he taught "Physical
Geography" to four sections of thirty men. He also offered a course
entitled "Physiography of the U.S.," and with Gregory offered a
seminar called "Physiography Research." He introduced a course
entitled "Forest Physiography" of which he wrote, "it is regular
systematic Physiography up to Christmas, and Physiography of the
U.S. and soils the rest of the year. . . . My extra year under Davis
assisting in the physiography of U.S. was just the very preparation I
needed for them."[8] He taught these classes on Monday, Wednesday,
and Friday. On alternate days Bowman was free to continue his work
with the U.S. Geological Survey in Connecticut and on Long Island.
That increased his income and contributed to his field experience. In
the following term he offered a course in "History and Social Science"
and another entitled "The Geography of America." Of this course
Bowman wrote:

I propose to make it geography and not physiography. With this
end in view I am collecting and roughly classifying all sorts of
responses to physical conditions: they certainly make an
interesting lot! Later on I want to do the same for the other

> continents with the view of giving a set of courses in regional geography.[9]

Bowman was becoming intrigued with geographic controls. He had been impressed with the work of Albert P. Brigham and Ellen C. Semple: "One course in 'Geographic Controls in American History' is regarded as hot stuff by the folks. It is one of the most fascinating fields I have yet found and during the past winter I collected stuff that seems to be taken for the real thing."[10] Bowman here referred to his course on "The Geography of America and Geographic Controls in American History," first offered in 1907 and described in the Yale catalogue as: "A study of the regional geography of North and South America in its physical, political, and commercial aspects, and of the control exercised by the physiography of America over man's distribution and conditions of life."[11] This description revealed Bowman's strong "regional" emphasis and the importance he placed on the seeking of controls. When Ellsworth Huntington joined the department in 1907, he and Bowman taught "Geographic Controls in History." In 1909 they offered "Anthropogeography," for which the writings of Ratzel, Supan, Kirchoff, Peschel, and Hettner were listed as required reading:

> Geographic environment and its regional qualities as affecting man's grouping and development. A systematic study of geographic responses is followed by research work upon selected problems in America and Eurasia.[12]

Other courses that Bowman offered included "The Geography of North America," "Geography Conferences for Teachers," and in 1914 both "Principles of Geography" and "Political Geography."

Bowman had already pondered the role of research in teaching, and the place of both research and teaching in the development of the discipline. "Without teaching there is no university and without research there is no teaching—worthy of the name of 'university' at any rate."[13] He firmly believed that a subject is what its creative scholars really make it. And he was fully aware that in creating a literature he, together with his geographer colleagues, was helping to fashion the discipline. He had already come to the conclusion that geography would advance through substantive contributions. He had little faith in pedagogical method to advance thought. In fact throughout his career he never developed much appreciation for method: "for every man who can impart an impulse there are a dozen who can impart a method."[14] As the years passed he became ever more concerned to make sure that teachers insisted on substance and not method. When the National Council of Geography Teachers awarded Bowman its Distinguished Service Award he wrote to Alice Foster, an official of that organization:

> Teaching that is not related to research is bound in the end to be formalized and barren. The text-book is a most useful adjunct to teaching. It is indispensable that someone should give attention to the organization of material for teachers who are not qualified to obtain it or who do not have access to library facilities....[15]

In a statement published later in the *University of Virginia Alumni News* he wrote, "I used to say to graduate students in search of a thesis subject: read the best papers of the frontiersmen in the field, and when you reach the phrase 'we may safely assume,' stop right there and set up your tent."[16] He suggested

> "good teaching" is a mis-leading phrase: it is all in the learning. When the learning process begins the teacher succeeds. By the process of learning we do not mean entertaining. We mean, rather, a taking hold of the mind.... The text-book simplifies: a sense of reality is gained by sensing facts or conditions in their complex environment.... We all know text-books of the anemic type that instruct by pale generalization. If higher education has any contribution to make to elementary or secondary education it is that experience with the stuff of the text-books, when possible through case histories tied to personal "field work," in one form or another, has no substitute. The more one practices education as evocation or a sense of reality to be attained, the more exciting and sound it becomes.[17]

Later Bowman wrote:

> we seem to have facts, processes of thought about facts, and third and equally important, a clear statement in English of these two

things, a statement that itself requires intelligence to prepare and intelligence to read. I used to pay a good deal of attention to this in the instruction of graduate students at Yale, so that a given problem was tackled from these three standpoints; and it is amazing what values students can get out of such analyses and how open-minded and judicial they become of a sudden as they see how much difficulty is created in science by muddled thinking about thought or by no thinking at all on the subject of thought and expression. . . .[18]

Not surprisingly, his classes are well remembered:

He was one of the few people who could revolutionize one's knowledge and thinking, and even more, to give a deeper understanding of the world, its physical resources and meaning and its possibilities. . . . I think our class at Yale was Bowman's first teaching experience . . . he spoke so fast and his subject matter was so compact and new to the students that it was indeed difficult to keep up with him. We used to joke that he would give the equivalent of a volume of the *Encyclopaedia Britannica* to digest over each weekend. . . . All of us, however, gained insight and learned lessons that lasted a lifetime.[19]

Another student recalled:

The fact that I was born in Sitka and lived there my first sixteen years intrigued him, so we had numerous delightful conversations. . . . Dr. Bowman was what I would term a delightfully enthusiastic teacher. The way he presented a subject held one's full attention.

For example, I can recall clearly the explanation about the weather in the Puget Sound area. He explained the reason for the heavy rainfall along the Washington and Alaska Panhandle coasts. Then showed us why cities like Seattle and Tacoma received medium precipitation and Victoria and Port Townsend very little.[20]

He was described as

a dedicated teacher. He always very carefully prepared for his

classes and with lavish use of maps and the blackboard really
made us visualize his subject. He had a good sense of humor not
often displayed, but often enough to make his students feel at
ease with him. I recall, too, he was most fair in the grading of his
students.[21]

Roy Nash, later known for *The Conquest of Brazil* (1926), studied under
Bowman in 1907-08:

Of his class in physiography for foresters at Yale, I recall only his
delightful field trips. Practically all of us were graduate students;
Bowman was not any older than one or two in the class. The
atmosphere was most informal. He was but the keenest intellect
among a group keenly interested in the shape and substance of
the surface of the earth.[22]

Of course, by teaching, the teacher breeds his own extension. Given
Bowman's attitudes toward research and teaching it is hardly
surprising to find that several of his larger ideas began to germinate in
these years. Yale was alive with intellectual discovery. As Bowman
later recalled, "The period 1905-1915 when I was at Yale still seems
like a Golden Age. There was such a tremendous stir in the life of the
place and so many glorious beginnings of things."[23] Departmental
offerings were being systematized in a way that nurtured and
stimulated the minds of all department members. Research and
teaching were inimitably intertwined. A magnificent example of the
relationship among teaching, field work, and research was provided by
the yearlong course which Bowman, Gregory, and Barrell provided for
the Yale Forestry School. "Physiography," "Lithology," and "Soils of
the U.S." were given in sequence to would-be foresters.

Bowman amassed notes, carefully wrote out his lectures, and
illustrated them with maps and diagrams which he drew on the
blackboard or had published by a local print shop. And he listened to
the lectures of the gifted Joseph Barrell. Bowman relied largely on
Davis for the physiography section, though he began to sympathize
with some of Salisbury's objections to Davis's style of physiography.
For the lithology and soils parts Bowman read King, Hilgard, reports of
the U.S. Soils Survey, and numerous articles. One of the many
students who took this course was Oliver E. Baker. Bowman wrote to

Albert P. Brigham, secretary of the Association of American Geographers:

> Just now I am very much excited over a Forest Physiography that I hope to complete during the summer. It will be chiefly soils and physiography of the United States with special attention to their relation to the distribution of forest trees, and will be based on the course in Forest Physiography that I have given for the last five years in the Yale Forestry School.[24]

Later Bowman wrote to Charles C. Colby:

> I am glad to see you carrying out the idea of a source book. You know that is the way I came to write my Physiography of the United States. The task of supervising the reference work of several courses in the absence of a textbook compelled me first to make abstracts, reference lists, outlines, etc., and presently, with six months of intensive writing, I had the thing done.[25]

The manuscript was completed early in 1911 and promptly published by John Wiley and Sons as *Forest Physiography: Physiography of the United States and Principles of Soils in Relation to Forestry*. In this 759-page book Bowman provided the first comprehensive physiographic description of the United States, to which he added a section on soils. He had combined the arts and virtues of "altogether explanatory writing" and "purely descriptive writing." In the preface Bowman revealed some of the thoughts that had prompted its writing:

> If the forest is accepted merely as a fact, and the chief concern is its immediate and thoughtless exploitation, physiography may indeed be the fifth wheel to the coach, although even so practical a view as the lumberman's must include some knowledge of topography and drainage if merely to put forest products upon the market. But forestry is more than lumbering, and if forests are to be conserved, if they are to be improved and extended, every direct relation of the tree to its physiographic environment is vital.[26]

Bowman dedicated the book to Eugene Waldemar Hilgard, Leader in

Agrogeology." Perhaps he had been led to this tribute by his continued use of Hilgard's work on geology and soils in the classroom. Hilgard, then a faculty member of the University of California at Berkeley, acknowledged the dedication.

> The great merit of your book is that it takes geology as the natural basis of all physiography, a feature the lack of which renders so many elaborate ecological treatises so unsatisfactory.... Your descriptions and liberally interspersed maps and diagrams give an excellent idea of the entire country, far beyond the forestal features.[27]

Production of so large and detailed a book had tired Bowman. He began to realize that exercise, fun, and social relations were also a part of life. He made friendships with men in other departments, many of which lasted a lifetime. Those relationships with Charles Upson Clark, Clive Day, and Charles Seymour were perhaps the most significant. He played tennis with Joseph Barrell and handball with Lull and various other members of the Geology Department. To Mark Jefferson he wrote:

> To finish the task before leaving for South America meant working late every night and every minute of my time that could be spared from classes, and only finishing the last of the page proof and the index at Panama on my way to Peru. The result was that I was practically prostrated....[28]

Bowman worked extremely hard and suffered "from an attack of nerves and tonsilitis due to overwork and had to spend my time in bed while not actually teaching. In fact had today off. Monday. I am well again and expect to take a week's vacation after the Summer School."[29]

He was ever anxious to help promising students undertake graduate study. Two of his most notable protégés were Gladys M. Wrigley and George M. McBride. When Wrigley arrived in the Deparment in 1911 after studying with Herbert J. Fleure at Aberystwyth, Wales, Bowman's course work on South America interested her most. Under Bowman's tutelage she wrote a dissertation entitled "Roads and Towns of the Central Andes" and in 1917 became the first woman in the United States to earn a doctorate in the field of geography. And when

Bowman discovered McBride teaching in a Chilean mission school, he encouraged him to enroll at Yale in geography courses, and to write a dissertation entitled "Land Tenure in Latin America" (1921). This study was revised and published by the American Geographical Society in 1923 as *The Land Systems of Mexico*.

At the end of ten years at Yale Bowman wrote, "There I got the fever of work, and by that I mean incessant, grinding toil, that leads to rheumatism, tonsilitis, and the rack. There is such a frightful abyss between A in college and an A in the work of life.."[30] But his contribution in the classroom had been noteworthy. Charles Seymour commented that when Bowman "came to Yale as a young instructor he found geography, so far as the undergraduates were concerned, the softest of the so-called snap courses. When he left ten years later, all too soon for us, it had become a stimulating discipline on a permanent basis."[31]

Herbert Gregory also recognized Bowman's worth:

> Geography as an independent subject of study at Yale is directly related to Professor Bowman's activities. In 1905 the subject was an outcast . . . but . . . became assured only after its subject matter was treated in a professional way by a man who had established a well earned reputation for scholarship and teaching.[32]

Word spread of Bowman's competence as a geographer and teacher of geography. Between 1907 and 1909 he offered courses in physical geography as a "special lecturer" at Wesleyan University in Middletown, only a few miles distant from New Haven. There he came to know and to be influenced by William North Rice.[33]

And at the University of Chicago Salisbury and his departmental colleagues had learned of Bowman's work for the United States Geological Survey and had heard him present papers before the Association of American Geographers. Salisbury invited Bowman to visit Chicago during 1908 with all expenses paid, about "a matter of importance." Bowman did so and Salisbury offered him a position in the Chicago geography department. But Gregory persuaded Bowman that his larger opportunity resided in New Haven. Nevertheless, the invitation was flattering. "It is so good to feel wanted by two institutions!"[34]

Salisbury also asked Bowman to teach at the University of Chicago summer school, from 15 June to 28 August. The pay was inviting, and he was to offer the "Regional Geography of North America" and a short series of South American lectures. An opportunity to live at Salisbury's house with an entire floor to himself, "and a chance to write on South America all I wish" secured Bowman for the Chicago department of geography much of that summer.[35] There he met Ellen C. Semple for the first time, renewed his friendship with Harlan Barrows, under whom he had studied briefly at the Ferris Institute nine years previously, and came to know J. Paul Goode and R.D. Salisbury. He also became acquainted with Thomas C. Chamberlin, Henry C. Cowles, and some of the sociologists. But at the conclusion of the summer session Bowman returned to Yale. Again in 1911 Salisbury invited Bowman to teach in the Chicago department of geography, this time in the spring quarter, but Bowman declined.[36]

Bowman's success in the classroom was, in part, the product of a commanding manner coupled with a pleasant and clear voice, carefully planned map work, self-taken lantern slides, and interesting lectures. Just as important was his selection of good articles and books as "required reading." To this end he searched the review sections of the many periodicals which the Yale library purchased. In this way he discovered Jean Brunhes' *La Géographie Humaine*. "I read it through and recognized it as a masterpiece ... and used it every year with successive classes," [37] Later with Richard E. Dodge he arranged and edited an English translation of this book, (translated by his Yale friend and colleague, Irville C. LeCompte), which was then adopted in classrooms throughout the English-speaking world. [38]

Bowman's classroom success was also the result of the research in which he steeped himself. He had replaced gazeteer and picture-book geography with a scientific approach. Davis at Harvard had given Bowman the discipline which Bowman was offering in the classroom, and which initially inspired his research. He believed stalwartly in the Davisian cycle, the Davisian emphasis on field work, and Davisian insistence on hard thought. When Bowman insisted that the emphasis was "placed upon the ontographic half of the subject," that too was inspired by Davis.[39] Later Bowman wrote, "One of the things that I used to dwell on with great insistence to graduate students ... at Yale was advice that no man could expect to get anywhere unless he became his own severest critic. Those of us who were trained under Davis are all pretty much of that sort."[40] He told Davis:

> You used to lay great emphasis upon the fact that interruption might come at any time in the uplift of a given mass and that following the interruption further uplift or depression could take place with all sorts of differing consequences, depending upon the rate and amount of uplift, etc., etc. This idea of the flexibility of all the elements of the problem is lodged in my mind as characteristically a part of your teaching and it was of infinite help to me in my own teaching at Yale and in my field work....[41]

Davis's inspiration was even more important to the energy and direction which Bowman imparted to research. Upon acceptance of an instructor's position at Yale in the autumn of 1905, Bowman filed papers with the dean of the graduate school in candidacy for a doctorate in geology.[42] During that year he studied geography with Gregory, history with Bourne, and colonization with Keller. The following year he studied further under Gregory, demonstrated the required proficiency in the reading of French and German, and began to structure a thesis concerning the Andes of South America. This was an interest which had been prompted by Mark Jefferson. Gregory urged Bowman to undertake field work in the Andes, and arranged the financing of what came to be known as "The Yale Peruvian Expedition." This was the first of three field trips Bowman was to make to South America. Of his thesis "The Geography of the Central Andes" Charles Schuchert wrote:

> The chapters treating of the physiographic features of the Bolivian Andes are particularly valuable and give the first comprehensive account treating of this side of the geology of northwest South America. The thesis shows that the candidate has excellent powers of observation and research along new lines.[43]

In 1909 Bowman was awarded the Ph.D degree[44] and promoted to the rank of assistant professor. At the same degree-granting ceremony Ellsworth Huntington also received a doctoral degree in geography.

But neither man was present for the occasion. Huntington was furthering his climatic research by taking soundings from a canvas raft on the Red Sea, and Bowman had just married Cora Goldthwait. These were among the earliest geography doctorates awarded in the United States. Bowman's was among the first to adopt the regional approach, and to include the word "geography" in the title. It was also the first doctoral study treating a part of South America. The academic exercise had helped establish Bowman at Yale and satisfied the geologists that his variety of geography was legitimate. Huntington did not write a dissertation, and may be unique in that regard in the history of American geography.[45]

Bowman took two more field trips to South America in 1911 and 1913, which resulted in much published research. Early in 1911, before his second trip to South America, he had tentatively arranged "a very ambitious proposition for the physiographic study of Newfoundland in the summer of 1912—a sort of Professor Schuchert—Smithsonian Institution combination."[46] When W. M. Davis announced his "Transcontinental Excursion" for that same summer and invited Bowman to be Third Excursion Marshal, Bowman changed his plans. The Excursion (which celebrated the sixtieth anniversary of the American Geographical Society and the occupation by the Society of a new building) lasted fifty-seven days, covered over thirteen thousand miles, and brought into daily contact forty-three European geographers and approximately seventy Americans. This travelling seminar was without comparison in the history of American geography. American geographers joined and departed the group at their convenience; the Europeans completed the Excursion.

Bowman met many of Europe's leading geographers for the first time, saw a great deal of the United States, and exchanged points of view with various savants. He came to know especially well Eduard Brückner of Austria; Albert Demangeon, Emmanuel de Margerie, Emmanuel de Martonne, and Lucien Gallois from France; the Germans Joseph Partsch and Harry Waldbauer; George G. Chisholm and Alan G. Ogilvie of Great Britain and Emile Chaix and Fritz Nussbaum from Switzerland. His personal friendships with these men lasted a lifetime and led to a substantial exchange of correspondence and publications. Perhaps the first visible benefit to accrue to Bowman from this Excursion was a certificate of corresponding membership in the

Geographical Society of Vienna, forwarded by Eugen Oberhummer in
1914.

Much of Bowman's research was presented initially in paper form to
the Association of American Geographers and to the Yale Geology
Club. He had been present on the occasion of the founding meeting of
the Association in 1904 and was elected to membership in 1906. At the
age of twenty-eight he was one of the youngest persons so honored in
the early history of the Association. He was elected second vice
president in 1912 and again in 1919, secretary 1914–1916, president in
1931, and councilor in 1932–33. In the first ten years of the
Association only William Morris Davis presented more papers to that
body than Bowman did. Some of Bowman's offerings were: "Partly
Submerged Islands in Lake Erie" (1904); "Hogarth's 'The Nearer
East' in Regional Geography" (1905); "The Deserts of Peru and Chile
in South American History" (1906); "Geographic Relations in Chile
and Bolivia" (1908); "The Regional Geography of Long Island"
(1909); "The Geographical Results of the Yale Peruvian Expedition"
(1911); "Lake Titicaca and the Rivers of Tiahuanaco" (1912);
"Nivation in the Central Andes and a New Hypothesis of Cirque
Development" (1912); and "The First Decade (of the Association of
American Geographers)" (1913).[47]

Bowman regularly presented geographic papers to the faculty and
graduate student members of the Yale Geology Club. Twelve to sixteen
meetings were held each year with increased attendances after
February 1909, when Charles Schuchert sanctioned smoking, pop, and
occasionally punch or beer. Included among Bowman's papers were
"Deserts" (1905–6), "Deserts of Peru and Chile in South American
History" (1906–7), "Karst Structure in Illinois" (1906–7), "The
South American Journey" (1907–8), "The Regional Geography of
Long Island" (1908–9), and the "Millionth Map of the World"
(1909–10).[48] These intrusions of the geographical into a geology
department were happily accepted, as were papers by Avard Bishop,
Herbert Gregory, and Ellsworth Huntington.

In his ten years at Yale Bowman published four books (*Water
Resources of the East St. Louis District,* 1907; *Forest Physiography,* 1911;
Well-Drilling Methods, 1911; *South America: A Geography Reader,*
1915), twenty-four articles (twenty of which relate to his South
American research), and some book reviews. He had seized hold of his

opportunity in splendid fashion. Yet at the end of that ten-year stay the geographical end of the geology department did not appear promising. The popular Angelo Heilprin had died in 1907, and William Graham Sumner in 1910. A revision of the Yale curriculum in 1911 reduced the number of students taking geography courses. In 1910 Gregory had been provided with some moldy supplies while trying to help Navajo and Hopi Indians in Arizona. Gregory came close to death, and although he recovered to lead a long life his strength for the immediate future had been sapped. In 1913 he relinquished the department chairmanship, which geologist Charles Schuchert then assumed.

That development sounded the death knell for geography at Yale. It was Gregory who had helped insert geography into the Columbia-Yale program established in 1905–6 for the purpose of preparing students for consular service in the Far East. It was Gregory who had brought Albrecht Penck, professor of geography at the University of Berlin, to give the 1908 Silliman lectures at Yale, where Albrecht's son Walther was studying. It was Gregory who had increased the number of geography courses offered, and it was Gregory who had arranged leaves of absence, salary increases, and field work expenses for the geographers. It was Gregory who had successfully invited the Association of American Geographers to hold their annual meeting in New Haven in 1912, having failed in 1908.[49]

Yet Yale did not separate geography from geology. The department was entitled "Geology Department," not even "Geology and Geography Department." Although in 1913 the geological faculty agreed "to request the University to appoint an Alumni Committee on Geography,"[50] nothing was accomplished. The issue had been prompted by inquiry from the patrons of the American Geographical Society when Bowman had requested funds for his intended 1913 expedition. By 1915 University administrative enthusiasm for such a development had become minimal.

When early in December 1914 Bowman was offered the directorship of the American Geographical Society, to begin 1 July 1915, he accepted. Ellsworth Huntington left Yale at the same time. The Yale Corporation appointed Loomis Havemeyer to the geology department, but his interests were sociological and anthropological rather than geographical. The dean and chairman then offered Bowman a professorship at $4,500 if he would remain, but he was not to be persuaded.[51] When the University administration asked Bowman to hire a geographer in his stead, he asked Salisbury if he would part with Wellington D. Jones. Finding that Salisbury preferred to retain Jones, he then recommended Charles F. Brooks. Additionally, Bowman sought to bring Eugenius Romer, living temporarily in·Vienna, from the recently destroyed University of Lwow in war-devasted Lemburg.[52] But that plan too failed. Criticism of the work of Havemeyer and Brooks quickly mounted, and the cause of geography at Yale faded after such promising beginnings.

Chapter Three

Eldorado Discovered:
The South American Expeditions

Isaiah Bowman's curiosity about distant places began in his early boyhood when he read of Captain James Cook's voyages and Henry M. Stanley's travels in Africa. His particular interest in South America had been initiated by study under Mark Jefferson at Ypsilanti's Normal School. As soon as he had arrived at Yale in 1905, he had offered a regional geography course on South America. The initial part of the course was constructed around Mark Jefferson's outline maps on which were plotted the distribution of population. Then followed climatic study and, most notably, readings from the work of Hahn, Humboldt, and Darwin. Soon Bowman drew his own maps showing distributions in South America. These he had printed in New Haven.[1]

This course offering revealed to Bowman the paucity of the literature available. He made his course respected at Yale, and in 1906 before the Association of American Geographers read his first contribution toward a geography of South America—"The Deserts of Peru and Chile in South American History." All the while Mark Jefferson sent him literature on South America from his own private library. With the granting of a leave of absence from Yale in February 1907, Bowman made final plans for a trip to South America. Archer M. Huntington, wealthy benefactor of the American Geographical

35

Society, contributed $1,000 towards the expenses of the expedition, and Herbert E. Gregory, then head of the Yale geology department, persuaded the Yale Corporation to continue Bowman's salary during his months of field work. A title was bestowed upon the venture: "Yale South American Expedition of 1907."

Bowman travelled to Washington to gather suggestions for a profitable trip. He spoke at length with WJ McGee, though perhaps he gained most from Bailey Willis and his topographer, who had both recently returned from China. Armed with numerous letters of reference, a sextant, a psychrometer, and a barometer, and accompanied on part of the journey by a companion named Zahm,[2] he embarked on the *Alliance* 1 April 1907. He explored portions of the Atacama Desert and the Maritime Andes, traced the shorelines of the ancient lake on the Bolivian tableland, and descended the Chapare Valley northeast of Cochabamba as far as the border of the Amazonian Lowlands. The work was hard; from Antofagasta Bowman wrote:

> Our first month's work was as profitable and adventurous as it could well be. I became thoroughly acquainted with a mule's back—after 600 miles of travel on it; and to our other comforts were added low temperatures, snowstorms, canned foods, dust, heat on the pampa, mountain sickness, etc.! Carried a topographic section away over into Bolivia where we take it up again and carry it east to Eastern limit of Andes if possible.[3]

Forty years later Bowman recalled the wonder and excitement of his first South American expedition in an address entitled "Discovering South America":

> Eldorado, the famous city of gold, is still there. . . . It is a curious city because it can be found only by those who personally hunt for it: no guide can show you the way. It can be seen only by those who are excited about finding it: it has never yet been glimpsed by a dull eye. It is a drifting city, never long in one place. . . . I first found Eldorado in the desert. It was on a moonless night on which we began a long journey to escape the intense daytime heat and glare of the Desert of Atacama in Northern Chile. At four o'clock in the morning we stopped and made camp and in the light of our brush fire we saw Eldorado. The sand was like gold, the dry

arroyo bed seemed to flow like liquid fire. Down from the rose-
tinted sky and snow of the Andes ran floods of gold. I filled my
pockets with it. I have been a millionaire ever since because I
would not take a million dollars for the memory of the night when
I first saw Eldorado in the desert. My panorama of travel memory
has never once been dimmed by time and work, never lost. The
desert is a land of color and excitement that I habitually patrol.[4]

It was Bowman's first extended field trip in which he had attempted
to make studies of the ontography and physiography of "The Central
Andes ... a proposed name for a group of closely related natural
regions that lie between 12 degrees and 26 degrees south latitude."[5] In
"Peruvian Physiography" Bowman wrote:

On my first visit in 1907 the "Central Andes," as I named them,
were practically unknown from the standpoint of modern
physiographic science. As a young man I had the rare
opportunity of making the first scientific interpretation of

Andean physiography based on modern analysis of land forms in the field ... I expected to see wild relief everywhere, and a disordered and picturesque landscape. Such were the pictures of the geography text-books that had excited my boyish imagination. ... The view from the coast as I sailed southward from Payta in 1907 provided distant glimpses of realities that matched the dream, though great was my disappointment when, having outfitted my expedition at Iquique, Chile, I travelled eastward to find a forty-mile stretch of Cordilleran skyline so level as to deny the promise of the text-books. Riding up over the piedmont and the western flank of the Andes I found beveled surfaces in cross-section on the high quebrada walls as well as at the top of the country. The Central Andes had been peneplaned and the lofty mountains whose altitude seemed so attractive on the map were but moderate sized cones perched on top of extensive lava flows (Western Cordillera) or residual remnants (Eastern Cordillera) rising above old erosion surfaces now in process of destruction.

How extensive were these surfaces? ... If the Andes was a vast up-arched block of the earth's crust, were its borders and its interior basins flexed or faulted? Had the surface come to rest in its present position in geologically recent times? ... Old shorelines had been described by a number of observers about the edges of main basin of the altiplano of western Bolivia. ... What was the history of the lake or lakes that occupied the basins at one time? ... Of course the relation of the life of the Central Andes to those varied physiographic features is a matter of special interest to the geographer, but in this paper I will not take time to go into details about the human geography of the region. ... To attack these large questions adequately one expedition was not enough. Two expeditions were inevitable, each directed into new territory so as to enlarge the picture and establish the interrelations of Central Andean physiography.[6]

This trip inspired Bowman to begin a doctoral dissertation which was concluded in 1909. Entitled "The Geography of the Central Andes," this study was later misquoted in the literature as "The Physiography of the Central Andes." It contained eight chapters: "The Physiography of the Maritime Andes"; "The Physiography of the Eastern Andes"; "Regional Population Groups of Atacama"; "The

Highland Dweller of Bolivia"; "An Anthropogeographic Interpretation";
"Trade Routes in the Economic Geography of Bolivia"; "Man and
Climatic Change in South America." In the preface Bowman wrote,
"All the chapters on the life side of the geography of the Central Andes
have been or are being published in various geographical journals. . . ."[7]

By 1911 he had published seven articles based upon chapters in his
dissertation. The exception was "The Military Geography of Atacama"[8]
(those based on the dissertation included: "The Distribution of
Population in Bolivia,"[9] "The Highland Dweller of Bolivia: An
Anthropogeographic Interpretation,"[10] "Man and Climatic Change in
South America,"[11] "The Physiography of the Central Andes: I, The
Maritime Andes; II, The Eastern Andes, "[12] "Regional Population
Groups of Atacama,"[13] "Trade Routes in the Economic Geography of
Bolivia").[14]

Of more significance than these immediate articles was the
experience and knowledge gained from gruelling field work. He had
taken Davis's precept, "process, structure and stage," into the Andes
and sought interpretive understanding. This exercise was a critically
important part of his education as a geographer. Later he called this
understanding his "capital." And Bowman had found an area which
fascinated him, and allowed the free play of his faculties to develop his
notion of regional geography. In his retirement, forty-two years after
this first trip to the Andes, he planned a book tentatively entitled "The
Five Courts"; the first of these courts was "the court of the dusty foot"
which he had visited at Cliza in 1907, and at which he had been asked to
officiate.

As a result of this trip the Rand McNally Publishing Company
invited Bowman to write a South America textbook for a series which
they were planning. Ellsworth Huntington was to write on Asia,
J. Paul Goode on North America, and Emmanuel de Martonne on
Europe. By 31 January 1910, Bowman could write, "The Reader on
South America is now all but ready to send to the Editor."[15] In fact
Richard E. Dodge, editor for the series, and the appropriate
representative of Rand McNally procrastinated and the book did not
appear until 1915. It was one of the first geographical textbooks on
South America in the English language. Used for many years in high
schools, normal schools, colleges and universities, it probably sold
more copies than any other book Bowman was to write. A New Yorker
named Rosales wished to translate the *Reader* into Spanish, but

although Bowman urged the Wiley Company to facilitate and publish the translation, Mr. Rosales had to settle for a private and unpublished translation which enjoyed a limited circulation. Atsushi Tsuyusaki, who had translated Ellsworth Huntington's *Asia: A Geography Reader* (1927) secured permission from Bowman to translate into Japanese, *South America: A Geography Reader.*[16] A privately printed Japanese version appeared in 1930.

By 1910 Bowman planned to return to South America for further field work. He wrote to his mentor Mark Jefferson:

> It is a very great secret and you must not tell anyone else about it, except Mrs. Jefferson, that I am going to South America again a year from this coming June, to complete the Central Andes, or as much of it as I can do in another journey. Then the work of both expeditions will be published in book form, probably here at the University.[17]

When the wealthy historian and geographer Hiram Bingham of Yale proposed a field trip to South America and offered Bowman the position of geologist-geographer on that expedition, Bowman accepted. The title "Yale Peruvian Expedition" was bestowed upon the intended work and Bingham was made director. The other members of the expedition were Dr. W. G. Erving (surgeon), H. W. Foote (collector and naturalist), Kai Hendriksen (topographer), H. L. Tucker (engineer), and P. B. Lanius (assistant).[18] The expedition proceeded via France, the Bay of Biscay, a one-day stop at Jamaica and another at Panama, and landed at Mollendo, then chief seaport of southern Peru, in June 1911. They journeyed at once to Cuzco, the old Inca capital, and commenced five months of field work. Members of the expedition were divided into three parties to undertake archaeological, geological, and topographical exploration. Bowman wrote:

> Fossils, erosion cycles, andenes or artificial terraces, folds, structures, climatic changes, glacial forms, mountain lakes, etc., are on my calendar. The region has been rather carefully selected and we have great hope for the results. After the report of the expediton has been prepared I wish to complete the writing of the other trip—and combine the results of both expeditions in a

single book "The Central Andes." If the opportunity presents itself to made a third expedition farther south and still in the central region I may not publish in book form until I have been down here a third time.[19]

In fact Bowman's major contribution on this, his second South American expedition, was to make a topographic map of the Cordillera from the junction of the Urubamba and Timpia Rivers, southward along the seventy-third meridian to Camana on the coast. He also constructed a topographical sketch map of the lower Urubamba Valley from Rosalina to Pongo de Mainique, a distance of about a hundred miles. The limits of past glaciation and of perpetual snow, cycles of topographic development, geological evidences of past climatic change, the history of the great coastal terraces—all were matters that commanded his attention. Harry W. Foote collected approximately three thousand specimens of insects and nonflowering plants and some hundreds of land shells. Hiram Bingham managed administrative details and discovered a number of Inca and pre-Inca cities, most notably Machu Picchu. Bingham's first communication to the outside world concerning this discovery may well have been the letter he sent to J. Scott Keltie, secretary of the Royal Geographical Society:

> Three days journey from Ollant-ay-tambo, not far from the left bank of the Urubamba River on an almost inaccessible ridge flanked by magnificent precipices I found the ruins of a wonderful Inca city. . . . I believe it to have been the ancient city of Pitcos (or Vitcos) or Pitchu. . . . It is so difficult of access that no one hereabouts has seen it. So far as I can discover only three Peruvians have seen it (except a few Indians).[20]

Near Cuzco Bingham found human bones under seventy-five feet of gravel. Bowman helped with the excavation and made geologic investigation. He concluded that:

> the gravel beds belong to the Pleistocene series and that the bones were deposited during a period of pronounced alluviation . . . while compelled to refer the gravel beds of this locality to the Pleistocene series I have yet to determine their place in that

series. When this is done the antiquity of the vertebrate remains may be more safely approximated than now. A provisional estimate would hardly be less than 10,000 years....[21]

Bowman urged caution on the matter of dating these remains in an article entitled "Yale's Results as to Early Man in South America,"[22] and offered further detail in another article.[23]

The members of the Expedition endured some harsh circumstances. Bowman's canoe was overturned and nearly lost on the Urubamba and he broke a bone in his right foot. One of the hired Indians was drowned while crossing that river, and two more hired Indians were accidentally shot. Bowman and topographer Kai Hendriksen suffered mountain sickness at heights of nineteen thousand feet and were obliged to camp at 4° below zero (Fahrenheit). Six months away from home and family—Bowman and his wife then had two very young sons—added to the loneliness of the work.

From this Expedition came several published articles by Bowman including: "A Buried Wall at Cuzco and its Relation to the Question of a Pre-Inca Race";[24] "The Canon of the Urubamba";[25] "The Geologic Relations of the Cuzco Remains";[26] "The Valley People of Eastern Bolivia";[27] and "Asymmetrical Crest Lines and Abnormal Valley Profiles in the Central Andes."[28] Much of his South American research had been presented in papers delivered before the Association of American Geographers. In 1911, however, he summarized his field work of that year in "The Geographical Results of the Yale Peruvian Expedition,"[29] and in the following year he contributed to physical geography his "Nivation in the Central Andes and a New Hypothesis of Cirque Development."[30] In 1916 *The Andes of Southern Peru* was published, revealing in detail Bowman's work on his two South American expeditions.

Bowman began to plan a third expedition to South America for 1913. Hiram Bingham was also planning another expedition and invited Bowman to join him, but Bowman was intent on pursuing a stricter variety of geographical and geomorphological field work than Bingham's proposed archeological sortie would permit. And he had come to feel that perhaps Bingham was just a little eager to claim credit for the work of others. However, it was not until Bowman had secured funds from the American Geographical Society that his expedition was assured. The Council of the American Geographical Society voted him

$4,000, one of the largest sums it appropriated for a single expedition in the first half of the twentieth century. The official title of the mission was "Expedition to the Central Andes under the auspices of the American Geographical Society."[31] Yale University continued his salary for six months, which was the anticipated duration of the expediton.

On 3 April 1913, Bowman left New York for Southampton. Before taking ship for Buenos Aires he travelled to Oxford where he probably talked with "Professor Herbertson and his assistants," then spent time in the rooms of the Royal Geographical Society examining maps and books "as bear on my problems." On 8 April he sailed for Buenos Aires, from where "I expect to conduct a little geographical expedition to Northwestern Argentina, and adjacent portions of the mountain and desert country of Chile and Bolivia."[32] An unsigned article in the *Bulletin of the American Geographical Society* commented:

> The expedition to the Central Andes will enable Professor Bowman to complete certain lines of investigation upon which he has been engaged since 1907.... The subjects of study in the projected field work are pimarily the anthropogeography of the region and its relation to the physiography. The investigation of topography drainage and climate will thus go hand in hand with the distribution and customs of the people....[33]

Bowman's essential purpose on this third expedition was to traverse again what he had termed "the Central Andes," with a view to writing at least one book on the ontographic response to the physical environment. His enthusiasm for the region was revealed in a report he wrote: "In the field of human geography the Central Andes form one of the most important groups of natural regions in the world. It is impossible to find elsewhere in South America an area of equal size with so great a variety of life."[34]

Bowman outfitted for this field trip in South America, at the nitrate plant of Central Lagunas east of Iquique in Chile. He and his companions travelled east across dry baked mud flats of the piedmont to Pica and Tambillo, through the desert margin with its enchanting oases, and then began the ascent into the Andes. They crossed the mountains with a stop at the Huasco Basin, encountered a severe snow storm, and reached the Puna de Atacama in the full severity of winter.

The cold wind dried and cracked facial skin and created excessive thirst. Altitude sickness gripped the party. This harsh experience continued many weeks. All the while Bowman was absorbing an enriching field experience, making notes at every stopping place, sketching the trails they travelled, noting settlements, and human practices. The whole was to be presented in *Desert Trails of Atacama*[35] and, earlier, in the "First Report of Professor Bowman's Expedition,"[36] and "Results of an Expedition to the Central Andes—Under the Auspices of the American Geographical Society."[37] The 1913 trip, however, had numerous consequences for Bowman and his career beyond the matter of publication. The efficiency with which he had conducted the expedition and the immediacy of result led to his becoming director of the Society in 1915. And the "One to One Million Map of Hispanic America" was also a product of this journey. As Bowman wrote:

> The Millionth Map of Hispanic America had its remoter origin in a personal experience of 1913 when for the third time I was preparing to go to South America.... A base map for field notations was required and though I searched the files of the principal collection in this country I could find no map suited to the purpose. It was necessary to construct one and a quick compilation was made to do ... it seemed to me that a base map for all of Hispanic America was a first desideratum if we were to do serious geographic work in that vast territory in the years ahead. Two short years after my expedition of 1913 I became Director of the American Geographical Society and found in its Council and members a spirit of enterprise that helped generate a feeling of happy accord with respect to future plans. The first world war interrupted these plans, but directly thereafter it was possible to launch a program of research in Hispanic America of which the Millionth Map played an important part.[38]

The 1913 trip confirmed Bowman's belief in the concept of region and his interest in pioneer settlement, and it helped to clarify his thought on the man-land relationship, all of which was to reveal itself quite clearly in his professional career. Participation in these three expeditions had equipped him as one of the most knowledgeable of geographers concerning South America. The knowledge had been won at the price of "ten thousand miles by muleback through the Central Andes. A year and a half all told. Three expeditions. Camp at temperature 4 degrees F. below zero. Fun? Don't you believe it. Leave your wife and kids for a month and it's hell. What do you suppose it is like for a half-year at a time?"[39] Three books resulted from his South America days: *South America: A Geography Reader* (1915); *The Andes of Southern Peru* (1916); and *Desert Trails of Atacama* (1924).*The Andes* was translated into Spanish by Carlos Nicholson in 1937 (a thousand copies were sold at reduced price, half to the Peruvian government and half for student use).[40] *Desert Trails of Atacama* was translated into Spanish in 1942 by Emilia Romero, in collaboration with the Executive of the President-Coordinator of Inter-American Affairs.[41]

Much more significant for the development of Bowman's career was *The Andes of Southern Peru*, which was immediately recognized as a notable addition to the literature. Bowman invented four Peruvians who told the story of their immediate physical environment in striking manner, defining the four regional divisions of the country: forested lowland, eastern valley, high plateau, and coastal oasis. Such treatment splendidly exemplified the way in which regional geography could be wrought. Bowman adopted the regional diagram revealing land type and land use, "constructed on the principle of dominant control. Each brings out the factors of greatest importance in the distribution of the people in a given region."[42] The book also made important contributions to the origin of coastal terraces, dune formation, the bergschrund hypothesis, and the climatology of Peru. Most important, however, was the topographic map of the seventy-third meridian.

The book was received with acclaim. G. B. Roorbach wrote in the *Annals of the American Academy of Political and Social Science:* "The originality of thought and content, the brilliancy of style, the many original maps and diagrams, the wonderfully beautiful half-tone illustrations, all combine to make this work a noteworthy contribution to geographic science...."[43]

The *Nation* commented that the Andes were "never so well described as in this book."[44]There were reviews in the *New York Times* [45] and *Boston Transcript.* [46] Distinctly unusual was the lengthy evaluation Theodore Roosevelt — explorer, historian, and former president of the United States — published in *The Geographical Review:*

> This is a really notable book; one of those uncommon books in which a man who has had the vision to undertake adventure and the hardihood to carry it through sets forth with wisdom what he has seen. Such a combination is rare. . . . The book is of high value from the scientific standpoint — and possesses the additional merit, not always found in scientific books, of being exceedingly interesting even to the layman.[47]

Roosevelt's review contrasted dramatically with the critical opinions of J. W. Evans, appearing in *The Geographical Journal.* [48] Bowman was perturbed by the unfair nature of Evans's statement and corresponded with confidants on the subject. Four months later, in the next issue of *The Geographical Journal*, there was a rejoinder by Mark Jefferson, himself a student of Latin America.[49] Jefferson took exception to Evans's review. With his caustic, incisive style, he had little trouble dispatching Evans's criticism. After all, Evans's opening sentence, "The present volume presents a compendium of the results obtained by the expedition sent out in 1911 by Yale University to Peru," was quite incorrect. Bowman's responsibility was a geographical reconnaissance along the seventy-third meridian. The other tasks of the expedition were neither Bowman's responsiblity nor fundamentally geographic, and it did not seem appropriate for Evans to opine that Bowman used the wrong sort of canoe for river descents. The editor of the *Journal* offered placation with an editor's note, but battle lines had been drawn.[50] The directors of the American Geographical Society and the Royal Geographical Society did not have a happy relationship for twenty-five years, and when at last Arthur Hinks and Bowman took a meal together in London during the Second World War, Bowman supposed that many an opportunity had by then been lost. The other consequence of this published exchange was that *The Andes of Southern Peru* became well read. It was largely from this book that, at the request of Jean Brunhes, Bowman culled "Types of Islands of the High Moutains: The Central Andes," chapter seven of the English translation of Brunhes's *Human Geography* (1920).[51] This chapter was then substituted for a chapter entitled "Le Val d'Anniviers" which had been published in the first edition of the book in 1910.

In the 1960 edition of *Physical Geography* A. N. Strahler mentions Bowman's thought on the influence of highland climate on landscape and life.[52] And even in 1966 on the fiftieth birthday of the book, a publication of the Association of American Geographers describes *The Andes* as "One of the finest regional treatments, based on a cross-section of the Andes along the seventy-third meridian carried out in the field. Original use of the 'regional diagram' as a method of geographic description."[53]

The third of Bowman's three books concerning South America, *Desert Trails of Atacama*, was not published until 1924. Bowman's directorship of the Society and war work had interrupted him. In fact, he wrote and published *The New World* before writing the *Desert Trails*. Bowman wrote to George G. Chisholm of his manuscript in 1922:

> You may be interested to hear that I have begun a book to be called *Desert Trails of Atacama*, which will be a field study in border settlements of the desert based upon the experiences of three expeditions in South America but more particularly that of 1913. My coming here and the War and Peace Conference have conspired to delay the completion of this work, to which I have just turned with great interest and enthusiasm. It will serve as a handbook to the Copiapo-Atacama sheet . . . and it will deal with the Desert of Atacama on the one hand and the Puna de Atacama on the other. There is an immense variation of life and of physical circumstance here and the region deserves modern treatment for that reason.[54]

In the preface to the book Bowman said:

> I have attempted herein to describe and interpret a region traversed on three field expeditions, which has more strongly attracted me than any other part of South America. . . . The narrative is brief, personal experiences being introduced, as a rule, only when they serve to complete the geographical picture. Near the southern end of the desert are the towns of Copiapo and Vallenar, and the longest chapter is devoted to their fascinating life and especially its pioneer character. Of equal interest to the geographer is the girdle of settled country that runs about the high and cold Puna de Atacama. I have not limited the story to

the desert country alone but have included a brief account of the
Chaco or grasslands of northeastern Argentina and adjacent
Bolivia, because the currents of business flow naturally from
these border settlements across the Atacama country and deeply
affect its life.[55]

The book was recognized at once as an authoritative source on this
part of South America. It became required reading in many South
America geography courses in the United States, and was read quite
widely by historians. It was released as Special Publication Number
Five of the American Geographical Society, and for that reason
Bowman discouraged extended review in the Society's own journal,
The Geographical Review. He considered that such attention might be
considered immodest, even improper. Consequently the *Review*
published only a brief objective description of *Desert Trails*, with a note
relating the book to the Society's forthcoming Millionth Map of
Hispanic America.[56]

The book was largely ignored by Hinks of *The Geographical Journal,*
who widened the existing schism between the directors of the two most
significant geographical societies in the English-speaking world. Albert
Demangeon published a thoughtful and appreciative article on *Desert
Trails* in the *Annales de Géographie.*[57] An anonymous review was
published in *The Geographical Teacher,* summarizing the work and
concluding that "the whole arrangement of the book is of a high
order."[58] More notable was the absence of reviews in the professional
literature. Not even the *Book Review Digest* referred to Bowman's
book, and yet it was unquestionably a work of considerable
geographical significance. Gladys Wrigley, who edited the book, wrote,
"It was a keen disappointment to Isaiah Bowman that the Society did
not reprint *Desert Trails* long ago. I think that this book and the
Mohammedan World article were dearest to his heart."[59]

The lack of professional reviews of this book was due to Bowman's
insistence that copies not be sent to magazine and periodical editors.
He had come to distrust those with the review mentality and he did not
want to see quick and hasty appraisal of his book which had been so
much a labor of love. In the last months of his life Bowman was
approached by the Duell, Sloan and Pearce Publishing Company
concerning the possibility of their publishing a new edition of *Desert
Trails.* He approved the idea and suggested that he rewrite the first

chapter, saying that "the old one may have been good in its time but it sounds today a little bit prosy." He wanted to reproduce the oasis of Matilla in color, adopt some of the prose and photographs of Light's "Atacama Revisited," and "make improvements in the English of it. These are already made in a copy from which the printer could work."[60] Bowman's death in 1950 ended this project. In the obituary Gladys Wrigley composed for *The Geographical Review,* she wrote of *Desert Trails of Atacama:*

> This book, best of all his writings perhaps, reveals the passionate devotion of the geographer ... the desert seems to inspire devotion in a unique way — witness the travel literature on Arabia. We glimpse his delight in the picture of the oasis of Matilla: 'The first and last impression of the desert towns is enduringly pleasant.... In the twilight of morning and evening the strong contrast of yellow plain and deep green foliage is most marked and lends to the view an indescribable charm.' To Professor Jefferson, who insisted on human dominance in geography ... he replied: 'I love the desert and everything about it. The desert doesn't have to teach me a lesson or stand for a great principle ... I just like it in every one of its moods.'[61]

In October 1937 Mary and Richard Light "detoured eastward across the blistering nitrate desert to the oases at the foot of the gorge-creased western slopes of the Andes. Our intent was to follow by air two routes taken on the ground earlier by Isaiah Bowman."[62] Richard Light had been fascinated by Bowman's *Desert Trails* and had determined to make a study in aerial photography while traversing the routes which Bowman himself had taken in 1913 and which were described in his book. That had required flights from three widely separated bases, and even then the hundred-mile reach of the Puna remained uncrossed. Light had appreciated the intricate analysis rendered by Bowman: "No better illustration of the irrevocable union of person and region can be found than that offered in Dr. Bowman's monumental analysis of Atacama."[63] Some years after Bowman's death William E. Rudolph published *Vanishing Trails of Atacama* (1963).[64] Rudolph had lived in the region as an engineer since 1922, and had been fascinated by Bowman's book. Bowman had persuaded Rudolph to join the American Geographical Society, then to contribute nine articles to *The*

Geographical Review between 1927 and 1951. Rudolph came to know the Atacama and its desert trails firsthand over a period of forty years, and to recognize that Bowman's horse, mule, llama, and caravan trails, footpaths and cart ruts were being superseded by other trails. Rudolph's book served as remembrance to Bowman's early work. But by this time *Desert Trails of Atacama* had become a collector's item, although three printings of the book had totalled ten thousand copies.[65]

The geomorphological significance of Bowman's South American researches is considerable.[66] Bowman's meteorology, although presented in an interesting fashion, hardly went beyond data already published by Peruvian, American, and German meteorologists. However, geographers came to appreciate his correlation of the physical environment with the human settlement, and later authors have frequently cited *The Andes of Southern Peru* for the portrayal of influence of highland climate on landscape and life.

Bowman's findings on high Andean physiography constitute a much more substantial contribution to geomorphology. At least three aspects of his work are worthy of special attention: his analysis of the complex nature of the Andean Cordillera, his study of glaciation within the Tropics, and his theory of the processes involved in the formation of cirques.

The detailed investigation of the complex nature of the Andes and of its geologically recent uplift, associated with much volcanism, was of considerable value. It formed the basis for the physiography in Alan G. Ogilvie's *Geography of the Central Andes* (New York: 1922) for which Bowman wrote an introduction and supplied field notes, maps, unpublished personal information, and nearly all the photographs. Even the title was the same as Bowman's doctoral disseration of 1909. *The Andes* was also given as a reference to complex mountains in A. K. Lobeck's *Geomorphology* (1939)[67] and would probably have been cited more frequently in the literature had not Old World authors been more concerned with the great wealth of detail available on the Alpine mountain system in Eurasia.

The remaining two thrusts of Bowman's research, glaciation within the Tropics and processes shaping cirques, attacted worldwide and lasting attention. Bowman demonstrated that the existing glaciers had undergone a large advance followed by a succession of periodic retreats, each of which deposited at its snout a terminal moraine that marked a distinct halt stage in its retreat. Such a succession of periodic halts in the glacial retreat could, Bowman averred, be explained only by climatic change and not, as rival theorists affirmed, by a steady lowering of the whole mountain summit by erosion.

The problem of the processes shaping cirques was dealt with at great length in the chapter of *The Andes of Southern Peru* entitled "Glacial Features." This discussion opened with an analysis of the height of the snow line and of its slope from the horizontal according to exposure to insolation and precipitation. Bowman then wrote on the process of nivation or snow erosion. His fieldwork led him to affirm unequivocally that on strong and topographically varied slopes where the snow is concentrated in headwater alcoves, there is enough downhill movement of snow masses to have discernible effects both of erosion beneath the snow and of sediment accumulation at its lower borders. With this claim Bowman repudiated the work of Matthes, who asserted that the snow masses remain stationary.[68]

Bowman was investigating the problem of nivation from a most advantageous viewpoint, as highlands with snow masses in the Tropics experience smaller seasonal changes and far more freeze-thaw oscillations than anywhere else on earth. His fieldwork convinced him that snow masses do erode or degrade, in spite of the absence of real abrasion which would cause glacial striae on boulders. The very distinctive qualities of nivated surfaces, together with the general absence of all but a thin coating of waste even in rock hollow, and the accumulation of waste up to boulders in size at the lower edge of the nivated zone, indicated to him that "compacted snow or névé of sufficient thickness and gradient may actually pluck rock outcrops in the same manner though not at the rate which ice exhibits."[69] Bowman compiled a graph of snow motion, in which snow thickness is related to slope gradient. He urged that it might be necessary to modify the graph for each individual case of application depending upon prevailing climate.

Bowman's final contribution to high Andean physiography concerned bergschrunds and cirques. He was skeptical of Willard D. Johnson's hypothesis, which dominated discussion of the problem: "as the final solution of the cirque problem it has several weaknesses in its present form."[70] Bowman knew Johnson personally, and discussed the subject with him at meetings of the Association of American Geographers. Bowman's hypothesis was a direct corollary of his theme of downward movement of snow masses with increase in depth and steepness of slope. Briefly summarized it states that the greatest depth of snow and névé in a pre-glacial river valley occurs at or near the spot which marks the center of the incipient cirque. Through self-stimulation of increase of snow, downward pressure, and névé motion, the floor of the cirque is flattened and the flattening proceeds until sufficient to offset through escaping uphill ice-flow the augmented forces of erosion. A bergschrund is not essential at any stage of the process though the process is hastened wherever bergschrunds exist. The remainder of Bowman's notions on the cirque met with widespread approval. Robert P. Beckinsale astutely observed . . .

> the appeal of the expositions on snow movement and cirque formation has tended to distract attention from the percipience of some of the other geomorphic or physiographic observations in *The Andes of Southern Peru.* For example, Bowman's account of the Vilcapampa batholith (granitic intrusion) and its topographic effects is masterly.... Yet the valuable observations that followed on the influence of rocks on surface relief attracted little attention presumably because geologists in their writings preferred to describe terrains and countries better known to them and their readers.[71]

Bowman's South America researches and writing were remembered in the work of others, and in honorifics bestowed by geographical societies. He was pleased that later workers had reexamined his thesis of Central Andean topographic evolution. Carl Troll followed the essentials of Bowman's thought in "Von Titikakasse zum Pooposee und zum Salar von Coipasa." G. Steinmann acknowledged Bowman's contribution in "Geologie von Peru," as did H. P. Moon in "The Geology and Physiography of the Altiplano of Peru and Bolivia." Otto A. Welter and J. V. Harrison accepted the principles and concepts of Bowman's early physiographic interpretation of the Andes in, respectively, *Bulletin of the Geological Society of Peru* and "The Geology of the Central Andes in Part of the Province of Junin, Peru." Norman D. Newell also added to the work of Bowman in a monograph on the geology of the Lake Titicaca Region.[72] W. Vaughan Lewis of Cambridge University investigated and approved Bowman's thought on cirque formation in South America from his own glaciological researches in

Europe. Lewis investigated snow patch hollows and cirque formation in high latitudes and corresponded with Bowman on the subject in the 1930s. Newell, J. Chronic and T. G. Roberts wrote in 1953, "To Bowman (1916) we are especially indebted for calling attention to the great sections of upper Paleozoic rocks in south-central Peru."[73] And in 1956 W. F. Jenks observed that Bowman had noted "the absence of granite boulders in basal conglomerate of Carboniferous or Permian age in the Apurimac Valley" and "faulting at the east front of the Andes."[74]

Bowman's findings still occupy a place in standard geomorphology texts throughout the world. *The Andes of Southern Peru* was added as a reference in the famous *Traité de Geographie Physique* by Emmanuel de Martonne (Paris: 1927). Bowman's ideas on cirque formation are described in the well-known standard text, *Principles of Geomorphology* by William D. Thornbury (New York: 1954) and also in the most recent detailed account of ice work by British geomorphologists, namely *Glacial and Periglacial Geomorphology* by Clifford Embleton and Cuchlaine A. M. King (New York: 1968). And in 1974 H. F. Garner cited Bowman's work frequently and weighed it in the contemporary geomorphological balance in *The Origin of Landscapes: A Synthesis of Geomorphology* (New York: 1974).

Bowman's interest in South America never abated. The Hispanic America research program of the American Geographical Society, a chapter called "Possibilities of Settlement in South America" in *Limits of Land Settlement*,[75] another titled "Population Outlets in Overseas Territories" in *Geographic Aspects of International Relations*,[76] "Discovering South America,"[77] a foreword to Carlos Monge's *Acclimatization in the Andes*,[78] and "Fisiografia Peruana"[79] are only some of the visible indices of a life and career nurtured on memories of Andean country. Bowman wrote in 1946:

> I am again looking at the beloved Puna de Atacama. I wonder if another person can quite understand the thrill I feel as I follow each ridge crest and slope and stream to be sure that I have not overlooked anything. These photographs remind me of the intensity of my feelings as I approached this great highland country from the east for the first time and wondered what I should find in it.[80]

Chapter Four

Director of the
American Geographical Society

Early in 1913 Bowman had sought financial support from the American Geographical Society for the third of his trips to South America, and more particularly to explore the Central Andes. The Council of the Society met on 20 February 1913 and established a special committee' of wealthy New York gentlemen to consider financial assistance. Messrs. Ford, Greenough, Huntington, James, Tuckerman, and Kahn liked Bowman's proposal so much that they granted him $4,000, more than he had requested. Bowman wrote of this occasion:

> Later I learned that at the close of the meeting Mr. Huntington said to Mr. Greenough, "I wonder if this isn't the man that we have been looking for some time as director of the A.G.S.? Keep your eye on him." Mr. Greenough told me this story later and I presume it can be put down as authentic.[1]

On 8 December 1914 the Council of the Society entered into a general understanding with Bowman that he should become librarian and director of the Society on 1 July 1915, at an annual salary of $7,000. Bowman was already secretary of the Association of American

55

Geographers; thus he had come to hold a position of dominion unique in the history of American geography. Bowman thought the title "director" was suitable; but Mr. Chandler Robbins insisted "on tacking on two words 'and librarian.' He insisted on this because he said that the Society was so small that a director would have nothing to do."[2] Initially Bowman's contract was for a five year period, and he was assured of $1,000 per year for an assistant, and $2,000 per year for publications.

> I did not know at the time that I was touching one of the mainsprings of action in Mr. Huntington when I stipulated as one of the conditions of my coming an annual appropriation of $2,000 for monographs. They asked me what monographs I wanted to publish and I told them they would have to wait and see. I suggested as a beginning Bowman's "Andes of Southern Peru" which had just been finished in manuscript. Dominian's book was also approaching completion.[3]

Bowman at once sought an assistant. After consulting with the Council he offered Gladys M. Wrigley, then a graduate student of geography at Yale, the position of research assistant.[4] It was a happy day for the Society when she accepted.

Bowman completed his responsibilities at Yale and acquired a house at 46 Lewis Parkway, Yonkers. The building at Broadway and 156th Street in New York where he had his new office was only four years old, and was described by J. K. Wright as follows:

> The building was then new and bright — not cluttered as it has since become. It had an air of spaciousness and dignity. Profound calm reigned in its uncrowded offices and halls. In cool and airy stacks some 47,000 fascinating volumes stood on the shelves, with ample room for twice as many more, and 36,000 equally fascinating maps did not nearly fill the handsome oak cases in the map room. No other geographer in the country had such material resources at his disposal or such an opportunity for increasing and improving them and making them "dynamic".[5]

Bowman envisioned a strong research program for the Society. He felt obliged to replace some of the existing staff with better qualified people, and by December 1916 had released six of the eleven male and eleven female employees. Later yet others of the original staff were to leave. Quick to recognize ability, Bowman chose workers carefully. In addition to Gladys Wrigley, his most notable new colleagues included Charles Krisch, Ena Yonge, John K. Wright, Elizabeth T. Platt, Alan G. Ogilvie, Raye R. Platt, Mabel H. Ward, Dorothea H. Hanatschek, Osborne M. Miller, Weld Arnold, Nordis A. Felland, and Charles B. Hitchcock. Throughout his twenty-year term of office Bowman retained the services of W. L. G. Joerg and the cartographer William A. Briesemeister, both of whom had joined the Society's staff prior to 1915.

> His relations with his staff were easy and informal, and he undoubtedly knew how to delegate responsibility. He left Wright to run the Library without interference and he left Joerg and Miss Wrigley the power of decision in all editorial matters, even to having Miss Wrigley edit his own MSS unmercifully. One day he complained to me that she had deleted another of his sunsets, but when he protested all she said was "Mr. Bowman, it isn't geography." She always called him Mr. Bowman.[6]

Bowman would often take lunch with Raye Platt, Wright, Ogilvie, Miller, and Marcel Aurousseau in those halcyon society years of the early twenties. He was never aloof, but very easy of manner, a man to whom staff members felt it easy to turn if the need arose. And if Bowman learned that any member of his staff was suffering a hardship he would bring the matter promptly to the attention of the patrons: twice indeed, even the custodian of the Society was so helped.

The intellectual strength of the personnel was the strength of the Society; capacity and will to conceive, nurture, and complete even the most formidable project made the Society a force to be reckoned with in geography. It is probable that Bowman created a staff whose academic talent was unequalled at that time by any university in the United States. He wrote to Emmanuel de Martonne:

> We . . . employ a sort of faculty which includes besides myself, Joerg, Wrigley, Wright, Miller and Platt. . . . Each one of these persons has a distinctive field of expertness. Together we constitute a balanced group able to take care of the work of the

institution in a manner comparable to that of a department of geography in a university. Freedom from all teaching . . . gives us time to attend to the routine work of the institution and at the same time do research work. The research work has two aspects, one which looks toward the production of scholarly books and maps and a scientific journal by the Society, and a second which looks towards outside agencies that find their work improved by the play of geographical thought upon their problems.[7]

And to Carl Shippee he wrote:

> We have a strong professional staff. . . . Six highly trained mature persons, besides technical assistants, constitute the strongest group of expert geographers in any one institution in the country, whether a society or a university.[8]

Recognition of a high order had already come to the Society by 1917, when it was encouraged to institute the Inquiry, a body of experts who assembled a vast quantity of data preparatory to the negotiation of peace at Paris (see chapter 5). The Society was about to enter its golden age. In 1920 Bowman relinquished the title of librarian to John K. Wright in order to concentrate his own effort on strengthening the Society's program. Both Wright and Bowman had been in Paris during the negotiations preceding the Treaty of Versailles (1919), and at that time Davis urged Bowman "to look up young Jack Wright."[9] In fact, it was there in Paris that Wright presented himself to Bowman in the Hotel Crillon. As an undergraduate at Harvard, Wright had studied physiography under Robert DeC. Ward, while his graduate studies, supervised by Charles H. Haskins of Harvard, constituted "a survey of medieval geography." Wright had gone to Paris to do research for his dissertation, but after Haskins had recommended him to Bowman as a suitable librarian for the Society he was so appointed. A dedicated bibliophile, Wright worked well with Bowman, who urged an acquisition program for the library as a first priority. Under Wright's librarianship large sums of money were invested in atlases, books, manuscripts, and brochures. By 1935 Bowman could write:

> Our library is the heart and center of the place. Scholarship on the part of the staff and the publications that are the product of

scholarship would be impossible without a first class library. Our building cost $330,000 and the land was given to us and there is no mortgage on either. But if we were asked to trade our library for the building and land we should have to inform the proposer that the value of our collections is probably three times that of the House in which they are stored.[10]

By the time Bowman left the Society in June 1935, the library was one of the finest of its kind in existence. And owing to the "Research Catalogue" compiled by Wright at the urging of Bowman in 1923, the previous system which Bowman characterized as a menace to research had been replaced by a system which permitted unlimited addition and widespread use.

William Morris Davis had not only helped direct Wright to the Society, but he constantly urged its publications on the attention of those who could appreciate them. Davis continually made suggestions to Bowman and provided him with encouragement. When Bowman informed Davis that the *Review* consumed much time at the Society, Davis replied, "I do not wonder that the Geographical Review takes a lot of work; it has made a strong place for itself; its career is clear."[11] And again, while Bowman was with the American Commission to Negotiate Peace in Paris, Davis wrote:

Let me say how greatly I rejoice in the development of your career. Only two days ago I was giving a sketch of your progress to a good friend . . . to whom I remarked that you hold the most important geographical position in America. . . . What I referred to was your position in the A.G.S. which under your direction is evidently destined to play a greater and greater part in our geographical future. I am figuring on your having 10,000 members in ten years or sooner; and with the income thus secure you will be doing great things.[12]

Davis's belief in Bowman's ability to manage the Society, and essentially the direction of American geography, was so firm that he resigned as chairman of the geography committee of the Geology and Geography Division of the National Research Council in order to pass the responsibility to Bowman.[13] History substantiates Davis's faith. On his return from Paris in 1919 Bowman assumed the position Davis had vacated, and by 1933 Bowman had been elected chairman of the National Research Council.

Of course no program of acquisition and development would have been possible without the support of a strong Council and the provision of funds. Of his days at the Society, Bowman wrote:

> There I was lucky enough to find sponsors for various research projects, and in the course of twenty years raised and spent about a million dollars. This was more free money than any other geographer in the world had at his disposal in that time. Naturally we were able to accomplish things that we think are of permanent value....[14]

As for the Council, Bowman found them a grand set of men, whom he admired and respected. Without their support, moral and financial, many accomplishments of the Society could never have been achieved. Bowman worked mostly with J. B. Ford and Roland Redmond, but it was for Archer M. Huntington that he developed an almost brotherly affection. As Bowman once put it:

> I have carefully refrained from asking Mr. Huntington for financial help.... He knows that help is needed, but he has always made his own choice of projects and degree of support. The point is rather a fine one and rests upon an intimacy of acquaintance that I cherish....[15]

The councillors and Bowman constituted a good team. The Council gave Bowman maximum freedom of decision. One of Bowman's earliest far-reaching changes was to revise in name and design the publication of the Society. He had come to perceive the *Bulletin* as a school-master's journal. He sought to convert it into a national scientific publication, and felt that achievement was not possible with the word *Bulletin* in the title. In conference mainly with Joerg and Wrigley, Bowman proposed the new title, *Geographical Review*. "One afternoon Mr. Huntington came in and I told him of our decision and that I wanted his help for a cover. He took a sheet of paper and drew the design in red pencil."[16] Thus the publication was reborn. Bowman wrote to those geographers whom he thought were representative of the emerging geography in North America, requesting their best contributions. To J. Russell Smith he wrote:

> What I have in mind in the way of an article for the Bulletin is that indefinite something that never was on land or sea! . . . A mixture of Tower's Argentina article in the Bulletin of the Philadelphia Geographical Society; Smith in Harpers; Huntington in the Yale Review; Albrecht in the February and April National Geographic. Don't let it be like anything else however — an article of real distinction — with punch, facts, charm of style, good photographs, all mixed in with Smith's ideas and Smith. It must be interesting but it must also be serious. Be one of my pioneers and push!
>
> Never mind our subscribers — liberate your imagination! We don't want them so much as new folks. We want to use your article for *exploitation*. On with the stylus! And let me have it for the October number — that gives you a month left in which to write it and you have nothing else to do anyhow, what?[17]

In an introductory note to the first issue which appeared in January 1916, Bowman described the purpose of the *Review* as "to broaden the range and deepen the intellectual interest of the articles, and to give its notes and reviews a more critical and scholarly quality."[18] The history of the *Review* indicates the wisdom of this dramatic departure from the *Bulletin*.

W. L. G. Joerg retained editorial responsibility for the *Review* until 1920, when Gladys Wrigley assumed that task. Joerg had been meticulous in his work. Wrigley was just as meticulous, but the play of her pencil was swifter. She developed a fine editorial touch, sensing what could be saved by rigorous editorial revision, and what was beyond the pale. And she began to plan numbers of the *Review*, occasionally grouping articles in meaningful sets, and occasionally requesting articles from authors whom she thought exceptionally able. Bowman would frequently give her advice on this latter point. Under her editorial regime (1920-49), the *Geographical Review* offered a remarkable example of scholarship to the geographical world. She always gave the first copy of the *Review* to Bowman. Snatches of her fine but little seen service are revealed only in "Adventures in Serendipity: Thirty Years of the *Geographical Review*."[19]

One year after the *Geographical Review* began its career, Bowman wrote, "in 1916 chiefly as a result of our unusual map illustrations, over twenty-one articles from the *Geographical Review* have been reprinted in other magazines."[20] The *Review* reached an all-time maximum of published pages in 1918, 1,040 pages exclusive of the indexes. In that year the Reverend Arthur A. Brooks compiled an *Index to the Bulletin of the American Geographical Society, 1852–1915,* which greatly facilitated use of the *Bulletin.* Bowman constantly sought articles from accomplished authors, occasionally sending two or three letters to the same person urging an article or monograph. It did not matter to Bowman whether the person was a geographer or not. Rather than method or technique, he sought large ideas, couched in non-technical language. He took great pride in capturing articles containing fresh thought and significant results of excursions and expeditions recently completed. But he, and the *Review* staff, always sought improvement. "As soon as the last number is out we gather around it like so many vultures and find more fault with it than all the other critics put together and we propose to maintain this attitude of humility and criticism."[21]

Notwithstanding the interruption caused by the tasks of the Inquiry and Bowman's absence at the Paris Peace Conference, the *Review* never failed to appear punctually. Already geographers in the English-speaking world, France, and Germany were reading the *Review* with newfound appreciation. While engaged in the work of the American Commission to Negotiate Peace at Paris, a delighted Bowman wrote to John Greenough, president of the Society:

> You will be gratified to know that the Department of Public Instruction of France has asked M. Emmanuel de Margerie . . . to supply a complete history of the American Geographical Society in order that the Department may print its report in the form of a special bulletin and distribute it to all the colleges, universities, normal schools, and higher grades of schools in France. . . . It would be difficult to exaggerate the degree of enthusiasm which Frenchmen have for the *Geographical Review.* Not only M. de Margerie but other professors in the Sorbonne have told me again and again that they regard it as far and away the best scientific

geographical magazine in the world.... Similar testimony has come from British geographers, and I think that in the face of it we may well be pleased with the progress we have made, though I should by no means say that we should be satisfied with it. Constant evolutionary progress must be made in order that we may push ahead farther still and gain added respect for scholarly permanent work.[22]

In January 1921 the *Review* became a quarterly periodical instead of a monthly. The change was made to relieve the editorial staff, reduce costs, and encourage a superior publication. However, when Bowman commented that the quarterly format was universally approved, swift rebuke came from Willam Morris Davis and from Mark Jefferson, who exclaimed, "I'll be bound you never thought of the reader's problem in your resolve to hand him three months in one."[23] Bowman wrote scores of letters to potential authors of many nationalities, and when he needed a map or article he would not hesitate to offer a special fee. In 1918, for instance, Bowman paid Jovan Cvijic $100 for "The Geographic Distribution of the Balkan Peoples" (with map), $125 for "Zones of Civilization" (with map), and $250 for a 1:1,000,000 ethnographic map.[24] Cvijic's work was needed by members of the Inquiry, and naturally was of interest to readers of war-related articles. Of Bowman's relationship with foreign geographers, Davis astutely observed, "The Western Excursion did well to lay the foundation of acquaintance that will now bear fruit."[25]

Perhaps the best-seller of the *Review* was an article that Bowman had prompted his brother-in-law, J. Walter Goldthwait, to write concerning his researches on the town of Lyme, New Hampshire, "A Town That Has Gone Downhill" *(The Geographical Review* 17 [1927]:527–52). J. K. Wright wrote that this essay "came to be regarded as a classic in its field."[26] And the *Review* could claim numerous firsts: the first world map of types of tides;[27] H. H. Bennett's first soils map of Cuba[28] and later his quantitative study of erosion technique (one of the first maps in measured analysis);[29] and Thornthwaite's climatic classification (1931)[30] with later revision.[31]

The *Review* was heavily used by academic geographers in the classroom. Occasionally, articles were entered on required reading lists, or sometimes a series of *Review* reprints would serve as a text for the course, as was the case in some years with Mark Jefferson's "Urban

Geography." Faculty members frequently had lantern slides made of maps or illustrations published in the *Review,* which were then used in the classroom. In January 1935 Bowman surveyed numerous professors of geography throughout the United States, who confirmed extensive classroom use of the *Review.*[32]

In addition to the *Geographical Review* Bowman initiated a Special Publications Series. During his administration (1915–35), fifty-two works appeared. It would be extremely difficult to overestimate the significance of these books in the development of geographical thinking in the English-speaking world. At least one volume a year was distributed free to Society members. The first volume published in this series was Bowman's *The Andes of Southern Peru* (1916). This was followed one year later by Leon Dominian's *The Frontiers of Language and Nationality in Europe.* Other significant titles included: *Battlefields of the World War* (1921) by D. W. Johnson; *Bering's Voyages* (vol. 1, 1922 and vol. 2, 1925) by F. A. Golder; *The Land Systems of Mexico* (1923) by G. M. McBride; *Aids to Geographical Research* (1923) by J. K. Wright; *Desert Trails of Atacama* (1924) by I. Bowman; *The Lesser Antilles* (1926) by W. M. Davis, *Peopling the Argentine Pampa* (1926) by Mark Jefferson; *The Coral Reef Problem* (1928) by W. M. Davis; *Richard Hakluyt & the English Voyages* (1928) by G. B. Parks; and *The Pioneer Fringe* (1931) by I. Bowman. Additionally J. K. Wright helped translate and edit six volumes on Arabian exploration by Alois Musil (1926–28), and R. R. Platt completed a remarkable four-volume *Catalogue of Maps of Hispanic America* (1930–33). This series is a swath of literary and substantive excellence in the discipline. The monographs published during these years constituted approximately three-fourths as much reading matter as was contained in the *Review.* Though none of these works was "popular,"all were the product of original scholarship. To secure a manuscript or a *Review* article Bowman might provide a desk, secretary, and library staff for authors such as Antevs, Jefferson, Stefansson and Teggart.

Simultaneously under Bowman's direction appeared some fine cartographic productions, most notably: *Map of Hispanic America on the Scale of 1:1,000,000* (in 107 sheets) (1922–45); *The Leardo Map of the World,* a reproduction of a medieval map (1928); *Physical Map of the Arctic 1:20,000,000* (1930); *Bathymetric Map of the Antarctic*

1:20,000,000 (1930); and a joint publication with the Carnegie Institution of Washington, C. O. Paullin's *Atlas of the Historical Geography of the United States* (1932). All of these publications cost a great deal of money. If the councillors balked at cost, Bowman would comment, "The recollection of quality is remembered long after the price is forgotten."

During the twenty years while Bowman was director he wrote six books: *The Andes of Southern Peru* (1916), *The New World* (1921, 1924, 1928, and *The New World Supplement*, 1923 and 1924), *Desert Trails of Atacama* (1924), *International Relations* (1930), *The Pioneer Fringe* (1931), and *Geography in Relation to the Social Sciences* (1934). He also wrote seventy-seven articles and notes, three introductions to books, three memorials, and sixteen book reviews. This in itself was a remarkable scholarly achievement, one which very few geographers anywhere would equal. He wrote on a large variety of subjects, revealing an extraordinary diversity of learning and interest. And his literary style was good. He worked indefatigably at the business of putting the right word in the right place, whether in writing a book or a letter, refusing to allow unfinished prose to leave his office. His vocabularly was extensive, and his reading was wide, including political history and poetry. He wrote much verse himself and produced an elegant prose whose cadence, rhythm and organization was frequently mentioned in reviews.

Bowman reckoned that he had more time at the Society to plan and undertake research than he did while on the faculty of Yale University. He was freed of classroom lectures and their preparation, grading, and university committee work. At the Society, once he had instituted a large and meaningful program, work went forward efficiently and little time was lost. Visitors who came to gawk were pleasantly but swiftly ushered out, and those who came on important business shared lettuce leaf sandwiches for lunch.

Although Robert Cushman Murphy has observed that Bowman "was of course very nearly a genius,"[33] the business of writing prose did not come naturally or even easily to him. He worked at the task. Frequently he would stay in his office late into the evening, writing or seeking an appropriate reference in the library stacks. He could become quite incensed at the suggestion that he exploited Society staff in the preparation of his own publications. He wrote to Richard Hartshorne:

> Hobbs once said to me that it was easy for me to write because I had a staff to help me prepare portions of the text. I circulated his statement amongst the staff of the American Geographical Society for their amusement. . . . Within the past few months I have had friends of mine actually ask me whether I employ a writer to help me with my addresses and they invariably say, "It is impossible for one man to write on so many different themes in so short a time in view of the other demands upon his strength." This statement is called forth by a little book of addresses entitled "A Design for Scholarship." I make no claims for excellence in my published material and I regret that it has to be done under pressure and in short intervals of time but, whatever its worth, I have written it if my name is on it.[34]

Perhaps some of his best writing was accomplished in the Wrens Nest, a small cottage which gave him privacy, and later in a shack which he built on Turtle Island, Lake Wentworth, New Hampshire. He had purchased the Island as a family retreat in 1915 on knowing of his increased salary as director of the Society. Each year he returned to it, enjoying family life and relief from the stifling heat of New York City. He shut himself off from administrative intrusions, reduced the discomfort he might otherwise suffer from hay fever, and appreciated the splashing of the bass and the call of the loon. When writing *Desert Trails of Atacama,* he wrote Davis he had "fixed up a shack with good light and every office facility — shelves, tables and the like — and am working here very comfortably, with enough play and diversion to keep me in good health. I think I must spend more time up here. . . ."[35] But he allowed himself only brief stays on the Island, before returning to the Society. There he would seek the references, statistics, and quotations not available to him in New Hampshire. Most frequently he would scribble his articles wherever he happened to be, at the Society, on the way home, or at home. If thoughts and material for an article had been in his mind for some time he would dictate it to his secretary, Mabel H. Ward.

He seemed to think best while pacing the floor, interrupting his perambulations to think while gazing out of the window onto upper Broadway. He dictated the article on "The Mohammedan World," printed first in *The Geographical Review* and later in the fourth edition of his *The New World*, in a couple of hours in a single session.[36]

On occasion he would deliberately seek thoughts and ideas from members of his staff. Aurousseau wrote:

During the afternoons Platt and I worked in a kind of gallery just outside the door of Bowman's office. Sometimes, when he wanted to clear his mind he would poke his head out and call us in, with such invitations as "Come in here, you two artists with words." None of us went long without a pat on the back with him, and Platt, as a matter fact, had literary aspirations. At one of these impulsive little meetings he asked what I thought of his new book, *The New World*. I said that I thought it to be an exhaustive account of the geographical changes brought about by the war of 1914-1918, in the Old World, but that there was nothing about the New World in it. He promptly set to work and produced a supplement, not so much on the Americas as on the United States.[37]

Bowman also liked to share his visitors with the other members of the staff. Aurousseau remembered a visit of Rosita Forbes:

She was very beautiful, very charming, and, at first, very grand. But Bowman subtly drew Wright out in a way that showed madame that she was dealing with a scholar who knew as much about Arabia as she knew herself. (He was then preparing Alois Musil's journals for publication.) Meeting her match in both Wright and Bowman the celebrity came down to earth and was soon amusing us with personal matters, which included an account of how she met Colonel McGrath and consented to marry him "provided that he let me go ahead with this Arab stunt." On another occasion we received W. M. Davis on his birthday.

Bowman had arranged for a cold luncheon to be served in his anteroom, and he got us all to sign a copy of an offprint from the Geographical Review entitled "A Conference on Cycles." Davis gave a quick glance and remarked "Um. A conference on cycles. What kind of cycles?" Climatic cycles, of course, answered Bowman. "Humph. Should say so," grunted Davis. We were all frightened of the old martinet.... Bowman's technique with celebrities was to let them do the talking.[38]

Mabel Ward recalled other visits from scientists and explorers.

Among those who came most often were Admiral Richard E. Byrd, when he was planning his Antarctic expeditions, Sir Hubert Wilkins, Lincoln Ellsworth, Merian Cooper (who made the film "Grass"), Captain Robert Bartlett, Louise Boyd, and others. Colonel P. H. Fawcett and his small party came in to see him just before their departure on the expedition to the Matto Grasso from which they never returned, as did Commander Dyott, leader of one of the several search expeditions that went to look for him.[39]

Before he developed policy and priorities, Bowman found himself and the Society caught up in tasks which were later rejected. Between 1915 and 1919 he planned for a department of education at the Society, which was to have its own publication series. He received letters from Lawrence Martin[40] and R. H. Whitbeck[41] in June 1915, asking if he would assume the task of continuing publication of the *Journal of Geography*, hitherto essentially a University of Wisconsin venture (at least the three main officers were from the Wisconsin department of geography: V. C. Finch was business manager, Whitbeck was editor, and Martin was associate editor). Bowman liked the idea and placed the proposition before the Council of the Society.[42] When the existence of the *Journal of Geography* was threatened in 1918, the Society took over its management from January 1919 to May 1920, and put the *Journal* on a sound footing. Then management of the *Journal* was passed on to the National Council of Geography Teachers.[43] That act of generosity saved the *Journal* and was recognized in 1936 when the Council awarded Bowman its "Distinguished Service Award."

Bowman came to realize, however, that his idea of an education department was not practical. On 18 March 1920 the Council of the Society resolved "that the Society regards its most important function as that of research and the preparation of original scientific matter."[44] Bowman retained very definite notions concerning the role of pedagogy and research in the development of the geographic discipline. He firmly believed that geographic education would follow in the wake of scientific research. But scientific research must lead the field.

He was frequently consulted on educational matters and was from time to time able to encourage the entry of geography into education. He advised Edward B. Mathews of the National Research Council on the need for increased instruction in geography in the colleges and universities.[45] On the direction of the Association of American Geographers Bowman wrote to Richard E. Dodge:

> You are right about sticking to pure science. Let the Meteorological Society make all the fuss and excitement it can. It deals with teachers. We are dealing with the creative aspects of our subject. Our big function is to produce original work. Let's keep our eyes on that; and let's stress it continually.[46]

When the administrative officers of Harvard University considered the establishment of a geography department in 1926, Kirtley F. Mather, professor of geology, wrote to Bowman requesting his support. Bowman replied, "I shall be delighted to consult and advise so far as I am able. The subject of geography is in a mature stage of development; perhaps the teachers are not."[47] Bowman urged the creation of a new geography department independent of geology. He also recommended the appointment of W. S. Tower as head, and urged that he be given free choice of his associates. But Bowman was always anxious that a first-class man not allow pedagogy to detract from his scientific work. In correspondence with A. G. Ogilvie, after the latter had assumed the chair of geography at the University of Edinburgh upon the retirement of George G. Chisholm, Bowman fiercely urged him toward research and not compilation. J. F. Unstead had proposed to Ogilvie that he write a regional geography text of South Africa. Ogilvie, independently,

had thought of undertaking a large study in the population distribution
of Africa. Of the proposed South African regional geography textbook
Bowman wrote:

> Is it research? It is fatal to get into the textbook writing business
> before fifty. Work out every great thought and new idea.
> Experiment widely. Dig deeply. Develop all the best that is in
> you, and then if you like turn to the other at a later stage.[48]

Bowman believed devoutly in the worth of geography. He studied
the subject and ancillary matters to comprehend man's "creative
experiment." A synthesis of the components man, land, and time was
forming in his mind. He was reluctant to work on undertakings that did
not produce intellectual growth, and consequently rejected numerous
offers.

> One day three tycoons were hardly admitted to his office before
> one of them said, "We've come to buy you, Bowman. We've been
> watching what you've been doing and we've decided that we need
> you in the City, now what's your price?" One of them got his
> cheque book out and said, "Come on Bowman, anything within
> reason." He told me that it took him an hour to convince them
> that he was not tempted. "And do you know," he said, "those
> chaps went away with a new idea, there were actually things that
> they just couldn't buy."[49]

One offer that Bowman rejected was the presidency of the
University of Cincinnati. He wrote to his friend Fenneman, who had
suggested Bowman's name:

> If I should accept the presidency on the basis of my present
> knowledge of the University and the kind of president it ought to
> have, it would be only because I wanted to be president — the
> lowest of motives. For I really know very little about your needs,
> your present educational position, your most promising line of
> future development.
>   But these things I do know of the American Geographical
> Society where I have experience and friends and an occasional
> chance to pioneer a new trail. The Council of the Society has

> done so much for my plans and I have such faith in the purposes
> of the institution and its present work that the thought of another
> job does not deflect the needle of my compass.[50]

The source of the Society's creative endeavor sprang from the large
themes which Bowman had provided for it. These themes acted as foci
for research, staff employment and publication. They included a Latin
American program whose main project was the construction of a map
of Hispanic America on the scale of one to one million; an ongoing
interest in advising, following, and publishing the results of Arctic and
Antarctic exploration; and the study of pioneers and pioneer lands (see
chapter 7.)

Bowman announced the plan for Latin American research at the
1920 meeting of the Association of American Geographers. He wrote to
Richard E. Dodge:

> Please put me down for a paper entitled "A Program of Latin
> American Research," which will take about fifteen minutes and
> can be worked in at any time. I have something exciting to say. I
> had not intended to speak, but since we wished to make some
> announcement of our plans, this seems to be the appropriate time
> and place to do it.[51]

The work of the program had been loosely defined by a resolution of
the Society's Council on 18 March 1920, "That the project as outlined
to the Council for the millionth map of Latin American be adopted as a
program of research which embodies the chief features of the accepted
policy of the Society...."[52] Archer M. Huntington and James B. Ford
each contributed $25,000 to the project and the Society's largest single
undertaking had begun. Bowman enjoyed the confidence and the
friendship of both of these gentlemen, and both responded generously
in spirit and financial support.

Bowman successively invited Mark Jefferson, Vernor C. Finch and
Alfred H. Brooks to take charge of the program, but each declined.
Bowman then approached Alan G. Ogilvie whom he had first met on
the occasion of the A.G.S. Transcontinental Excursion of 1912, and
with whom he had become reacquainted at Paris in 1919.[53] Ogilvie
accepted the post and held it for three years, at which time he accepted
the Chair of Geography at the University of Edinburgh. Meanwhile

Bowman had asked Mark Jefferson to find a research assistant who would participate in the Latin America program. Jefferson chanced to have a student named Raye Roberts Platt, older than the class average and experienced in the First World War. Jefferson arranged with Bowman to provide Platt with special tutoring, if the Society would hire him into its Latin American program. Jefferson taught Platt Spanish and mapmaking. Platt assumed his post in 1921, and when Ogilvie left in 1923, was appointed head of the Department of Hispanic American Research. With the assistance of cartographers and draftsmen William Briesemeister, Charles Krisch, Norman MacCleod, Osborne M. Miller, Gregor Noetzel, and Gustav Schweizer, the "Millionth Map" and other related cartographic work began to emerge. In 1923, after three sheets of the map had been published, the title of the map program was changed from "Latin America" to "Hispanic America" because Bowman had learned that the Brazilians had undertaken coverage of Brazil on the sheet lines of the International Map of the World on the scale of 1:1,000,000.[54] Aurousseau recalled:

> The day when the first Brazilian sheet arrived in New York was one of general excitement for us, because the sheet adjoined one of Bowman's sheets. The adjoining edges of the two sheets were carefully folded back and the map margins were brought together. They fitted almost perfectly! Bowman looked as excited as a schoolboy.... But was the correspondence evidence of accurate work by both compiling authorities — or was it just the result of using identical sources? Quien sabe? Which reminds me that Bowman's Spanish was said to have been almost without foreign accent and he certainly resolved all our linguistic difficulties during the compilation of the sheets with masterly decision.[55]

Work on the sheets of the great map continued. Nine more appeared in 1927, four in 1928, four in 1929, fourteen in 1930, three in 1931, five in 1932, two in 1933, seven sheets in 1934, and ten in 1935, the year in which Bowman left the Society. From 1936-45 another forty-four sheets were drawn to complete the epochal 107-sheet "Millionth Map." For twenty-five years a team of seven or eight compilers and draftsmen were kept at the task. The map was completed in 1945, at a cost of nearly half a million dollars. When the cost of the project was called into question, Bowman retorted, "What a small part of a battle cruiser this would buy!"[56] In December 1945 the Society held a commemorative dinner attended by members of the Latin American diplomatic and consular corps, government officials, and representatives of educational, research, industrial, and financial institutions. On that occasion Bowman was presented with the Society's David Livingstone Centenary Medal. The principal speaker, Spruille Braden, then assistant secretary of state and a personal friend of Bowman, stated that the map had helped remove simple ignorance, one of the sources of fear and suspicion. He knew that map data had been employed in the adjudication of six boundary disputes: between Guatemala and Honduras (1919), Chile and Peru (1925), Bolivia and Paraguay (1929), Colombia and Peru (1932), Colombia and Venezuela (1933), and Peru and Ecuador (1941). Bowman well knew the details of these settled disputes, and was writing about them in "Where the Forces Strive," the first chapter of an untitled manuscript in progress at the time of his death.[57] And certain sheets of the map were used extensively during World War II. Bowman thus had the satisfaction of seeing a project brought to completion after a quarter of a century, a project which had enabled the Society to maintain a force of compilers and draftsmen for this span of time. He was aware that the Society would receive international recognition for the map. But it was the beauty of the finished product which most inspired him.

> The Millionth Map will bear comparison with the illuminated books of medieval time for it was drawn by hand and is embellished with color.... The lithographic art has been developed to the point which permits a very high standard of beauty to be coupled with mass production. Each sheet of the Millionth Map can be enjoyed for its aesthetic qualities. Indeed these overshadow the utilitarian in my mind as I pick up each new sheet....[58]

The map and associated publication program was for Bowman one of the three main intellectual thrusts which he provided for the Society. The second of these thrusts was the interest and research which Bowman visited upon explorers and men of science, and exploration of the polar world. Again this was a personal interest which Bowman institutionalized. His interest in polar lands may have begun with his friendship with Vilhjalmur Stefansson during their Harvard days. During his Yale years Bowman was excited by the epic conquest of both poles. When he assumed the directorship of the Society one of his first tasks was to read of the Society's interest in Arctic exploration from the years of Elisha Kent Kane to Robert E. Peary. Bowman had already become familiar with much of the detail of Peary's twenty-three years' devotion to Arctic exploration and eventual attainment of the North Pole in 1909. Later Bowman's interest in, and knowledge of, Peary, was to be of great value: in 1935 he was asked by Peary's daughter to adjudicate the deceased Peary's claim of North Pole attainment.[59] Meanwhile Bowman had become a member of the Explorers Club which included a number of Arctic explorers. Bowman urged the award of the Society's Charles P. Daly medal to Stefansson in 1918, and occasionally gave the latter office space in the Society's building. The medal provided Stefansson with support from attacks from Rudolph M. Anderson and Roald Amundsen, who had labeled Stefansson's method of travel over the ice as "harmful and dangerous nonsense." Bowman also befriended Knud Rasmussen, whose ethnographic and archaeological researches in the Arctic were facilitated by dog teams. Bowman regarded Rasmussen as the man who was most at home on the Arctic ice.

In 1925 polar exploration by boat and sled became obsolete wth remarkable advances in technique provided by the airplane. With apparatus available to record data in unprecedented quantity and accuracy, Bowman was able to offer the services of the Society to those in need. Explorers came to him for advice, data (frequently maps), and financial help. The Society became a clearinghouse for plans and schedules of several polar explorers. Later Bowman wrote to J. K. Wright that in the twenties and thirties he "knew personally and was consulted by practically every Amercian exploration leader and by a number of foreign expedition leaders with respect to work in both the Antarctic and the Arctic."[60]

Bowman presented Sir George Hubert Wilkins's 1927 flight plan to the Detroit Aviation Society, to secure funding for the flight. Wilkins had discussed with Bowman the plan of taking a sounding five hundred miles northwest of Point Barrow to add to Chamberlin's notion of a hollow Arctic and a humped Antarctic, in further search of land distribution. When one of the Detroit businessmen asked Bowman, "Could you give me a business answer to the question: what is a single sounding out there worth?" Bowman replied, "A single sounding 500 miles northwest of Point Barrow is worth the price of an airplane." Bowman said the man "was satisfied with his immediate and specific reply and the money was raised in the next five minutes."[61] The plane was provided, and Wilkins took a spot sounding of 5,440 meters some 330 miles north of Wrangel Island, then the greatest depth recorded in the Arctic basin.[62] Bowman helped procure money from the *New York Times* through the good offices of J. H. Finley and in 1928, in further pursuance of the problem of whether or not land existed in the Arctic Sea, Wilkins flew again from Point Barrow to Spitzbergen. Upon his return Wilkins proposed an Antarctic flight over Palmer Land; Bowman assisted him by securing funds from William Randolph Hearst.

Results of many such undertaking were published in the *Geographical Review*, and in books, pamphlets, and especially maps published by the Society. Expedition support by newspapers began to bother Bowman. He recognized that funds for large expeditions could be found in no other way, but was concerned that only the spectacular features of exploration would come to public attention. To offset this he gave a talk on Antarctica to the American Philosophical Society in 1928, part of which had been radioed to Little America, and also across the United States.[63]

What was lacking was an assembly of all of the concepts that entered into polar exploration. The public should be told why scientific men, not adventurers merely, were interested in polar exploration. The serious side of the business should be emphasized. I thought we could make the proper impress only by producing a book written by a group of authorities who themselves were good newspaper copy.... I burst in upon Joerg with my grand idea and he took fire immediately.... It may interest you to know that we had no declinations, as I remember it, when we sent out invitations to contribute.... I think it is significant that every important polar expedition in the 20's published results in *The Geographical Review* and I think that all of them published their first accounts in the *Review*.[64]

In 1928 *Problems of Polar Research* and *The Geography of the Polar Regions* were published by the Society, and proved of enduring value to any study of the polar realm. *Problems* was of special joy to Bowman, with its thirty-one essays contributed by leading explorers of the polar regions. But the latter work was also valuable and the first book of its kind available in the English language. It consisted of translations of *Polar Nature: A General Characterization* (1918), written by Otto Nordenskjöld and translated for the Society by Ernst Antevs, and *Die Polarländer* (1925), written by Ludwig Mecking and translated for the Society by W. L. G. Joerg.

When the Depression struck in 1929 the effect upon the Society was traumatic. At once Fellows were lost and by 1932 expenses of the Society exceeded receipts. Salaries were halved in April 1933; the purchase of a coal supply for the next year was delayed by order of the Council. Bowman secured money from the Rockefeller Foundation to continue the Millionth Map. He recognized that the Map was near completion, the polar program had accomplished much of what it had been organized to do, and the pioneer studies sortie had entered the applied stage from the theoretical (see chapter 7). New money and new objectives were needed, and he proposed a general world atlas, an atlas of international relations, an atlas tentatively entitled "America's Prospects," and a popular magazine to supplement the *Geographical Review*. Each of these suggestions failed to secure support. In 1933 he accepted chairmanship of the National Research Council. He wrote something of his concern to W. M. Davis:

> Of course the arrangement is experimental in view of the fact that it has hitherto been a full-time job. It very distinctly remains to be seen whether I can commute between New York and Washington and be responsible for two institutions. I am mainly interested in policy ... having the matter constantly before me in the development of this Society. Under other circumstances the decision would have been an extremely difficult one for me to make; but the Council of this Society were so hospitable to the idea and the Nominating Committee and officers of the National Academy — Campbell, Millikan, Merriam, Howell, Jewett, and others — were so cordial that I had no alternative but to accept.[65]

In the same year President Roosevelt appointed Bowman vice-chairman and director of the Science Advisory Board. He was invited to assume the chairmanship of this Board, but declined since he had proposed creation of the Board itself to the president. Karl T. Compton, president of the Massachusetts Institute of Technology, then assumed the chairmanship. Bowman and Compton worked well together; the Board's fundamental task of restoring the belief of the American people in the worth of science was in good hands.

In part he accepted these two appointments in order to reduce Society expenses, and probably in part his action was prompted by the instinct for self-preservation. His two sons were both attending college, and Bowman in his middle fifties viewed the Society as financially troubled. He had grown somewhat pessimistic concerning American geography. He felt that within the discipline trivial measurements were replacing large ideas and that small technical pieces of work had become commonplace. He began to think carefully about his own future.

In the early thirties, Bowman had become less tied to the Society. People there knew their function and work proceeded with little direction needed from Bowman. He had been elected one of five vice-presidents of the International Geographical Union at Cambridge in 1928, and became president of the Association of American Geographers for 1931. It is interesting to note that by this time he had declined the latter office on six occasions. With one of his declinations in 1926 he offered the following explanation:

> I appreciate very much indeed your thought of me for President of the Association of American Geographers. It is true that I have several times declined the proffered honor of being President and I have done so with no lack of appreciation of either the offer or the work of the Association.... Doubtless you know that this Society in the past published the Annals for quite a number of years for the Association and turned over the whole of the joint research fund to the Association so as to support the Annals in a critical period. It is very largely because of the help that we have given the Association that I feel it unwise to accept the Presidency. Some time in the distant future, when all thought of the help that we gave the Association has passed I could accept such an offer.[66]

His acceptance of this office in 1931 was prompted by his election as president of the International Geographical Union. He felt it

inappropriate to accept the international honor prior to the national
office. He had already received numerous corresponding memberships,
honorary degrees, and medals, and had become weary of accepting
some of the lesser accolades. In 1932 he was elected to the American
National Committee on International Intellectual Cooperation.
During his participation in the International Geographical Congresses
of London and Cambridge (1928), Paris (1931), and Warsaw (1934),
he made rigorous yet diplomatic attempts to encourage the German
geographers to return to the congresses following their expulsion
resultant to the First World War. Following his 1931 stay in Paris as
president of the International Geographical Union, he travelled in
Germany and spoke with several of the German geographers. He
repeated his trip to Germany following the Warsaw Congress (1934),

and corresponded with numerous geographers including Albrecht
Penck, Gerhardt Schott, Robert Gradmann, Fritz Machatschek, Carl
Troll, and Otto Maull. He revised some of the statutes of the
International Geographical Union. But his work seemed in vain.

Gerhardt Schott summarized the thinking of German geographers:

> You will please differentiate (1) joining the International
> Geographical Union and (2) the special case of Warsaw. . . But
> every German geographer is naturally sovereign as to whether he
> in a given case will go to a Congress or not. I for my part, can
> under no conditions visit Warsaw so long as the "Corridor" and
> eastern Upper Silesia, two regions robbed of the Germans, are in
> Polish possession. . . . With one exception I have heard the same
> opinion everywhere. This senseless corridor, which was created
> at Versailles in 1919, is particularly for geographers an eternal
> provocation. . . . If it is desired to have the Germans not only in
> the Union but also in practice, after Paris another country than
> Poland should have been chosen for 1934.[67]

Personal meetings and abundant correspondence with German
geographers helped to ameliorate a sore condition. Bowman proposed
to the National Research Council, Division of Geology and Geography,
that the International Geographical Congress to follow Warsaw should
be held in the United States. The Council approved this plan and
Bowman presented the invitation to the Warsaw Congress, but high
travel costs forbade an American venue and the next congress was held
in Amsterdam.

In the United States the economic depression lingered. The Society
began to atrophy. Bowman's proposals were too frequently tabled for
want of funds and he became dissatisfied. When an invitation to
preside over The Johns Hopkins University was presented to him,
Bowman accepted. When Archer Huntington asked Bowman why he
had made such a decision, Bowman replied, "I am tired of being a
mendicant."[68] His secretary, Mabel Ward, felt that it was a "joyless
move."[69] Five years after leaving the Society, Bowman wrote wistfully:

> I am conscious as I look back along the road, of the importance
> and spiritual value of friendships. No group of people with whom
> I have worked drew out so much affection from me and
> established so firm a position in my heart as the staff at the A.G.S.
> We were indeed a happy family.[70]

Chapter Five

The Inquiry and
Paris Peace Conference

"In the early autumn of 1917 it was proposed by Archibald C. Coolidge of Harvard to Edward M. House (President Woodrow Wilson's agent in preparing material for an eventual peace conference), that a geographer should be associated with the 'Inquiry' and that I should be invited to collaborate in studies that bore on peacemaking at the close of the war then in progress. This led to my participation in the Peace Conference of Paris in 1919."[1] So wrote Bowman in 1947 when Nordis Felland of the American Geographical Society requested him to record the circumstances which had led to the writing of *The New World*.

It is unclear whether the idea of the Inquiry originated with the Department of State, or in the mind of Colonel House.[2] In April 1917, the month in which the United States entered the First World War, a committee composed of Sidney Mezes (Colonel House's brother-in-law), Walter Lippmann, David H. Miller, and Colonel House undertook the preparation.[3] Lippmann, as secretary, directed the work. The project was transferred on 10 November 1917 from the New York City Public Library to the spacious third floor of the American Geographical Society, where access to needed maps and materials was immediate. Soon "more than half of the entire space in the building and later the whole third floor of the Indian Museum was turned over to the work of the Inquiry."[4] When the work began to founder Bowman was approached by individuals wishing to divorce themselves from this arrangement. In July of 1918 Lippmann received a commission in the army and went to Europe as a member of the Intelligence Section, leaving the direction of the work to Sidney Mezes. Mezes, president of City College, did not know how to make the investigative machine function. Signs of disarray swiftly appeared. Bowman had foreseen this circumstance and had taken his wife and children to the family vacation spot of Turtle Island in Lake Wentworth, New Hampshire. He did not return to New York until the middle of July, making this the longest vacation he had ever taken. His canny political sense served him in good stead.

Bowman replaced Lippman on the committee, which now comprised Mezes, Miller, and Bowman. But Mezes's notions of direction were at variance with those of Bowman and Miller. Miller spoke to Colonel House of the situation, and in August House offered Bowman "the running of men, money, and plans."[5] Bowman promptly created a "Research Committee" composed of Haskins (chairman), Shotwell (editor), Young (secretary), and Bowman (executive officer). Morale immediately improved.

> The map collections of the Society were drawn upon freely in the preparation of memoranda for the President, scores of maps being sent to the White House and the Department of State. Upon these were drawn lines illustrating matters connected with the war and the secret treaties as well as tentative suggestions respecting future territorial settlements. Some of these first maps were specially and quickly drawn for occasions as they arose, others were commercial maps upon which were drawn special interpretive lines and shadings, in color or otherwise.[6]

The map work of the Inquiry fell into three main categories: maps accompanying current reports and memoranda; base maps for use in research and at the Peace Conference; and distributional maps and cartograms for analyzing boundary propositions. Maps of the first group were sent to President Wilson on 21 December 1917 and 2 January 1918. The report of 2 January was entitled "A Suggested Statement of Peace Terms," and was the most extensive of the class of general reports. "It was accompanied by a collection of maps, about twenty in all, and was employed by the President in the framing of the so-called 'Fourteen Points' that were later to become a basis of peace negotiations with the Central Powers."[7] When later Bowman read a manuscript by Charles Seymour, he commented:

> it is also true that 'the settlement finally approved by Mr. Wilson' was at variance with the Paris settlement. The implication is that Wilson was wise in *not* following the Inquiry Report. The Inquiry was the most astonished group in the world when the President's speech was read.... We found wholly delightful in naiveté the resounding phrase "by friendly counsel along historically established lines of allegiance and nationality.".... It seemed to us the one profoundly weak spot in the Fourteen Points. At least the Inquiry Report was nearer realities than that.
>
> These things are not said in defense of the Inquiry report. That Report was an unguided affair, so conceived and so managed that the President did well not to follow it too closely.[8]

Bowman ordered completion of the 1:1,000,000 map of Europe, and the 1:3,000,000 base map resumed. Mezes had previously not approved work on these maps, which were completed just in time to be taken to Paris. For regions where the boundary problems at one time threatened to be very complex, block diagrams were made.

> Those constructed for the Inquiry were made with great care, and according to the principles of perspective drawing.... Nearly all delegations at the Peace Conference requested a series of these as well as of the base maps.[9]

The 1:3,000,000 map of Europe (with relief) was unquestionably the most used base map at the Peace Conference. It was reprinted at the army base printing plant and used extensively in the preparation of the territorial settlements as recommended by the American experts. A total of over sixty base maps, drawn on scales varying from 1:250,000 to 1:14,000,000 were in use by the Americans at Paris, as were over seventy maps centering on big towns of the world, all on the scale 1:1,000,000. Bowman had correctly reckoned that at Paris maps would be of far more value than volumes of memoranda.

By this time the Inquiry fairly dominated the American Geographical Society building whose resources now included fifty thousand books, over forty-seven thousand maps, and a large number of periodicals. From November 1917 until December 1918, approximately 150 men and women labored at the task of intellectual preparation for the peace conference. To facilitate the work of the Inquiry the Society secured from European scholars a series of papers which were relevant to territorial settlements, and which were published in the *Geographical Review*. Especially useful were "The Geographical Distribution of the Balkan Peoples"[10] and "The Zones of Civilization of the Balkan Peninsula"[11] by Jovan Cvijic; "Albania and the Albanians"[12] and "The Balkans, Macedonia, and the War"[13] by H. Charles Woods; "German Colonization in Eastern Europe"[14] by Jean Brunhes and Camille Vallaux; "Central Hungary: Magyars and Germans,"[15] "The Peoples of Austria,"[16] "The Rumanians in Hungary,"[17] "The Slavs of Northern Hungary,"[18] and "The Slavs of Southern Hungary"[19] by B. C. Wallis; and "The Regions of Mixed Population in Northern Italy"[20] by Olinto Marinelli. Mark Jefferson was dispatched to study German colonization in Chile, Argentina, and southern Brazil.[21] Bowman arranged to have Douglas W. Johnson, who had published a series of articles concerning military campaigns on the eastern and western German fronts and in the Balkans and who wanted to supplement these articles with field study, comissioned a major in the Division of Military Intelligence. The National Research Council provided a grant for Johnson's assistant, Lieutenant Knight. The results of their research were sent to the Inquiry via the diplomatic pouch of the State Department. On 15 November 1918 Bowman requested Secretary of State Lansing to attach Douglas W. Johnson, Lawrence Martin, Stanley K. Hornbeck, and William C. Farabee to the peace delegation. Bowman also had Lansing successfully propose to the president that Mark Jefferson be appointed geographer and cartographer to the American Commission to Negotiate Peace.

Yet in October 1918, the politics of personality again erupted. Colonel House had sailed for Europe on the sixteenth, and from shipboard sent a radiogram to Sidney Mezes informing him he must take control of the Inquiry.[22] Mezes immediately drew up a list of personnel who would be included in the American delegation to Paris. Bowman's name was not on the list. Later Mezes suggested Bowman could go to Paris as a clerk; then invited him to scratch off the list the name of any man he wished and take his place. Bowman refused both offers. Learning of this circumstance, President Wilson wrote to

Secretary Lansing, who then consulted Mezes. Mezes then requested Bowman to lead the specialists and assistants of the Inquiry.

The councillors of the Society had demonstrated their faith in Bowman when they allowed the Society to be invaded by the Inquiry despite the "necessity for working in secret [which] made it impossible to make more than a general statement to the board of trustees of the Society, though a full statement was made to Messrs. Greenough, Ford, Huntington and Dr. James."[23] Under Bowman's direction the Inquiry began to assume the proportions of a formidable brains trust, with expert witnesses gathered from the universities of the United States.[24]

Together, the members of the Inquiry labored to prepare in readily usable form information which might be needed at Paris. Serious cartographic work began in May 1918, following the visit of Secretary of State Lansing to the Society. Lansing requested a large-scale map of Latin America to be financed by the Department of State. Lansing approved an outline which Bowman prepared, which then became the basis of the map and research program of the Latin American Division of the Inquiry. Bowman hired Bailey Willis to administer the work of the division, which included a staff of map draftsmen and research assistants. Numerous reports were made: of especial note were those concerning the Tacna-Arica dispute, the Guatemala-Honduras boundary zone, and the Rio de la Plata region. A map of Latin America on the scale of 1:5,000,000 was hastily drawn and a second map in twenty-nine sheets on the scale of 1:2,000,000 was compiled for more detailed work. Yet neither the map nor the memoranda satisfied Bowman. When Mark Jefferson returned from his assignment in Argentina, Brazil, and Chile in August 1918, Bowman made him director of the Inquiry cartographic program.[25] Much of the information prepared during these months was reduced to map form to make it more accessible. Bowman helped with this work, spending "three quarters of my time . . . in doing plain clerical work, but that too was necessary."[26]

Bowman had placed Captain James Truslow Adams in charge of the photostat room, both in New York and at Paris. Bowman helped with the machine, became acquainted with Adams, and soon began a correspondence which lasted until Adams's death in 1949. Another young historian, Samuel E. Morison, was attached to the Military Intelligence Division which exchanged information with the Inquiry.

One lasting memento of the Inquiry which Bowman secured for the Society was the signatures of the commissioners plenipotentiary. In a letter written much later to Gladys Wrigley, Bowman provided both a photograph and the detail of this accomplishment, which was to be deposited in the Society's archives. Each minister, and finally Woodrow Wilson, climbed onto a filing cabinet to sign his name on the wall behind Bowman's desk. Bowman had the signatures covered with a glass.[27]

In December 1918, three army trucks carried the Inquiry material to the U.S.S. *George Washington,* which sailed for Brest. Though Bowman was anxious about the welfare of the American Geographical Society, he had faith in the ability of his secretary, Miss Cornelius, and W. L. G. Joerg to manage the Society's affairs in his absence. The *George Washington's* departure was accompanied by "a terrible din as we left. Two airplanes circled and swooped about us and ten destroyers were running parallel at every quarter. The 'Pennsylvania' led us out and is to continue on the whole voyage."[28]

The sea journey lasted ten days and provided those members of the Inquiry staff who had been invited to the Paris Conference with an opportunity to relax. Bowman chatted with President and Mrs. Wilson from time to time, and with other members of the delegation, notably White and Lansing. Numerous photographs were taken of the Inquiry, Military Intelligence Division, yet the Inquiry members were

> excluded from the main dining room where Army and State personnel dined in evening dress. We ate at a long table in the second class dining room, and we ate at narrowly fixed hours, until George Crees ... spoke to the executive Officer or to the President whereupon some of us were moved to the upper deck staterooms (we were all on D. Deck at first!) where meals could be obtained on a more reasonable schedule.[29]

On Tuesday 10 December, President Wilson met with twelve members of the Inquiry in a historic occasion. Bowman sat very close to the president and, realizing the significance of the occasion, "the President's remarks seemed so important I risked his displeasure by taking a sheet of paper out of my pocket and began to take notes."[30]Immediately following the meeting Bowman reconstructed his notes and had the 1,200-word statement typed. "This is the first and only expression of Wilson's views as to the nature of the job at Paris. It is a unique document. He had said that his remarks were confidential and I hesitated a moment before beginning my notations, but only for a moment. From the first we were all aware that he was in good form and that he had definite views."[31] Charles Seymour, David H. Miller, and James Shotwell each cited Bowman's notes and particularly his last paragraph:

> The President concluded the conference by saying that he hoped to see us frequently, and while he expected us to work through the Commissioners according to the organization plans of the conference, he wanted us in case of emergency not to hesitate to bring directly to his attention any matter whose decision was in any way critical. He concluded with a sentence that deserves immortality: "Tell me what's right and I'll fight for it; give me a guaranteed position."[32]

Later that day,

> Mezes dropped in and suggested a walk on deck. As we strolled

along he commented on Wilson's remarks saying, "Did you notice the form of one of his remarks? He said, 'Show me what's right and I'll fight for it,' and that means he's from Missouri and it's up to us to 'show' him, no easy task. "Did you notice," said Mezes, "how he bore down on the 'show.'" I replied that neither the words nor the meaning of Wilson were correctly interpreted by Mezes' remark. I pulled out my notes with this very sentence included. Wilson had said, "Tell me what's *right,* etc.," with no use of show or accent on "tell" but accent on "right.".... Other members of the Inquiry ... had as many versions as persons and none of them was right when compared with my record. Yet all were trained to observe, remember, and record accurately. My method in taking notes was to shut my ears after a key sentence was spoken and write down exact words *on the instant* very rapidly. The result was accuracy as high as a stenographer's *for those phrases written down.* Afterward I supplied the run of the argument from memory.[33]

This practice of taking notes at the critical instant, or immediately thereafter, was a Bowman characteristic. Throughout his lifetime, he thus accumulated hundreds of such memoranda. Some of them, as in the case of President Wilson's address on shipboard, were unique. Bowman was proud of the record produced in this way, and on numerous occasions remarked, "I am accustomed to speak with historical accuracy."[34]

On other occasions Bowman met with White and Lansing to discuss in detail the work that lay ahead in Paris. Then at ten o'clock on the morning of Friday 13 December, the *George Washington* was

met by a great fleet of battleships and destroyers until 32 American ships were in line, airplanes and a dirigible overhead.... Then French fleet of 10 ships came out and each gave us 19 guns.... A dozen motor launches came up with civil officials, including Tardieu and the Mayor of Brest and military and naval big wigs. Half dozen American admirals came aboard, including Sims and Benson, and generals, including Pershing and Bliss. President and the big ones got away in a special boat, the rest of us in a later one.[35]

The following day there was a large procession through the streets of

Paris, which had produced "no such crowd for King George or King Albert. Wilson wore his best smile and apparently deeply touched by the reception.... Streets jammed full of people from curb to curb."[36] What the enthusiastic public did not realize was the difficulty of formulating a peace that would endure.

Work began in earnest for Bowman and the American delegation on 15 December. "Worked on memos for President on 1) the economic aspects of the devastated areas; 2) the compromise between the Jugo-Slav and Italian claims on east side of Adriatic. Called in Young, Haskins, Shotwell, Jefferson, Lunt, Day, Seymour, Martin."[37] But it was not until a week later that Bowman was able to organize matters: "The day of the great storm! I cut loose right and left and got our men established in rooms, threw out desks and men everywhere and got all rearranged so that we could get to work. Only chaos reigned until we took hold of the whole situation and made changes."[38] The Inquiry staff in the French capital was:

> reorganized by me at the request of the Commission after we got to Paris in late December 1918. The individual Commissioners quickly learned the special capacities of the 18 division Chiefs, most of whom were former Inquiry members. The result was a direct communication between individual specialist and any given Commissioner who wanted information and advice on current questions.[39]

Establishing the cartographic section headed by Mark Jefferson was perhaps Bowman's most critical and the most difficult task. Considerable amounts of equipment were brought in to what had once been a suite of elegant bedrooms in the Hotel Crillon fronting the Place de la Concorde, despite the apprehension of the hotel management. The American delegation was the best equipped, able to be objective to a degree not possible in some of the other twenty-six delegations as the United States had not been close to the theatre of war. But the Americans could not work independently of the other delegations, and evidence of atrocities on all sides stimulated an urgency to bring about solutions swiftly. Twenty years later Bowman wrote:

> The representatives of the Powers on all of the boundary commissions were of one mind with respect to the trimming of

Germany. It is so easy at this distance to forget that the Germans destroyed an entire British army as late as March, 1918 when they broke through the western lines. We forget that in May, 1918 the Germans took the impregnable Chemin des Dames and pushed south occupying a salient that extended past the south bank of the Marne. We did not dislodge them from that salient until mid-July. On November 1, 1918, at the pre-armistice conferences, Foch and Haig both said that their losses were higher than at any time since the beginning of the war and that they were facing a "well-organized, powerful and determined enemy." Only a few weeks after this we were in Paris making peace terms on the principle of viability for a future Europe. We could see only trouble ahead if we left Germany powerful. By "we" I mean everyone at the conference, and I think one can say everyone in the world who had a voice in public affairs. One can imagine what would have happened in those times if someone had arisen to say, "Let us be tender and gentle with Germany and set conditions that will make her powerful again." There were ten million dead who were staring in through the windows![40]

At Paris Bowman's title was Chief Territorial Specialist of the American Delegation and Executive Officer of the Section of Economic, Political, and Territorial Intelligence. This section was composed of approximately one hundred men divided into eighteen units, each headed by a scholar, nearly all drawn from the Inquiry staff. Bowman returned to the United States on 12 May, but at the direct personal request of President Wilson, he went back to Paris in October 1919 and remained there until December when the American delegation returned to the United States.

During the period of my service I was at one time or another a member of the Polish Commission, the Central Territorial Commission, the Rumanian-Jugo-Slav Commission, and I was the sole civilian member of the Polish-Ukranian Armistice Commission which arranged the terms of the Armistice between the Polish and Ukrainian troops during the siege of Lemberg. During the first half of 1919 I also acted as executive officer of the section of political, territorial, and economic intelligence in the appointment of personnel on the various commissions and organizing the work of preparing memoranda for the various commissioners plenipotentiary.[41]

At Paris Bowman was frequently a liaison between his superiors and his regional experts. Mark Jefferson, with Charles Stratton and Armin Lobeck as chief assistants and several other helpers, prepared maps to specification quite swiftly. "Both General Bliss and Secretary Lansing spoke of our reports as just the thing."[42] The Paris Conference was essentially about boundary lines, and it was said, "one map is worth ten thousand words." The maps of the American delegation were reduced and entered into two books, the "little black book," containing maps relating to Europe, and the "little red book," containing maps dealing with colonial matters. It was Bowman's task to control the flow of map requests going to Jefferson and to arrange an order of priority. Bowman also had to arrange to have maps produced for allies if it suited the American point of view.[43]

The Conference proceeded on two levels. The more visible of these was at the Quai D'Orsay where all the ministers plenipotentiary were gathered. It was there that formal discussion took place, and that final decisions were suggested and frequently adopted. But it was in private meetings, at meals, or in the privacy of hotel rooms that members of the delegations came to know each other. Bowman held such informal discussions with delegates from Latin America, Rumania, and other countries.[44]

Bowman was called upon to exercise a detailed knowledge of Europe in his work, especially with regard to Poland and Rumania. He studied the history, the rise of urbanization and industrialization, the ethnic composition, and the physical environment of these and adjacent countries. He was well equipped to discuss settlements with regard to these countries, and to understand veiled ambition in the form of proposals within the Commissions.

The first meeting of the Polish Commission, composed of Jules Cambon, Sir William Tyrell, Marquis della Torretta, and Bowman, was convened at 3:30 P.M. on 20 February 1919. In the next few weeks Bowman attended several sessions of the Commission and met with numerous Poles and Polish geographers. Bowman's reports were discussed, and invariably found acceptable. When Poland was discussed by the powers, he "sat behind the President, Lansing and General Bliss, and gave suggestions and answered questions relating to the Polish situation. By direct appeal to the President I got through the shipping motions. . . ."[45] His comments were all accepted by

> the President . . . [who] "followed through" magnificently. Lloyd George was fearless and careless in his use of arguments and facts particularly. The President was cautious and strong and made much the better showing. Much of the information he sought himself and the rest he listened to closely and accurately. Asked me to get after Lloyd George's advisors and convince him. I also talked with Lloyd George and Balfour, Pichon, Tardieu, General LeRonde, General Weygand and Marshall Foch, J. Cambon, General Bliss, Colonel U.S. Grant, Sir Maurice Hankey, and others.[46]

Danzig, the Polish Corridor, the Teschen, numbers of Germans in Poland, the Armistice and Truce in Eastern Galicia, were all matters which engaged Bowman and occupied much of his time. Later, James Shotwell wrote: "The restoration of Poland by the Paris Peace Conference owes much—if not indeed most—to the American Delegation; and its frontiers were largely determined by Dr. Bowman, who traced them with scrupulous care on the basis of exhaustive surveys."[47]

The Rumanian Commission work was less difficult and was resolved more readily, though it too, demanded the time and patience of the commissioners and Bowman. It might have been better for Bowman and the American delegation if he had not been involved in commission work, where he could be accused of favoring one side against another. Doubts of his objectivity occasionally arose, as when "Paderewski said before the others that he wished to talk with me as he believed I thought Poles unwilling to conclude an armistice."[48]

Bowman was frequently invited to advise President Wilson:

> With Haskins and D. W. Johnson went to the President's house and was in conference with him for one hour. Talked very frankly about the difficulties yesterday in the Council of Four re the Sarre Coalfields.
>
> He spoke of the acceptance by the Allies of the 14 points and subsequent addresses as a basis for peace. . . . Sent us to see

British to fix up a workable scheme but no annexation. Should not be an old-fashioned peace.[49]

Bowman was called to the president's apartment again on 1 April. The following day Wilson appointed him and Colonel Embick as American representatives on the Armistice Commission designed to stop the war in Eastern Galicia. And on 3 April Bowman called again on the President, who "gave no instructions. Conference lasted 40 minutes and most of the time we were kneeling or sitting on the floor with the maps."[50] Often Wilson sought Bowman's advice on territorial matters, and occasionally requested his presence at meetings held at the Quai D'Orsay. The importance of Bowman's opinions was demonstrated when his room in the Hotel Crillon was chosen as the site for the first Anglo-American meeting in Paris on the changes in the frontiers of Germany which should form part of the Preliminaries of Peace.[51]

Although Bowman worked seven days a week at Paris, and quite frequently twelve hours a day, he was able to visit local theatres, the Eiffel Tower, Chartres Cathedral, Versailles, and some of the battlefields. On one trip, "the carpenter at Veaux ... gave me a German rifle as a souvenir.... The railroad embankment near Veaux, the 'foxholes' of the men in the July fighting, the whole story of the Belleau fighting were all as if the struggle had ended but yesterday."[52]

On 26 February Bowman's wife Cora arrived, leaving their two sons and daughter with her aunt and uncle. At Paris she was introduced to notables of several delegations with her husband. On many of these social occasions Bowman naturally encountered other geographers, including Jean Brunhes, Emmanuel de Martonne, Emmanuel de Margerie, Lucien Gallois, Albert Demangeon, Alan G. Ogilvie of England, and Eugeniusz Romer of Poland. Bowman and Brunhes, who had not met before, talked of the latter's *La Géographie Humaine,* an English version of which, edited by Bowman and Richard E. Dodge, would appear in 1920. Bowman quickly developed an appreciation of Ogilvie's capacity and not many months later invited him to head the Hispanic American Research Program of the American Geographical Society. Bowman encouraged most of the geographers he met at Paris to send him articles for the *Geographical Review.*

It would be hard to overestimate the significance of these meetings in the history of geographic thought. The regional and possibilist point of view of the French helped reinforce Bowman's own feelings concerning the ontographic departure from the physiography of William Morris Davis, and helped strengthen his belief that the crudest forms of determinism were outdated. And, too, he learned of the plans for publication of *La Géographie Universelle*. He was most impressed by the French geographers, "an extraordinary gathering of scientific men. One could not get together such a group of the same distinction so easily and naturally in any city in the United States."[53] He was invited to a stag dinner on Saturday night—eight Paris geographers: Brunhes, Gallois, Demangeon, de Martonne, de Margerie, Grandidier, Raveneau, Rabot."[54]

Among the other luminaries Bowman met in Paris were T. E. Lawrence, the Emir Faisal, General Pershing, General Le Ronde, Henry Bergson, and Bernard Baruch. He also made firmer acquaintances with some of the plenipotentiaries in the American delegation. Colonel House approached him about an

> October 1 meeting of League of Nations in East Wing of White House. Wishes me to undertake, now, to prepare a program for the work of the informal committee that must operate until the Council of the League comes into being with the ratification of the Treaty.... Will have salary of 10–12 thousand a year and rank of Minister. Told him I would try to arrange matters with Council of American Geographical Society."[55]

In further conversation House spoke to Bowman of his appointment as secretary of the League. Cora Bowman was well disposed to the idea of life in Geneva, but her husband was not unaware of drawbacks to the life of the professional politician, neither was he unaware of his promising future as director of the American Geographical Society. The matter was seemingly dropped by early May; in September 1920 Bowman was writing to Charles Seymour inquiring if he would be interested in assuming the League of Nations post of chief of the Section on Mandates.[56] Bowman later supposed House had made the overture to him for political reasons, at a time when he was correcting House's prejudiced information to President Wilson on whether Fiume should belong to Yugoslavia. Bowman regarded House's "offer as a bribe to get me to run along with him on the Adriatic question.... When he subsequently heard of my participation in the letter to

Wilson there was no further occasion to court me!"[57]

Bowman's effectiveness and efficiency had been much appreciated by the heads of the eighteen sections of the Division of Economic, Political and Territorial Intelligence. On his last evening in Paris, as yet unaware that President Wilson would urge him to return at a later date, Bowman was given a dinner by the section heads, who were largely drawn from Inquiry staff. Bowman greatly appreciated the "intimate affair, almost like a family party. There was no speech making, but a frank exchange of confidences."[58]

Meanwhile a boundary dispute had erupted between Guatemala and Honduras, and the two governments had appealed to the secretary of state of the United States to act as mediator. Secretary Lansing approached Bowman, who proposed an economic survey of the territory in dispute. The American Geographical Society sent Major Percy H. Ashmead to undertake the work, and by careful use of the resultant maps and reports the matter was brought to a peaceful conclusion in January 1933.[59]

Bowman returned to the Society in May 1919, and soon began thinking of ways to further develop its program. In particular he wished to establish a research and mapping program for Hispanic America. At the same time he began to write a manuscript on the "New World," as it had been remodelled at Paris. He declined an offer from General Leonard Wood, who had aspirations to become president of the United States, "to be his adviser and intelligence officer in his campaign before the nomination and afterward."[60]

While Bowman was taking his annual vacation late in August at Turtle Island, the secretary of state sent him a telegram requesting that he return to Paris to render further expert assistance to the Peace Commissioners. Bowman wrote to President Greenough of the American Geographical Society, who thought that Bowman should not absent himself from the Society. But when Bowman returned to his office on 6 September he found a personal letter from President Wilson saying, "it is absolutely essential that a man of knowledge and experience in the negotiations should go and there is no one so well equipped for that service as you. I sincerely hope that you will find it possible to render this service to the government."[61] Neither Bowman nor the members of the Society's Council wished to see the Society without a director again for at least several weeks, but this direct request from Wilson determined the matter. Bowman left for France on 28 September 1919. He studied French on the voyage, but found the language difficult.

Back in Paris, Bowman was plunged into work. On 4 November he wrote to Greenough:

> My functions here have become clearer . . . I have been appointed a member of the Polish Commission and what is more important, of the Central Territorial Committee. Our chief business up to the present has been—
>
> 1) To handle the question of the Treaty between the Free City of Danzig and the Government of Poland.
>
> 2) To study the population conditions in Teschen, and on the basis of these studies to arrange the terms of the plebiscite that is to be held there to determine ownership as between Poland and Czechoslovakia.
>
> 3) To study and report on the Bulgarian counter-proposals to the Conditions of Peace as presented last month.
>
> 4) To carry toward near-completion our studies and recommendations for the disposal of Thrace.
>
> 5) To conduct negotiations with reference to the vexed Adriatic problem.[62]

He was asked to address the Supreme Council on the terms of the Bulgarian Treaty. The Americans were not in agreement with the other delegations on this matter, and it was necessary to place in the record a minority report. Bowman believed that ratifying the Bulgarian and Turkish Treaties would lead to

> quarrels and wars that will occur out of the unjust settlements that the British and French are forcing us to accept in Southeastern Europe and the Turkish Empire. To guarantee these settlements is to bring ourselves in on the wrong side of some future war. Our hands ought to remain free.[63]

Bowman realized that the delegates at Paris were "all vastly impressed with the fund of information we control and the responsiveness of the organization to them. We were able to deliver the real stuff. Moreover our old geographical society staff of the Inquiry is the brains of the American crowd outside the plenipotentiaries."[64]

Foch himself embraced Bowman, then presented him with the rifle of the Unknown French Soldier, which Bowman fired every Fourth of July in America until he exhausted his ammunition in the 1940s. And at Bowman's departure,

> our French and English acquaintances came to the railway station to see us off and frankly confessed that they would have made worse settlements if the American delegation, about whose views they said they were often impatient, had not been present to qualify the agreements. [65]

Bowman returned to the United States aware of the treaty's inadequacy. To Eduard Brückner of the University of Vienna he wrote:

> We are all agreed that some of the settlements are bad. I personally feel that the settlement in the Tyrol is extremely bad. But the work of the peace conference was done under conditions wholly new to the statesmen of our time and under great pressure, because the whole world had fallen into disorder. Added to these difficulties was the supreme difficulty of delay, and in my opinion this delay contributed almost as much as the war itself to the present distemper of the peoples of Central and Eastern Europe.[66]

Twenty-seven delegations, each with its own preferences and point of view, and numerous interest groups, had grappled with the problems of the world. The resultant compromises could not please everyone. Rather than complain about what was, after all, a remarkable accomplishment, Bowman decided to elaborate many of the difficulties in all their intricacy. The result was *The New World: Problems in Political Geography*.

Chapter Six

The New World

Quite frequently in the history of geography the publication of a single book has focused on its author the attention of a large audience drawn from many fields of interest and study. This attention presents the author with new acquaintances, increased awareness, and greater career opportunities. For Bowman such a book was *The New World: Problems in Political Geography*.

It is probable that this attention would have come to him sooner or later. But the publication of this one book brought him the respect of historian, economist, political scientist, politician, and reader interested in the peace settlement, not merely in the United States but as it affected relations between peoples of the world. This respect was additional to that of the geographic fraternity, who already knew of his work. Perhaps for the geographer *The New World* was of especial interest as representing a genre which came to be known as "political geography." Indeed, one later book was dedicated to Bowman "in recognition and appreciation of his leadership in the field of political geography."[1]

The idea of the book came perhaps more naturally to Bowman than to anyone else at the Peace Conference, for he was one of only a few professional geographers in Paris, and perhaps the only geographer occupying high enough office to enable him to speak with the leaders of other delegations. Certainly he was aware of the difficulties of changing national boundaries and creating a new world.

He began to write *The New World* in his spare moments at the Hotel Crillon. Some of it was scribbled during his private meals, and some was dictated to his secretary, John Storck. The material of the Paris Peace Conference preparation was so much a part of his life that writing about it came easily to him. The manuscript was an account of the way Bowman perceived the newly emerging political world. Yet he insisted that his book was not solely the product of his Peace Conference association. When J. Russell Smith referred to Bowman's use of Peace Conference material in his *Geography and Our Need of It*, Bowman wrote him:

> Not a line of "The New World" is based upon the material prepared for the Peace Conference. That material is utterly useless for the purposes of the book. Naturally, I learned much from my association with the men who prepared the reports, and vastly more from the experience of the Peace Conference,... "The New World" was written on the basis of an examination of a vast body of printed material, most of which is acknowledged in the bibliography at the end.... To acknowledge the help I received from association with scholars in the Inquiry I put a statement to that effect in the preface to the first edition. That statement does not occur in the second edition because the second edition (so-called fourth editon of the publishers) represents a state of development far beyond the Inquiry days.[3]

And when Richard Hartshorne referred to *The New World* as "consisting in large part of the materials gathered for the American Commission to the Peace Conference,"[4] Bowman suggested correction of the statement. Consequently, Hartshorne wrote in *The Nature of Geography,* "actual materials used (for *The New World*) were all gathered after his return to this country and did not include the materials brought back by the Commission from Paris."[5]

Dissatisfied with the first draft of his manuscript written between June and September 1919, Bowman destroyed it to the last sheet. It was only when he returned to the American Geographical Society late in 1919 that the book began to take on its definitive form. There he had access to the Society's library, and the assistance of Mabel Ward, who helped him gather statistical material and treaty texts. Gladys Wrigley read the completed manuscript and offered helpful suggestions. Remarkably the whole was ready by April 1921, though owing to a printers' strike the book was not available until October of that year. Bowman did not choose to have the manuscript published in the Society's Research Series, as the work contained some political opinon. Instead, he accepted the services of the World Book Company, whose owner Casper Hodgson lived only a brief walk from Bowman's house. The two men could discuss in the evenings such manuscript details as how many maps to include in the work. The published book of 639 pages included 215 maps and 65 engravings from photographs; the map work cost Bowman $5,000. *The New World* was the first geography book published in the United States to make repeated use of maps and to use them as an integral part of the text. Bowman even thought of his work as an atlas:

> There are thousands of people who want to know about these matters, but who cannot go to a library or buy many volumes, so we gave them a new atlas, and then strung along some historical, economic, and geographical observations on the maps and other things that are troubling people today.[6]

To Mark Jefferson he wrote:

> You will be interested to know that one of the objects of the book has been achieved—to get historians to illustrate their texts with speaking maps. Quite a number have mentioned the fact that they are going to use maps in this way, and Harcourt, Brace and Company of this city have recently accepted a manuscript on the Balkans by Professor Ferdinand Schevill of the University of Chicago History Department, which calls for maps to be made on the model of those in Bowman's "New World."[7]

Bowman was in communication with many of the leading American historians of the day, including James T. Adams, Charles Beard, Charles Seymour, James Shotwell, and Frederick J. Turner. But while each of these historians was sympathetic to the idea of cartographic illustration, Bowman remained uncertain of the reception *The New*

World would receive at the hands of the historians. He confided to Jefferson:

> I expected a storm of criticism (from the historians) on the ground that the history was scrappy and only brought in incidentally. On the contrary, the loudest protestations of delight have come from historians. Their welcome has been unqualified. . . . Between thirty and forty of them are going to use it as a text book . . . and in additon to that there are at least a hundred who are using it as supplementary required reading. . . . I hope that the geographers will do likewise![8]

Richard Hartshorne commented that the book's "extraordinarily effective use of maps has made it a well-nigh unique contribution."[9] Later, the Committee on Political Geography which deliberated on the appropriate chapter in *American Geography: Inventory and Prospect*, felt that *The New World* contained "no method or system demonstrating a distinctive character for political geography, with the important exception, generally recognized as the most outstanding contribution of the work, that an extraordinarily large amount of material was presented on maps."[10] Carl Sauer's opposition to the book was thinly disguised:

> Political geography is particularly hard to fit into the idea of a general discipline for all geography; of it we should perhaps say that it is the wayward child of the geographic family. It is certainly the least scientific. Method and material are free to the choice of the student. Interest can be translated promptly into action and expertness is more easily claimed than judged.[11]

Bowman wrote the book fundamentally to help educate and form intelligent public opinion. He did not seek methodological or disciplinal advance. He recognized that the United States had "never had a trained and permanent office-staff; and however lofty our intentions, we work, so far as scholarship goes, on administrative principles little different from those of a hundred years ago."[12] To James Shotwell he wrote, "I build no rainbows of hope nor have I attempted to prove a case. I have simply done the bricklayer's job of putting the stuff together in such form that a thoughtful person has a basis for judgment."[13]

Certainly the book constituted a comprehensive survey of problem areas throughout the world. It was the only contemporary study of international relations available in the English language so soon after the end of the First World War. Widely and favorably reviewed, the book had been on the market only one month when Bowman wrote to Jean Brunhes, "I hope to bring out new editions and so correct the perspective of the story."[14] Bowman collected the reviews and assembled constructive criticism, with a view to improving his book. He also culled criticism from the many letters he received, and made a file of the whole which he consulted for later revisions of the work. He received hundreds of letters, "and they came from all parts of the world. I was almost persuaded to write a novel or a book of poems! It shows that humanity is interested in life rather than technology...."[15]

Additionally Bowman asked fifteen or twenty friends to give the book a careful reading and point out any mistakes they found, for correction in the next edition. He accepted an invitation from Ellsworth Huntington to read critically the latter's *Principles of Human Geography* in exchange for Huntington's critical reading of *The New World*.[16] And he sent a copy to Jovan Cvijic of the University of Belgrade for criticism and correction concerning the chapter on Yugoslavia.[17] William Morris Davis, one of the first people to receive a copy, wrote Bowman:

> Your compendious *New World* was received a short time ago, and Mrs. Davis is now reading chapters aloud in the evening. I will soon send you comments, in addition to the admiring thanks that go herewith. You must have spent some time on it anyhow.[18]

In 1923 a supplement (in fact Chapter 35) to *The New World* was published, which dealt largely with the United States. This supplement was added to the 1921 edition of the book and notes were appended to fourteen of the original chapters; this constituted the 1924 edition, which was slightly revised and reprinted in 1926. In 1928 the fourth and very much revised final edition of *The New World* was published.

The book had now grown to a length of 803 pages, and included 257 maps. In the preface to this edition Bowman wrote:

> I have undertaken a complete revision of *The New World* to conform with the events of the period since 1921, when the first edition appeared. To make room for many additional maps and the discussion of the latest treaty developments, I have omitted the photographs that appeared in the first edition.[19]

Bowman sent Shotwell "one of the first copies of the wholly revised *New World* . . . . Russia, Italy, Germany, and the introductory chapter are among the parts that gave me special concern. I spent three years on the job."[20] Shotwell replied:

> The book has come and if you spent thirty years at it instead of three it would still be an achievement. . . . It was well worth every minute put into it, for it is simply magnificent. Your style is pictureful as well as clear in its narrative; a world full of problems, one can look at them in these pages without having himself dragged into them any farther than he wants to go, and yet even the difficulties are alluring here.[21]

Though *The New World* was not further revised, as late as the Second World War the United States Government reprinted it for use in its service schools and libraries.

Walter Fitzgerald of the University of Manchester called the book "one of the formative factors in my own education. In my own small way I am now preparing a book to be called 'The New Europe,' whose title is suggested by your great work, as you will see."[22] Frank Debenham, professor of geography at the University of Cambridge, wrote that his department used *The New World* as a textbook in classes of forty students per session and that "it is rapidly becoming a Bible."[23] Nicholas Spykman of the Institute of International Studies at Yale University wrote that he had "been a steady user of 'The New World' for my large class for quite a number of years now . . . and every year I make a patient investigation of the new literature to see if I can find a substitute. So far nothing has appeared."[24] Bowman replied, "*The New World* nearly killed me. It grew beyond the proportions of a one-man job and in 1928 I decided not to revise it again but if occasion demanded, to write an entirely new book along somewhat different lines."[25]

The New World enjoyed a substantial circulation. Four hundred copies were purchased by the Department of State and placed in consular offices throughout the world, and an equal number were placed in the "International Mind Alcoves" fostered by Nicholas Murray Butler, president of Columbia University.[26] The Board of Education of Indiana adopted the book for its Reading Circle in the school year 1924–25.[27] Eight thousand copies were sold in its first year, and approximately ten thousand more were sold in the English language version.

Bowman had hoped to see his book adapted for use by seventh and eighth grade, and possibly high school, students. He asked if Derwent Whittlesey "would care to take my book and get out a small one entitled 'Political Geography'.... it would have to be really elementary to suit the publishers."[28] But Whittlesey was not interested in the project. In 1924 Bowman suggested the undertaking to Rose B. Clark, of Nebraska Wesleyan University. A specialist in geographic education, Clark agreed and invested much of her time over the next five years simplifying *The New World* and reducing it to a smaller manuscript entitled "Elementary Political Geography."[29] But by 1931 the World Book Company had become very slow to return chapters, and very slow to answer letters. Bowman, quite exasperated, severed his relationship with the company after securing a settlement for Clark and leaving the manuscript in her possession. It was never published.

The New World appeared in Chinese, Braille, and French editions. The editor and translator of the Chinese version, Chang Chi-yun,

> had called on Chiang Kai-shek just before coming to America ... the Generalissimo had asked him what book by an American had the most influence on political thinking in China, and ... he answered, Bowman's *The New World*.... Dr. Chang ... said that it was used everywhere in China and that thousands of copies are bought each year. This is the pirated edition published by the Commercial Publishing Company of Shanghai.[30]

But it was the French edition that most concerned Bowman. In 1922 the French publishing house of Payot agreed to consider publication of

The New World, and Jean Brunhes agreed to write the introduction for the book. Bowman wrote to Brunhes:

> I could think of no better person to introduce it to French scholars. . . . Of one thing I am sure, and that is that France is not getting a proper hearing in this country and elsewhere . . . I hope that some such presentation of it in a revised edition of my book may have an educative influence in this country and promote better understanding. . . . It is . . . of the utmost importance that [students] should have a non-partisan and really honest presentation of the outstanding political problems of the time.[31]

The matter of a French translation was temporarily suspended as Monsieur Payot questioned the demand for it.

Relations between the French and the Germans were not good, and relations between French and German geographers were no better. Indeed, the German geographers were forbidden to attend the International Geographical Congresses that followed the First World War. A form of political geography developed in Germany, organized around a preconceived system, was revealed in Fritz Klute's review of *The New World*.[32] Bowman wrote to Brunhes:

> If Klute thinks that I have taken an English-American point of view in the development of "The New World," what will he say when the French edition appears? I think that some of our friends east of the Rhine are going to be very much shocked at the thought of a French edition and I think they will be still more surprised to find that it contains just the same queries and cautions that the English edition contains with reference to the Great Powers. . . . No, we are aware of the systems of the Germans but we discard them consciously as lacking in objectivity. Furthermore, we are prepared to discuss one state after another in the light of its own needs and problems. This is because we have a different viewpoint concerning geography as a science.[33]

Brunhes wrote a fascinating introduction to *The New World* which was finally published by Payot in 1928. The idea of a German edition of *The New World* had occurred to Bowman, for his friend Vilhjalmur

Stefansson wrote to F. A. Brockhaus of Leipzig:

> Dr. Bowman and I were lunching together recently and he spoke
> of seeking for a German publisher through an ordinary agent, for
> he felt, as I did, that the book was even more likely to appeal to
> the German temperament than any other. I then suggested that I
> send this copy to you.[34]

But *The New World* never did appear in German.

After World War II Bowman reflected on the history and
accomplishment of his book. When Nordis Felland of the American
Geographical Society invited him to compose a statement about the
book which would be kept with the library copy of *The New World*,
Bowman wrote:

> The method of the book is to take real problems of the post-war
> world and give them an historical setting—doing the history
> backward, as it were. Economic considerations were introduced
> whenever they seemed to have critical value or provided
> insights.... I particularly desired not to introduce a preconceived
> system of thought or set of doctrines between a problem and its
> analysis. I tried to keep in mind the truth that historical accident,
> not design only, has played its part in the creation and solution of
> problems of both rivalry and cooperation among the nations.
> Above all I tried to avoid justifying any one nationalistic policy in
> conflict with the policy of another nation.
>
> If the book has a "morality" it is that of responsible world
> association based on justice defined as "fairness". One element
> of successful international association is *gradualness*. Men can
> not learn to think and act together in foreign affairs without
> patience.... As a people we knew so little about the rest of the
> world in 1919! My book was designed to show in panorama what
> vast diversities had to be kept in view as we sought to rear a
> structure of world peace. It was a panorama sketched with great
> difficulty for there were no models....[35]

When he retired from the Presidency of The Johns Hopkins
University in 1948, Bowman wrote to G. Halliwell Duell of the Duell,

Sloan and Pearce Publishing Company that "my first task this fall should be the preparation of a book along the lines of *The New World*. Since the earlier book was published by the World Book Company, it is best to continue there."[36] The World Book Company continued to press Bowman for a revision of *The New World*.[37] He had in mind a series of books concerning varieties of awareness and a large work on United States foreign policy, but did not live to complete these, nor to see the 1956 publication of *The Changing World: Studies in Political Geography* by W. Gordon East and Arthur E. Moodie. East wrote that "for the world a generation after *The New World* Moodie and I offered *The Changing World* as a comparable review for the mid-1950's—and clearly such an attempt might be made again...."[38]

Chapter Seven

The Pioneer Fringe

In the lives of most intellectuals there emerges an idea or theme, perhaps inspired by childhood, some noble ideal which has great abstract appeal, or an ambition which becomes a goal. Whatever the circumstances, some men develop lifelong, sustaining enthusiasm. Isaiah Bowman was one of these men. He developed an intense intellectual enthusiasm for the study of lands marginal to settled areas, the pioneer fringe.

Bowman himself was born on a pioneer fringe. He grew up knowing the people and the ways of land and environment on the economic margin, where adz and ax still might begin one's lexicon and one's day. He worked for his father until he was twenty-one years old. The young Bowman helped raise two barns and two cabins, broke the land with a chilled steel plough, sowed the seed, learned to read the weather, and came to know the grasses and the flowers, the fireflies and the whippoorwill, the prairie chicken and the fox. In the evening his family would crowd around the kerosene lamp with apples, gingersnaps, and fresh bread, listening to father recite stories of his youth in a booming voice which shook the rafters. Hard work, isolation, and simple pleasures built strength of character. One ate what one grew, and what one grew was dependent upon a variable physical environment.

Bowman's "boyhood was spent in that earlier world ... in which the downright necessity of infinite and incessant toil was a condition of even mean living. That's what makes me so deeply interested ... in the problems of present-day pioneering."[1] Later he wrote:

> The idea of systematic and concentrated study of contemporary pioneer life on the active border of settlement throughout the world began to take form in my mind in 1905, while I was engaged in hydrologic work for the U.S. Geological Survey and first saw the surprising realities in the drier parts of Kansas and Oklahoma both on and beyond the discontinuous fringe of the wheat belt.[2]

In the following year Bowman included a lecture on pioneer settlement in his North America course at Yale, perhaps the first lecture of its kind in the history of American geography. During his three field trips to South America in 1907, 1911, and 1913, he witnessed a stationary frontier, and pioneering. Regional examples of his discoveries may be found in *South America: A Geography Reader, The Andes of Southern Peru, Desert Trails of Atacama,* and published articles resultant to these trips. Bowman wrote that his early interest in pioneers and pioneering "took fire in 1913 at Copiapo and when I visited San Pedro de Atacama."[3]

His work at the American Geographical Society in 1915 and the Paris Peace Conference and the writing of *The New World* kept him too busy for sustained work on pioneer studies. But these years enabled him to grow intellectually. His earlier ontographic studies were now more nearly a part of a human geography that was regionally inspired. After contact with determinist philosophy, and the possibilism of French geographers, he had emerged with a concept of geography large enough to embrace the idea of environmental limitation and to recognize the possibilities provided by a conditional conquest of nature by man. Bowman's work in seeking a science of settlement was recognized by the committee responsible for the chapter entitled "Settlement Geography" in *American Geography: Inventory and Prospect:*

> It now seems correct to say that when the pioneer studies were initiated in the 1920's the settlement of new and marginal lands

by small, independent farmers was already outmoded as an economic process of world-wide importance. Yet the interest in the settlement of new areas continues and is actively promoted in several American countries. . . .[4]

Bowman proposed to guide pioneer settlement scientifically, and to avoid the economic and social waste of unregulated and uninformed movement into unfamiliar areas. In 1925 he sought financial support for the pioneer settlement program through his association with the National Research Council. The American Geographical Society had been represented in the Division of Geology and Geography of the Council since its creation in 1919, and Bowman had been appointed to the Geography Committee prior to his return from Paris. By 1925 he was vice-chairman of that division in addition to being on the executive committee, the nominating committee, the committee on abstracts and bibliographies, the committee on editing Fremont's Reports of 1842–43, the committee on securing quantitative data of geological processes, and the committee on shoreline investigation of that division. He had established himself as one of the most active men in the National Research Council. David White, chairman of the Council, was impressed with Bowman's concept of the "pioneer zone" as it had been elaborated in conversation between the two, and as it had been revealed in an extemporaneous statement by Bowman to the Council in April 1925. White felt the subject was "an investigation profitable to mankind. . . . The preliminary committee for the consideration of the pioneer zone project, as named in Vaughan's motion, I have listed in my notes as follows: Bowman, Colby, Fenneman, Martin, Joerg, and Baker. This is a bright galaxy in geography."[5] Only five weeks later White wrote to Bowman:

> The more one ponders on the "Pioneer Belts" problem the more he is impressed with the complexity of the study on the one hand, and with the benefits to humanity on the other. It is a tremendously far-reaching project which can be handled only after very mature deliberation, thorough, one might say almost exhaustive, planning and consideration of the cooperative or coordinative relations with the other branches of science.[6]

In December 1925, Bowman informed White the best support for the project "I can think of is the National Research Council plus the Social Science Research Council, and I hope such a marriage can be brought about."[7] At a meeting of the Committee on Problems and Policy of the Social Science Research Council held early in 1926, Frederick J. Turner was appointed "to represent the Social Science Research Council in any conference that might take place with the National Research Council regarding the subject of Pioneer Belts. Professor Frederick L. Paxson was selected as his alternate...."[8]

Bowman invited other geographers to participate with him in the scheme. He invited Vernor C. Finch of the University of Wisconsin to lead and develop the work, but Finch recognized that disciplinarians with many points of view would have to be assembled, and the team would have to rise above differences of professional and personal persuasion. While Finch conceded that a geographer could "see the inter-relationship of the outstanding facts in all these fields and can synthesize them quickly into a usable document of considerable immediate value,"[9] he declined Bowman's proposal that he head a group of geographers in a study of the pioneer fringe in Rhodesia, as a test case.[10]

In August 1926, representatives of the Social Science Research Council met at Hanover, New Hampshire. Robert E. Park, professor of sociology at the University of Chicago, was chairman of the "Pioneer Belts Committee," on which Bowman also served. Park felt one of the problems was the lack of

> any clear generally accepted conception of what a pioneer belt was. It was not clear that the geographical conception of a pioneer belt would in all respects coincide with the use of the term frontier as used by historians, nor with the concept of "areas of open resources," an expression more or less familiar to sociologists.[11]

Bowman had attempted to bring some unity to the thought of the conference, but had not been successful. While he had been thinking for two decades about the pioneer belt theme, many of the other participants had not previously considered the matter. Following Bowman's statement to the National Research Council he placed a similar statement in the *Geographical Review,* soliciting "suggestion and comment."[12] A further expansion and elaboration of this article was published in *Foreign Affairs* as "The Pioneer Fringe."[13]

By September 1928 the Pioneer Belts Committee of the Social Science Research Council had agreed to help sponsor a Canadian-American Pioneer Belts Project. Dean William J. Rutherford of the University of Saskatchewan was suggested as director of the work, while the funds and the ultimate control of the Canadian and American project were to be vested in the American Geographical Society. An advisory committee was appointed: Frederick Merk (chairman), Oliver E. Baker, Kimball Young, William A. Mackintosh, and W. L. G. Joerg (secretary). The Council made funds available conditional upon a pledge from Canadian authorities that they would complete the Land Classification Survey in the northern portion of the Prairie Provinces (the estimated cost of which was $100,000).[14] When Rutherford declined the directorship of the Canadian project, Professor W. A. Mackintosh of Queens University, Kingston, Ontario accepted it.[15] Joerg joined with Mackintosh in editing the series. Between 1934 and 1940 eight of nine projected volumes had been published by the Macmillan Company in a series entitled "Canadian Frontiers of Settlement." The third volume of the series was inexplicably never published. Bowman contributed a foreword to the series and offered considerable advice to several of the thirteen authors, none of whom were professional geographers. The three thousand pages of the eight books constituted a vitally important contribution to the growing literature on frontier settlement and the exploitation of unsettled areas.

Of these books Bowman wrote, "They included studies far in advance of any previous thinking and affected Canadian government policies, especially in the fields of immigration and land settlement."[16] The first aid for the project came in January 1929, when the Problems and Policy Committee of the Social Science Research Council, supported with funds from the Rockefeller Foundation, gave $15,000 for the first year.[17] Additional help came from the National Research Council and several members of the American Geographical Society's Board. The Society produced five books, including *The Pioneer Fringe* (Bowman, 1931) and *Limits of Land Settlement: A Report on Present-day Possibilities* (prepared under the direction of Bowman, 1937, and published by the Council on Foreign Relations).

His work with these "pioneer projects" enabled Bowman to leave his administrative desk and return to the field. He spent six weeks in the summer of 1930 and a longer period in the summer of 1932 travelling in his own car with his son Robert, looking for evidence of contemporary pioneers and the pioneer spirit in the United States. The 1930 journey was spent in Montana, central Oregon, and western Kansas and Nebraska. His 1932 trip was more extended and took him nearly eight hundred mile northwest of Edmonton, covering nearly thirteen thousand miles in eleven weeks. The two trips were exciting to Bowman, who wrote:

> The six weeks that I spent in the West were more interesting than almost any other field expedition that I have taken, even in South America. I was looking for communities far from the railway and studying pioneer conditions in general. By concentrating on three selected regions ... I was able to get some very useful material for my book, the "Pioneer Fringe." I am also able to use some of the material in an address that I am to give to the Social Science Research Council at its annual meeting at Hanover, New Hampshire.[18]

Of his trip west in 1932 he wrote to Mark Jefferson:

> When I returned home after the summer's work in the West and the Canadian Northwest I felt that I never wanted to ride in a wheeled vehicle again.... I ran my legs off seeing people who could give information about settlement and other things of a geographical nature besides carrying an aneroid to scores of strand lines about the borders of lake basins in the Great Basin ... Peace River was the most exciting part of the journey. I got well up toward the northern boundary of British Columbia to the last settlements 90 miles from the railway where they are growing wheat that would cost 45¢ to haul to market where 22¢ is paid by the elevator. It's a strange fever that leads men so far.[19]

The 1930 trip inspired him to combat the notion that frontier life no longer existed in the United States. He published "Jordan Country," an analysis of a Montana community,[20] of which Gladys Wrigley wrote:

This model case study in the pioneering theme was based on field work in 1930, when he found frontier living still the rule in a 1000 mile belt of territory. It set him on fire: ". . . my notebook and head are filled with impressions as novel and exciting as any that I found in South America ... I keep finding the most astonishing things."[21]

On this journey he gathered fifty-four samples of lake sediments in thirteen different basins of the Great Basin province, and attempted to correlate these sediments with climatic changes, water supply, tree rings, and so forth. The results were presented in "Correlation of Sedimentary and Climatic Records,"[22] and harked back to his days of physiography.

These trips. transported him back to the days of his youth, and inspired a statement delivered as president of the International Geographical Union and his 1931 presidential address before the Association of American Geographers.[24] The latter presentation left quite an impression on the geographers present. Bowman began his address on New Year's Eve at 9:00 P.M. At midnight, still reading of pioneer settlement, he paused to wish the assembled geographers a happy New Year, then continued for another hour. He used the address to restate the totality of his researches on the theme:

> The ultimate purpose of the plan of research in pioneer settlement described . . . is to influence the makers of government policies in the direction of a reasoned approach to land questions . . . scientifically to study a life process that involves millions of people, vast acreages of good land, increased production of agricultural commodities in a world already cursed with overproduction, and the abandonment of once productive land of appalling extent. . . .[25]

In the preface to *The Pioneer Fringe*, dedicated to his father and mother, Bowman wrote:

> Pioneering today does not conform to the American frontier traditions of the nineteenth century. . . . The tools of conquest no less than new fields of conquest are now in the mind of the enterprising settler. Mere land is no longer a boon. No one is

looking for rough fare and homespun. Nowadays even the pioneer wants to have. To produce and to sell are the forerunning conditions of having.... The pioneer belts of the world are regions of experiment—"experimental zones" we might call them.... It is the purpose of this book to sketch the outlines of a "science of settlement," to set forth ideas that have moved men to take such diverse paths, and to provide a description of the different environments in which so many men elect to meet destiny.... A science of settlement is not desirable merely to provide means by which to attract men to new land. The ultimate withdrawal of the borders of settlement in the least favorable situations is also one of its objects.[26]

This book was one of Bowman's largest intellectual contributions to geography. Carl Sauer felt it was

really a curious book, shot through with a certain kind of fire, a sort of epic mood that transfers itself to the reader. I hope you will give us the pageant of the whole northwestern frontier. At the southwest it seems to me such a study would already be historical geography.... It is a grand theme you've got, and it will provide invaluable documentation for future generations.[27]

And Rudyard Kipling wrote to Bowman:

Very many thanks for "The Pioneer Fringe." Quite apart from its interest as a tale, it's a valuable book of reference for the history of the universal trekking instinct of mankind, which must have begun before the oldest amber-route was opened. But, to get emigration, we have, worse luck, to begin with the mere timber-or-land exploiter. He does the propaganda by material exhibits— just as the Red Indian used to come back to his tribe with raw scalps....[28]

Bowman was pleased to receive letters such as these from men of accomplishment, but he did not have the book widely reviewed. He appreciated the opinion of one young Englishman, L. Dudley Stamp, himself particularly interested in use made of the land, that the book "is probably one of the most important contributions made by scientific geography to the elucidation of world problems that have appeared within the last decade. . . ."[29]

Bowman toyed with the idea of sending Frederick Jackson Turner a review copy. He had read Turner while at Yale and in 1914, as secretary of the Association of American Geographers, had invited him to offer a paper to the Association concerning geographic influences in history. Turner had accepted and spoke on "Geographical Influences in American Political History." In the following year Bowman successfully nominated Turner for membership in the Association, and again came into direct contact with him in 1917 and 1918 when Turner was a member of the National Board for Historical Services and the Inquiry. Bowman thought Turner had perceived of the frontier as process, whereas he conceived of it as demarcation between regions. He felt that Turner was perhaps too much the documentarian and had not spent enough time in the field assaying in detail the quality of a physical environment as human habitat. However, he decided to send Turner a copy of *The Pioneer Fringe* and inquired, "Would you not like to review my book for the *American Historical Review* or the *New York Times*, if they have made no other arrangements?"[30] Turner was already too ill to review the book[31] but he did exchange letters with Bowman on the matter of the frontier and the frontier line in the United States. Turner wrote:

I have no desire to prove my consistency in the matter of a pamphlet written some forty years ago, but I notice that . . . you emphasized the fact that the frontier is far from having vanished; and it might be inferred that that early paper of mine had had some influence in spreading an error. Not, therefore, in the way of criticism, but simply from a desire to be understood, I should like to say that, in that paper, I quoted the remarks of the Census Bureau regarding the frontier *line* and dealt with that phase of American history that resulted from the continuous westward extension of a line having masked continuity. I tried to suggest that this continuous progress of the nation into vast areas of unoccupied land had been more fundamental in the shaping of our history than historians had as a rule perceived. . . . As the paper itself shows, I was aware that considerable areas of the country had not yet lost their frontier characteristics. My point was that, as an effective factor in shaping American history, the end of the frontier line, as described by the Census, marked the end of a real chapter in our history.... With regard to such regions as some of those dealt with by you in your book and in your article, where frontier conditions still show themselves, it seems to me, from my point of view, that they are local indications of survival rather than factors in the fundamental course of American development.... I would wish a scholar like yourself to understand that we are in agreement as to the distinction between frontier line and frontier....

Bowman replied:

My spear was leveled not at you but at those who use the phrase in an uncritical sense.... It was your penetrating study of the frontier in American history that gave the subject its proper place, and like hundreds of others I am profoundly grateful to you for the stimulating ideas you advanced in that epoch-making paper. In 1890 the problem took on a different aspect, as you clearly state. We have had since then the fixed type of frontier, if I may so term it—that is frontier conditions fixed in place and only very gradually ameliorated, if at all.... From the standpoint of geography the later advances have been extremely important; from the standpoint of history much less important. In other countries, e.g. Canada, and in other continents, notably in southern Africa, the advance of the pioneer has been much more striking. These countries exhibit phases of development later than ours. They are reliving some of our periods but under quite different conditions of race, material equipment, cultural standards, and political set-up. A comparative study is what we have in mind so that we shall see the process in all of its aspects... I sent you one of the first copies that came from the binder, because like so many other students of American history and geography I feel that you are the pioneer in pioneer studies.[33]

This pointed exchange resulted from Bowman's statement that "the commentators ... kept repeating so often the error that pioneering in the United States ended in 1890, that it was as if they walked about with closed eyes in a world where there were still 3,000,000 square miles of land capable of settlement, and wrote as if no such land lay in the United States."[34] In fact the error arose out of a misreading of two sentences in *The Compendium of the Eleventh U.S. Census:*

> Up to and including 1880 the country had a frontier of settlement, but at present the unsettled area has been so broken into by isolated bodies of settlement that there can hardly be said to be a frontier line. In the discussion of its extent and its westward movement it can not, therefore any longer have a place in the census reports.[35]

The moment that a line was no longer shown on a census map, the frontier was thought to have disappeared. Bowman found it necessary to write to several other authors distinguishing the American "frontier" from "the frontier line." One person he so addressed was Henry A. Wallace, then United States secretary of agriculture and soon to become vice-president. Wallace had published an article in the *New York Times* stating, "Just a century after the Federal Government was formed the Director of the Census announced that the frontier no longer existed."[36] Bowman wrote:

> I tried to correct this error but it keeps coming up again and again into public view as one writer copies it from another. I suppose that nothing can stop it now. . . . The frontier did not vanish: only the line of the frontier was omitted from the maps. The frontier has been with us from the beginning and is with us still. I have travelled in recent years through miles and miles of it.[37]

Historian Wilbur R. Jacobs believes that *The Pioneer Fringe* "pleased Turner because it suggested that his theory could be applied on a world wide scale," but that he was "annoyed" by Bowman's article "Jordan Country."[38] It does seem a little surprising that in "Jordan Country" Bowman did not mention Turner by name. Even in his fullest statement on this subject, *The Pioneer Fringe*, Bowman mentions Turner only once, and then in a footnote to an article Turner had written called "The Children of the Pioneers."[39]

Turner conceded in 1932 that his approach was "not as a student of a region but of a process,"[40] while the concept of region was very much in evidence in Bowman's approach, as indicated by his use of the terms "pioneer belt," "pioneer fringe," "pioneer zone." But while Bowman arrived at his concept in part through regional study he strove systematically to reveal laws of action or behavior in the science of settlement he wished to develop. Knadler astutely commented: "It may be that we have a basic problem in the philosophy of geography here, for Bowman seems to be hoping for the nomothetic characteristic of a systematic science to emerge when in the final analysis the problem may be simply one with the specific regions having mainly idiographic characteristics."[41]

When Turner died in 1932, Bowman wrote his obituary for the *Geographical Review:* "In Professor Turner was the rare combination of historical originality with geographical insight. His death is a loss no less severe to American geography than to the study of American history."[42] Yet of course the two had not always agreed. When Roy F. Nichols reviewed *American Historians and the Frontier Hypothesis in 1941* by George W. Pierson for the *Geographical Review,* he wrote that Pierson "wonders why more attention has not been paid to contrary findings by men like Bowman in his 'Pioneer Fringe.'"[43] Gladys Wrigley, then editor of the *Review,* sent Nichols's article to Bowman, who commented that Nichols

> is a good man and the review as a whole is O.K. I have no objection to his use of the word "contrary." Turner's ideas were curiously wanting in evidence from field studies that could easily have been made even in Wisconsin, as well as Montana, Texas and Utah. He represents a type of historian who rests his case on documents and general impressions rather than a scientist who goes out for to see. If I had been asked to say whether my views were contrary to Turner's I should have said that they were not so contrary as *variant.*[44]

Wrigley changed the wording accordingly.[45]

Bowman's interest in the frontier was international in scope and utilitarian in intent, while he viewed Turner's work as an investigation of American experiences. Bowman's conceived science of settlement was eminently practical. Yet he was also interested in the history of the settled margin, and observed that in the Bible "the 'pioneer fringe' was clearly recognized. . . . The migrants of that time had an equally clear purpose: 'That ye may live, go in and possess the land.'"[46]

He also had a substantial interest in the history of land occupance, land use, and the migration of peoples. His own forebears had come from Europe to North America, then migrated west across the Appalachians on the frontier. Perhaps this sense of participation in the history of frontier life prompted him to try to correct the historian's perspective by distinguishing frontier living from a frontier line on a census map, and by attempting to substitute field work for documentary analysis. Of his own pioneer work he wrote: "A certain professional urgency marked these studies. The historians of the Turner school were producing a genre of writing marked by sound research, that was distorted by popular commentators ... with imaginative or inferential elements that in many cases outran the realities."[47]

Fundamentally, however, Bowman's work was an inquiry into the way in which hitherto unsettled land might be settled and removed from the economic margin. He knew that the world's marginal lands were indefinitely investigable, but it was on the frontier of settlement that he perceived a priceless laboratory, from which he hoped to create a science of settlement. He viewed his pioneer research as practical, as filling a void in the intellectual world and a need in the real world. In the wake of *The Pioneer Fringe,* he co-opted twenty-six experts who wrote *Pioneer Settlement,* a collection of essays which "constitutes a world survey of pioneer problems by specialists who have an intimate personal knowledge of the regions they discuss."[48] Once again Bowman's very considerable international acquaintance served him well: eight of the authors were American; six were Canadian; three each from the Soviet Union, South Africa, and Australia together with New Zealand; two from the United Kingdom; and one from France.

The Pioneer Fringe and *Pioneer Settlement* represented a statement of the general principles and regional exemplification of an impending "science of settlement." These were Bowman's last contributions to original research in the field. He was not yet aware of the practical value and utilization that his studies were to enjoy.

Chapter Eight

'The Science of Settlement' and Resettlement Schemes

The world settlement problem as Bowman had perceived it, of population pressure vying with economic resources, became even more urgent in the 1930s when a political refugee problem began to emerge. When President Franklin D. Roosevelt established an Advisory Committee on Political Refugees with headquarters in New York City, Bowman became informally involved in its affairs. He had known Roosevelt for many years; it is possible that they met at Harvard during undergraduate days, as both attended geographical functions. During the teens Bowman had become well acquainted with Theodore and Kermit Roosevelt, and he had met Franklin Roosevelt at Paris in 1919 when the latter had been assistant secretary of the navy. In 1921 Franklin Roosevelt was elected to the Council of the American Geographical Society, and from that time until November 1928 when he was elected to the governorship of New York, he was an occasional visitor to the Society's rooms. As governor he continued to receive invitations to participate in the governance of the Society and, although he could rarely participate, Bowman kept him informed of events at the Society, which included a long-term project concerning the "Pioneer Belts of the World." Indeed in 1931 Bowman had sent a copy of his book *The Pioneer Fringe* to Roosevelt, and in an accompanying letter referred to "the western zones of experiment in the United States ... where I travelled in 1930 and where I found sentiment running so strong in your favor." Bowman urged Roosevelt to look at pages 140-142 "where there are some political implications."[1] At this time Bowman's research was academic. He wrote with the intent of helping the contemporary pioneer, but he had no idea how relevant his studies were to become.

In 1936 Bowman was invited by the Committee of the Ninth Conference of Institutions interested in International Affairs, held in Madrid, to prepare a monograph on the problem of "Peaceful Change." The text was prepared as a data book for the Tenth International Studies Conference held in Paris, in June 1937. Bowman hired as research assistant Karl Pelzer, who had recently completed a doctorate at Bonn under Waibel, and had then spent a year at the University of California, Berkeley. Bowman learned of Pelzer's presence through his son Robert who had begun a doctoral program there, and through correspondence with Carl Sauer. Bowman promptly invited nine other authorities in the subject to collaborate in a work which was published the following year by The Council on Foreign Relations as *Limits of Land Settlement: A Report on Present Day Possibilities.*[2] The several chapters were prepared at very short notice.

Only Bowman's great number of intellectual acquaintances made possible a publication such as this. The authors and their contributions were: Carl O. Sauer, "The Prospect for Redistribution of Population"; Carl L. Alsberg, "The Food Supply in the Migration Process"; W. A. Mackintosh, "Canada as an Area for Settlement"; Bruce Hopper, "Population Factors in Soviet Siberia"; Owen Lattimore, "The Mainsprings of Asiatic Migration"; Chen Han-seng, "The Present Prospect of Chinese Emigration"; Karl J. Pelzer, "Japanese Migration and Colonization"; Griffith Taylor, "Possibilities of Settlement in Australia"; J. H. Wellington, "Possibilities of Settlement in Africa"; and "Possibilities of Settlement in South America" by Bowman, who also wrote a preface and an introduction. But it was Karl Pelzer who did much of this work behind the scenes. Bowman "sent Pelzer to the American Geographical Society and arranged for the loan of the secretary Mabel Ward and the cartographer Stanley Smith, both members of the staff of the Society. The human resources and material of the A.G.S. made it possible to complete the book in time. . . ."[3] The theme of the work was timely, and it may have been the first of a new genre of research in pioneer settlement studies for Bowman. The study was distinctly utilitarian. United States Senator E. K. Cubin wrote to Bowman:

> At the request of certain members of the House and Senate I have recently prepared a memorandum giving a condensed picture of settlement in the past and the opportunities for settlement in the future. . . . The reason for this request is the problem of European refugees which will soon come before Congress. In the preparation of this confidential memorandum I have drawn freely from your recent book, *Limits of Land Settlement,* and have recommended it as a "must" book to be read by all legislators interested in land settlement for European refugees.[4]

During the thirties increasing concern was evidenced on both sides of the Atlantic regarding displaced persons, of whom most were Jewish and non-Aryan. The clamor of these people to enter the United States naturally increased in proportion to growing anti-Semitism in Germany, and especially after Adolf Hitler became chancellor on 30 January 1933. In America restrictionists, nativists, and workers protested against allowing large numbers of these people asylum. Unemployment was already high with eight to ten million people out of work during parts of 1938 and 1939, and many thought the admission of refugees could lead to further unemployment. When it was asserted that Jewish-owned stores were hiring Jewish refugees, Macy's, Abraham and Strauss, Stern Brothers, and Bloomingdale's issued public denials. Other people felt ethnic problems would result if new groups were admitted. Propaganda concerning a Jewish-Communist financial conspiracy was widely circulated. Anti-Semitic groups including Father Coughlin's Social Justice movement, William Pelley's Silver Shirts, and the German-American Bund were formed.

Roosevelt was keenly aware that the League of Nations was severely overburdened, and could not cope with the refugee problem. Consequently in the wake of the extreme persecution of Jews and anti-Nazis which followed German annexation of Austria in March 1938, Roosevelt had convened a conference at Evian in France, in July 1938. Representatives of thirty-two countries participated, but only the Dominican Republic offered to contribute a substantial piece of land for agricultural colonization. Soon after the Evian Conference,

General Rafael Trujillo offered to receive fifty to one hundred thousand refugees as agricultural colonists. Eventually some five hundred settled on the northern shore of the Dominican Republic at Sosua.

Roosevelt summoned Bowman, to talk of resettlement possibilities for displaced people. He had already corresponded with Bowman on the subject, occasionally writing in longhand, presumably to guarantee privacy. On 14 October 1938 the president wrote:

> I have been reading with great interest your *Limits of Land Settlement*. I wish I could get some information about settlement areas in Venezuela and the plateau lands north or south of the Orinoco. Do you suppose you can give me a line on sources of information for that territory?[5]

Bowman replied the next day that he was "taking steps immediately to gather together some material on the Orinoco country,"[6] and on 31 October he sent the President a four-page letter and a map enumerating the difficulties of settlement there.[7] Roosevelt thanked Bowman for the letter and wrote:

> Frankly, what I am rather looking for is the possibility of uninhabited or sparsely inhabited good agricultural lands to which Jewish colonies might be sent ... say fifty to one hundred thousand people in a given area ... do you think there are any possibilities in Colombia?[8]

Again Bowman drew up a report which included maps and summary explanations and sent it to the president.[9] Then in early November came *Kristallnacht*, the Night of Broken Glass. A Jewish youth had shot the third secretary of the German embassy in Paris, and in Germany as revenge Jews were assaulted, synagogues were burned, Jewish store windows were shattered and other property destroyed, and many thousands of Jews were put in concentration camps. German Jews were excluded from theaters, concerts, cultural exhibits, and public libraries, and prevented from driving their cars. Reaction against this outrage was immediate.

Bowman received a handwritten note from Roosevelt requesting a report on settlement possibilities for European refugees in Africa.

Bowman called Pelzer from Berkeley, and the two men spent the larger part of Thanksgiving Day discussing the report which had to be written in less than six weeks. Pelzer prepared twenty-six pages, two maps, and a summary; Bowman added a covering letter and sent the package by special messenger through Treasury Secretary Henry Morgenthau to the president.[10] Roosevelt suggested that Bowman keep Pelzer in Baltimore and New York, and told Morgenthau to raise the necessary funds for the Johns Hopkins University to add Pelzer to its faculty. Pelzer was appointed research associate of the Walter Hines Page School of International Relations.

In February 1939 Leo Waibel, formerly chairman of the Department of Geography at the Friedrich Wilhelm University in Bonn, who had lost his position because his wife was subject to the Nürnberg Anti-Semitic Laws, came to New York. Pelzer recommended Waibel highly to Bowman, who then appointed the latter to the Page School.[11] Both these men were to work on the project known as "The Scientific Study of Settlement."

Other letters from President Roosevelt requested information concerning settlement possibilities in Costa Rica, West Africa, East Africa, and Southeast Asia—already demonstrated opposition discouraged him from suggesting any programmed and substantial refugee resettlement in the United States. Pelzer and Waibel were set at these tasks under Bowman's supervision. To each of the president's requests Bowman responded with either a letter or an extended report complete with maps. He was realistic in presenting the hardships and limitations of life in marginal environments, yet as he was the only presidential advisor knowledgeable of the environment, his evaluations were frequently considered pessimistic. Politicans still had to learn that it was easier to compromise with a government and a political, economic, and social environment than with excessive or deficient rainfall, high temperature and humidity, lateritic or leached soils, ticks, fevers, *et al.* The spectre of a theoretical determinism had to be considered, as Stanton Youngberg wrote to Bowman about the island of Polillo, off the east coast of Luzon in the Phillippines. "It is one of the rainiest sections of the archipelago with no dry season. This, of course, can be quite depressing to a people from the northern part of the temperate zone."[12]

If the president needed a particular report very swiftly, Bowman was obliged to call upon his former associates Gladys Wrigley and John K. Wright at the American Geographical Society for help, commenting that "a request from the President is an order."[13] Bowman wrote Roosevelt something of his philosophical approach to the problem:

> The net conclusion . . . is that the refugee problem must be solved by settlement planning on a world scale with absorption of settlers in limited numbers . . . everywhere, so as to produce no shock to the economic structure of the receiving country . . . the absorption must be on such a limited scale in any one area that the people already established in the area will welcome the new settlers.
>
> I believe that money of the order of $500,000,000, expended on sound advice and based on the best detailed information, will put the refugees into new homes with more than a fair chance of successful absorption. . . .[14]

Roosevelt acknowledged the work on the Americas and Africa with gratitude and wrote, "I feel that we are now wholly implemented in discussing the general refugee problem with other nations."[15] Bowman was also approached by Morgenthau on the subject.

> Secretary Morgenthau called at 4:45 p.m. November 16, 1938, and said that he had seen the President and they had a laugh together over the fact that each had gone after the same man for information on settlement for refugees. He said the President volunteered information on his inquiries to me concerning northern South America.[16]

Bowman's suggestion that approximately $500 million would be needed for resettlement is an interesting and bold venture in cost accounting. It is not known what number of refugees Bowman had in mind, though Charles Liebman (president of the Refugee Economic Corporation) and Bowman had agreed that the cost of settling each refugee family would vary from $1,000 to $5,000. Of course as the war progressed, the calculated number of refugees increased. Estimates of the number of persons displaced by World War II supplied to President Roosevelt varied between three and twenty million.

Bowman, while intensely interested in migration and settlement problems, apparently did not feel that the issue was one that could take priority during armed conflict. In a letter to Lionel Curtis of Balliol College, Oxford, he wrote:

> The refugee problem has stirred a section of the American people but I do not think that it has stirred the masses so deeply that it will affect the war issue. The scale of the refugee problem is clearly beyond private resources, a matter for government to handle. It took a large part of the world's shipping to transport several millions of soldiers from America during the World War and provide a service of supply. No such vital need is felt in connection with the placement of refugees so far as the man on the street is concerned. It is generally felt here that the refugee problem will have to be settled in Europe, whatever sympathy and whatever help small-scale settlement in limited areas may contribute towards the bolstering of hopes.[17]

Bowman sent the president a copy of this letter, and wrote to Roosevelt about settlement possibilities in Costa Rica on land procured by the Refugee Economic Corporation:

> I have not spoken of the political difficulties which a large foreign immigrant group would create if planted in this small Latin American country, assuming that Costa Rica is willing to receive them. The effect of such a group upon the state, and the possibility that through the presence of the group we might become seriously involved in European quarrels, are matters upon which reflection is needed.... Do you want to run that risk? Do we wish to confuse our position and dilute our argument respecting the Monroe Doctrine?[18]

This was Bowman the politician, the realist, writing. Yet he worked to the limit of his capacity in attempting to "bolster hopes" with small-scale settlement of the dispossessed. Toward the end of the thirties there were a variety of organizations in existence, all with the avowed purpose of helping the refugees. Perhaps the most notable of these groups were the Refugee Economic Corporation, the Joint Distribution Committee, United Palestine Appeal, National Coordinating Committee for Aid to Refugees and Emigrants Coming from Germany, and the President's Advisory Committee. Bowman worked with the Refugee Economic Corporation and the President's Advisory Committee, though he concentrated his efforts on the former. The Corporation had appealed for aid relating to "geographic studies of localities throughout the world suitable for development by European settlers," and had already purchased land or settled Jewish refugees in Australia, Costa Rica, Bolivia, the Philippines, and North Carolina.

Charles Liebman of the Corporation and Bowman had become well acquainted following publication of *Limits of Land Settlement.* Liebman proposed a reprinting of *The Pioneer Fringe,* but Bowman suggested instead that Liebman continue to support active research on the subject. Consequently, in 1938, Liebman granted $25,000 to the Walter Hines Page School of International Relations, of The Johns Hopkins University, so that under Bowman's direction a selected team of investigators could rapidly make feasibility studies for suggested resettlement locations. For these purposes Bowman secured the services of Robert Pendleton and the director of the Page School, Owen Lattimore. Major investigating commissions were sent to British Guiana, the Dominican Republic, and the Phillipines. Teams of investigators tested soil, gathered climatic data by talking with the local population, and assessed the survival chances of refugees.

All three commisions submitted extensive reports, but perhaps the most exhaustive was that completed on the island of Mindanao, the second largest and southernmost of the principal islands of the Philippine group, during April and May 1939. The field investigation was officially led by O. D. Hargis, who had founded the Goodyear Rubber plantation in Mindanao and remained in charge of agricultural work there for twenty-five years. Accompanying Hargis on the mission were Stanton Youngberg, former director of the Philippine Bureau of Agriculture; Robert L. Pendleton, an authority on soils and technical advisor to the Government of Siam; Howard F. Smith, health and sanitation expert and Chief Quarantine Officer at Manila; and Captain Hugh J. Casey, hydro-electric expert of the U.S. Engineers Corps. A report of approximately eighty pages emphasized the feasibility of the project. The Philippine Commonwealth agreed to admit ten thousand refugees for settlement in the regions selected, but as World War II escalated, British Guiana and later Angola were proposed as the new Jewish homeland. Charles Liebman insisted on a Jewish homeland, preferably in Palestine, at critical junctures in this development.

Other investigations were conducted in Australia, New Zealand, Madagascar, former German colonies in Africa, China, Ecuador, Chile, Costa Rica, Alaska and southern California. These investigation were reviewed by the President's Advisory Committee, which came to realize that each government requested to absorb some of the refugees should be approached with regard to that government's needs. For instance, Ecuador could be offered a road-building program in exchange for accepting refugees.[19]

Liebman arranged a second grant of $25,000 from the Refugee Economic Corporation in May 1941 to The Johns Hopkins University. This was invested in feasibility studies especially in Peru, Ecuador, and Colombia. Bowman wrote of these investigations to James G. McDonald, chairman of the President's Advisory Committee on Political Refugees:

> A file of settlement materials has accumulated which deals with any and all aspects of settlement questions in many areas.... Special maps have been accumulated bearing on the same subject.... As soon as interest is concentrated in a region, or possibilities arise through political changes, more intensive work is done upon a given area and a more extensive report submitted. The theory back of this file, and its continuation, is that we ought to be able to give an almost instant reply to the question of settlement possibilities in any part of the world. Only a file that is kept alive and that represents the growing edge of current investigation will enable one to meet the constant demand for quick information.[20]

He revealed to Liebman that he was already thinking about the postwar world.

> In view of the control of the means of production in war-time we shall have the whole post-war economy controlled to a higher degree. This means inevitably the control of settlement that is a job for international agreement. The dreamers and the theorists will swarm around any possible peace conference that may be held. They will not have much respect for facts. I want to be loaded with them![21]

President Roosevelt continued to concern himself with the refugees. After considering South America and Africa south of the Sahara, he requested from Bowman a memorandum on refugee placement in Libya. This memorandum and ensuing meetings between the two men did much to create Roosevelt's Palestine policy. Bowman pointed out that political reactions throughout the Arab world would be violently adverse and that the number of Palestinians who could be accommodated immediately would be small.

> The Arabs are a group of peoples that may become united by a common distrust and hate of us. No internal uniting force is so powerful. Therefore, my advice is to keep the Palestine question or Libyan settlement in abeyance, so far as possible, until the end of the war.... In my opinion it would be most unwise to announce a Libyan settlement plan without saying that no other settlement project in the Arab world will be considered. Scattering the refugees here and there in the Arab world would have disastrous effects. It would confirm the propaganda, persistently broadcast by the Nazis, that the Allies have a deep-laid plan for giving the Jews dominance over the Arabs generally....[22]

On 10 August 1943 Bowman was called to the White House to talk further with the president, who:

> opened the conversation ... with the question, "Isaiah have you found places enough all over the map for refugees that we will have to look after?" This gave me the opening I wanted, to tell him two things: 1) that we were ready to give advice with respect to settlement on any question regarding refugees, in any place, at any time; 2) that he should avoid Libya.... I told him Angola was still the preferred place ... he responded immediately and said, "I got your good report and the maps that went with it, and gave the extra copy that you sent me to Churchill as you suggested. They are now informed as well as we are. I followed your advice in the matter." I told him I was pleased with this because settlement at any place in the Arab world would make terrible trouble at this time and that this was getting more intense in the Arab world, especially in Saudi Arabia with respect to Jewish immigration. He

again repreated that he agreed and was following my advice.[23]

Bowman's position was that Jewish admission to Palestine should be restricted and not brought up to parity with the Arabs. Of his report on the subject to the president, Bowman wrote:

> he told me he would follow and continue to follow [it]. He "broke training" in October, 1944, as an election dodge when the Zionists were on his neck. This left both the Zionists and the public confused as to what the President's position was. With this one exception his actions were consistent up to the time of his death and closely followed the line which I advocated personally to him and embodied in a report that he adopted as the basis of his policy.[24]

Eleanor Roosevelt also called Bowman to the White House. She had received reports from Zionists and others optimistic of the carrying capacity of Palestine, who had apparently named Bowman as one of the president's advisors on the Palestine problem. Bowman perceived the importance of Mrs. Roosevelt's summons, and reported the matter to the State Department.

> Mr. Hull sent for me this morning at ten minutes of one, and among other things asked me if I had "talked with the lady." I told him that I had not done so but was anxious about the interview not knowing the origin of her request. I added that I had made no special preparation for a talk with her on Palestine but that I was relying on quick foot work; and that I had decided to be a little rough with her if necesary in order to find out who had turned her attention to me. Hull said, "Why don't you do that? I think you have a right to know."[26]

Mrs. Roosevelt had been reading literature sent to her by Rose Luria Halprin, chairman of the Post-War Planning Committee of the Zionist Emergency Council. In a covering letter to some reports sent to the first lady, Mrs. Halprin wrote:

> Several experts, renowned in their respective fields, have of recent years reported on the absorptive capacity of Palestine and

have indicated that the country could, through scientific development, absorb a population several times the present number.[27]

Mrs. Roosevelt asked Bowman if "the convincing statements" which she had seen concerning the absorptive capacity of Palestine were true.

> She wondered ... could so large a population really be maintained under post-war conditions. ... "I told her I thought her question went to the heart of the problem. There is room for several million more Jews in Palestine, I told her, but only if they are supported from the outside. The larger the population gets however the more precarious it is politically and defensively. ... I told her that there was a more serious element of the problem, namely the resemblance of Zionism to Hitler's policies that group themselves around the principle of *lebensraum*. I asked her what difference there was between Hitler's using force to elbow non-Germans out of the way and take their land and the Zionist program of packing millions into Palestine and then crying out for more room, the force in this instance being applied by the United States and Great Britain.[28]

Bowman gave Mrs. Roosevelt specific examples of the reluctance of Colombia, Australia, and Canada to accept refugee Jews, and told her that at the president's request he had been studying the problem for several years.

> I concluded by telling her that under these circumstances, political and military help for an artifically enlarged Zionist state would be impossible to obtain except from Great Britain and the United States where the Jew is powerful politically; but help given to the Jew because of political pressure in time of stress would only increase the anti-Semitism that had risen in America during the past five years or more. It would flare up and be in the end disastrous for the Jew both here and elsewhere.[29]

On 24 January 1944 Bowman sent Mrs. Roosevelt a written statement summarizing what he had told her. It was a subject upon which he had firm opinions, based on scientific fact, and he was adamant in his denial of Zionism which he saw only as a force which could disrupt the future world order. Some of his Jewish friends felt likewise, including Charles Liebman, who was prepared to finance a search for places that could accommodate Jewish colonies.

Late in February 1941, Henry Field was assigned to the White House. "The President had said, 'I need an anthropologist on my staff during this war and afterward for there will be many human problems to solve.' "[30] By the end of the summer of 1942, Field had concluded that the displaced persons would prove a vital factor in the postwar world. With the help of John Franklin Carter, who was both confidential aide to the president and Field's superior officer, Field drafted a memorandum to the president incorporating these ideas for a research project:

> We did not know that this same idea had long been germinating in the President's mind.... Back came an order from F.D.R. to discuss the project with Dr. Isaiah Bowman, geographical adviser to the President and President of Johns Hopkins University. By Presidential Directive I drove to Johns Hopkins to talk to Dr. Bowman ... to try to persuade him to direct the work on Population, Migration and Settlement. Dr. Bowman in his most friendly manner listened carefully as I outlined the proposed researches continent by continent, country by country—each Study arranged along the same lines.[31]

Bowman approved, and by November 1942 the project was underway, entitled "M" for migration.[32] The project finally included 152 reports, 103 translations, 328 memoranda, 47 lectures, and 17 Administrative Series—a total of about 20,000 pages. Roosevelt emphasized that "because we would be dealing with political dynamite," the utmost secrecy concerning the establishment and the work of "M" Project must be observed. Financing would come from White House unvouchered funds. Special arrangements would be set up with John Carter by the Bureau of the Budget. Dr. Bowman's suggestions should be followed.[33]

The unvouchered funds provided by President Roosevelt amounted to approximately $50,000 a year. Bowman was chief adviser, though the details were left to Henry Field. On 23 April 1945, Field and Carter drew up an "Interim Report on 'M' Project."

> The areas of concentration in accordance with our Presidential Directives were:
>
> A. From November 1, 1942–April 30, 1943 preliminary studies were made on a world-wide basis, excluding the United States.
>
> An archive and small reference library were begun.
>
> B. From May 1, 1943–March 8, 1944 studies were written and obtained on selected areas throughout the world.
>
> C. From March 9, 1944–to date the areas designated were the Far East, U.S.S.R., and the other American Republics, including the Caribbean.[34]

In addition to some 666 reports, the "M" Project produced two hundred copies of the *Atlas of Population and Migration Trends* on 15 November 1945. The assembled "M" staff (some fourteen permanent members and as many associates) were to constitute the brain trust for making intelligent decisions about the postwar world. They paid special attention to the history of previous resettlement attempts and the immigration laws of many countries.

The "M" project bore a curious resemblance to the Inquiry of World War I days, and Bowman had that in mind as he influenced the direction of the project. Yet perhaps the matter of the displaced person was a larger and more pressing problem in the Second World War. Ladislas Farago wrote that Roosevelt

> regarded the victims of the war as representing but one of the three groups. In the second group were the surplus populations of certain European and Asiatic countries, while the third group was made up of so-called "geopolitical problem children," minorities whose presence in certain countries is traditionally exploited for power-political purposes.
>
> Roosevelt believed that the post-war necessity of a large-scale resettlement of refugees would enable him to solve the interdependent problems of all three groups simultaneously.[35]

Roosevelt told Henry Field he intended to use the "M" project "studies as a basis for discussion and implementation of post war projects."[36] But when Roosevelt died on 12 April 1945, the project also died. Truman officially terminated it in October, having ordered Henry Field

> to deliver by guarded truck all the files to Dr. Bowman's office at Johns Hopkins. With an armed Marine guard, I rode on a truck to Baltimore where the files were deposited in the attic above the President's office.... Following Dr. Bowman's death the "M" project files were sealed with all his papers until 1975.[37]

The "M" studies were in fact barely utilized. The Nazis had liquidated several million Jews who might otherwise have been the postwar beneficiaries of the "M" project. So many people had been killed and so much destruction had been wrought that the matter of organized resettlement was given a low priority. Not until 1960 were the studies finally declassified. Truman's Point IV Program for underdeveloped areas became the single practical application of much of this research.

> [A] friend of President Truman's from Kansas City ... left him some notes.... These notes contained the basic idea that the United States could export technological assistance to many nations of the world. When the bell rang Clark Clifford gave this note to President Truman. After reading it carefully the President thought that this was an important new suggestion. With the scissors he cut between Point III and Point IV and inserted these notes with a memorandum to write this out more carefully. All the numbers following were changed by one number. Thus this idea became Point IV which is known throughout the world. In conversation later, President Truman told me that because of the flow of "M" Project Studies in a special file which he had happened to look at early that morning, he was convinced that this was a very excellent proposition. Thus Point IV benefited both then and later from the Studies.[38]

Bowman was approached by government officials and urged to take charge of the Economic Cooperation Administration, one of the institutions through which Point IV was to be implemented. He refused to head the Administration in Paris, and accepted an assignment in Washington on the condition that he could retain the title and duties of consultant. Harland Cleveland, George Hoffmann, and Averill Harriman each talked to Bowman of the need for his services but he declined to assume too much responsibility. He was tired, and wished to reserve his strength for writing a book on U.S. foreign policy "similar to what Mahan had done for U.S. naval policy."[39] Even so, he did

> accept responsibility for certain studies in this field that relate to the underdeveloped areas of colonial powers. I have agreed to give a certain amount of time to it. It is broader than pioneer settlement which relates to land chiefly.[40]

One of his first tasks was to write a report concerning "Reclamation of New Lands for Agriculture," which had been specifically requested by Trygve Lie, secretary general of the United Nations." In a letter to Hugh H. Bennett, chief of the U.S. Department of Agriculture and a friend of many years, he wrote:

> I agree with you on the too-hopeful view that many persons have of "new lands." In my writings of the past twenty years I have stressed the marginal character of most new lands. The one big exception has been the interior of Brazil, and there we have a social system that neutralizes Brazil's principal opportunities. The tzetze fly region would be a second. I know of no comparable third. The Arctic fringe was in fashion some years ago but its spectacular qualities now being understood, the slugging period of settlement has begun and it is not pleasant.[42]

Bowman felt that a fatal gap existed between scientific findings and social programs. He urged not less study of resources but increased study of processes, a recognition of a new composition of forces, the need for thinking from acts to consequences, and the endowment of chairs at universities staffed by scholars who studied the totality of the problem.

It was a great satisfaction to him to see the pioneer studies which he had commenced in the twenties at the American Geographical Society put to such use. He wrote to J. K. Wright, "I . . . realize more fully than ever what tremendous effects pioneer settlement studies have had upon thinking in action centers. None of the work was lost. It has grown to be President Truman's point four, and it is the E.C.A. share of that point four enterprise that I have been asked to be responsible for. . . ."[43]

Chapter Nine

President of The John Hopkins University

On 1 July 1935 Bowman assumed the presidency of one of the most prestigious universities in the United States. The emphasis upon research, the exchange between graduate student and professor, and the sense of intellectual community were all facets of a way of life which Bowman knew and enjoyed. In their thorough search for a new president, the Board of Trustees of Johns Hopkins had sought above all an accomplished scholar, an individual who was a man of affairs, and one experienced in the art of raising funds.

Bowman's predecessor, Joseph S. Ames, had been unable to cure the economic ills of the institution which had accumulated as a result of the economic depression. Notwithstanding a voluntary reduction of ten percent in faculty salaries during Ames's last year in office, the deficit amounted to $183,000.[1] Bowman had confronted the same problem since 1929 as director of the American Geographical Society. With unusual candor, Ames wrote Bowman several letters enumerating mistakes and errors of judgment which he felt he had committed as president; he also revealed remaining campus difficulties. Personal squabbling in the administrative ranks, finances, and the gulf which yawned between the academic campus and the Hopkins Hospital loomed as the largest and most immediate problems confronting the incoming president.

141

Bowman eliminated much of the squabbling by assuming a very firm control of matters immediately upon arrival. His incisive administrative manner once again proved invaluable to him. He visited the hospital, talked and corresponded with the physicians, watched some operations performed (including the first "blue baby operation"), facilitated and encouraged the work of part-time doctors, and in 1946 appointed Dr. Lowell J. Reed to the newly created office of vice-president of the Medical Division of the University. But the financial problem persisted throughout Bowman's presidential tenure, and he was obliged to devote much of his time to it.

On the day Bowman assumed office as fifth president of the University it was arranged that one million dollars would be taken from the unrestricted funds of the Academic Division of the University to reduce the deficit of the Division. Then Bowman began the task of raising funds and "the adjustment of the work of the Division to the need for further economies."[2] After an intense campaign of only six weeks, half a million dollars had been raised for a "three year Sustaining Fund." Bowman had met frequently with members of the Board of Trustees before becoming president, and had decided that he could work with them. With their support he placed numerous statements in newspapers (especially the *Baltimore Sun*), investigated the financial policies of Hopkins investments, and made speeches to a wide variety of organizations.

These talks, sometimes given at the rate of two a day, covered all sorts of subjects. Bowman had adopted a policy of putting Johns Hopkins on display. Many of his addresses were written, revised, and then rewritten. Of his typical schedule Bowman wrote to Frank E. Williams:

> In addition to the talk at the Geographical Society, I spoke on the Barnwell Foundation at the Central High School on December 8th. I must give the inauguration address at Vanderbilt on February 5th. In six days between Christmas and New Year's I must prepare six addresses which I give in January. One man has too few ideas to spread himself out more thinly by taking on new engagements. My strength is taxed to the limit....[3]

Generally avoiding the subject of geography, Bowman's addresses emphasized the social relevance of university research, and the nature and purpose of university development throughout the world. He brought Anson Phelps Stokes, whom he had known at Yale, to Hopkins to lecture on university history. He became increasingly fascinated by the history of higher education, and developed an interest in biography.

Bowman's initial curiosity in Daniel Coit Gilman, president of Hopkins 1876-1901, perhaps lay in the manner and style in which Gilman had managed Hopkins. But there were similarities in the careers of the two men.[4] Both had taught geography at Yale, had held office in the American Geographical Society, had helped arbitrate boundary disputes in South America, had physical features in the Arctic named after them, had a fondness for poetry, and had studied European educational forms in hopes of improving the educational system of the United States. And both men had become presidents of The Johns Hopkins University. When Abraham Flexner wrote *Daniel Coit Gilman: Creator of the American Type of University*, Bowman read the book at once and reviewed it for "From the Bookshelf" of *The Evening Sun*.[5]

Curiously, Gilman did not found a department of geography at Hopkins. But three of the earliest doctoral dissertations which might be regarded as geographic—by Cleveland Abbe, Jr. (1898), Oliver L. Fassig (1899), and J. A. Bonsteel (1901)—came from The Johns Hopkins University Department of Geology. Fassig, who continued detailed study of the climate of Baltimore, assumed charge of the State Weather Service and was appointed Baltimore representative of the U.S. Weather Bureau. Hopkins faculty and students attended meetings of the Geographical Society of Baltimore and the National Geographic Society.[6] However, when Bowman arrived in Baltimore, few remnants of this early activity were in evidence.

Bowman had less opportunity, though perhaps more determination, than Gilman to introduce geography. Senior members of the Hopkins faculty had visited Bowman shortly after he came to Baltimore and firmly announced their opposition to the creation of such a department. Perhaps they had in mind the unhappy example of Wallace Atwood's regime at Clark University, and what the institution of a geography program had meant there. Atwood had created a large department of geography and the first graduate school of geography in the United States—it was supposed at the expense of other departments, most notably psychology. The matter had become nationally known. Bowman consequently did not attempt to create a geography department at that time, but was content to wait.

He was obliged to declare a policy for Hopkins in the wake of President Ames's insufficient definition of University objectives. In 1925 President Goodnow had announced the anticipation of a time when the university would cease to give instruction in most of the subjects then taught in the first years of college. The plan had not seemed effective, but it had been approved by the trustees and adopted by the University. Bowman steadily assailed the plan, quieted doubting alumni, and before his retirement had thoroughly reestablished the place of the undergraduate in the University. He announced this policy in his inaugural address, and then found and cited documentary support for his position in the writings of Gilman. His emphasis upon undergraduate instruction rather surprised the faculty, who had come to regard the fundamental mission of Hopkins as that of research coupled with graduate instruction.

Bowman declined an inauguration of public ceremony. Nevertheless he gave an inaugural speech, "A Design for Scholarship," on Commemoration Day, 22 February 1936. This address, together with twelve others which he had given since accepting the Hopkins presidency, was published in that same year by the university press.[7] Several of the included essays revealed Bowman's social philosophy, which had hitherto been little publicized. He wished to mobilize the resources of society and invest them in the public good, using institutions as the instruments of such a mobilization. The shift in his thought from primary emphasis upon geographic scholarship to the social good seems to have been a product of the depression years.

While the essays revealed a wide and various learning, they did not exhibit the discipline, balance, and organization of Bowman's previous work. Recognizing that he did not have sufficient time to give each of the essays the care he wished, Bowman was a little uneasy about the book's composition and appearance. But there were just too many tasks to be accomplished.

In his inaugural address he reaffirmed his intention to encourage the undergraduate at Johns Hopkins. However, his enthusiasm for the interchange between faculty member and graduate student both engaged in research was unbounded: "In the long view the most valuable, most expensive, and least understood intellectual enterprise of a university is the graduate school."[8] He preferred to work for the possibility of high attainment by the few, rather than programs established for large numbers that were less intense. The thrill of study with Davis and Shaler and the milieu of the Yale geology department came flooding back to him. He knew the excitement of intellectual discovery and its application, and could now help others experience it, too. The particular role of the graduate school fascinated him.

In his second "Annual Report of the President" he devoted himself to the matter of graduate study, and especially that at Hopkins. He was concerned that "higher education was only more education rather than the discovery and development of talents through independent work." Knowing that education in the United States was designed to facilitate "a better if not new social order," he warned of the "only . . . real danger—centralized national control and ensuing deadly uniformity of indoctrination to suit the government of the day."[9] This extended statement, also urging closer ties with the town and recognition of those who sought part-time study, was further elaborated and revised, then sent to a variety of his correspondents and friends in university administration. It was embodied in a memorandum which was published in 1939 by the Federal Office of Education as *The Graduate School in American Democracy*. Bowman reverted to the theme again in his 1939 "Annual Report of the President," noting that "all educational institutions . . . [should] review their programs and results . . . in the light of swift social and political movements that challenge the methods and purposes of education."[10]

Bowman was not content to allow graduate education to continue at Hopkins without investigating its purpose. He wished to demonstrate to the Board of Trustees its purpose and function, and benefit to Baltimore. He met with the trustees frequently, usually individually and privately, and quickly won their confidence. But he encountered other problems.

At the American Geographical Society, Bowman's staff had been concerned solely with research and matters geographic, and had been selected by Bowman. At Hopkins the situation was quite different. Bowman was the newcomer, and he faced a faculty which felt that they should govern and direct the institution. Inevitably and occasionally there ensued a clash of will between segments of the faculty and President Bowman. These clashes were tactical skirmishes rather than structural incompatibilities, but they did not make Bowman a popular president. His efficiency and performance were recognized, but some friction was generated by his policy of hiring and firing, his insistence in chairing or sitting on large numbers of committees, and what appeared to some as his arbitrary action in expanding or eliminating academic departments.

Invariably Bowman worked at least twelve hours a day, and often fourteen hours. Saturdays were frequently spent in university business, in the quest for financial support. Sundays he reserved for less formal correspondence, for writing addresses, scientific articles, and a large book whose form was beginning to take place in his mind. Fatigue took its toll. He suffered two bouts of influenza, followed by hospitalization with stones in the kidney. Daniel Willard, president of the Board of Trustees, wrote to Bowman during his convalescence:

> My latest from Dr. Tom Brown is that while you have been busy doing more things than perhaps any one man should undertake, you have also been developing at the same time a stone quarry in one of your kidneys which while more or less annoying is not necessarily, in fact not usually, fatal. . . . I think you have been trying to do more than you are physically justified in doing . . . I think it highly desirable that you should place a check on [your activities] for a time and let some of our younger colleagues do a little more. . . .[11]

Bowman did not reduce his work schedule but did maintain a close relationship with his physician, Dr. Brown. At first only professional, the relationship became personal, and Bowman began to take an interest in human anatomy that was later revealed in the functioning of The Johns Hopkins Medical School, and in studies of physiological climatology.

Bowman was extremely reluctant to sever his relationship with scholarship which he maintained in addition to his complex administrative responsibilities. His keen interest in pioneers and pioneering was revealed in *Limits of Land Settlement* (1937)—for which he was responsible—and in a contribution toward some studies of refugee settlement possibility.

He also continued a close relationship with the American Geographical Society. He advised John K. Wright, who was then director, on a variety of matters including the ever-present financial problem, and he frequently wrote to Gladys Wrigley about articles and authors for the *Review* which she edited. They exchanged information on books and articles either had recently discovered, and word forms and poetry which both so enjoyed. More importantly for Bowman's career, he came to rely very much upon Wrigley to provide him with books, articles, references, and apposite quotations. She edited his writings swiftly and deftly, returning them usually within the week. Indeed the help she gave Bowman in the years 1935–50 can hardly be overemphasized. Bowman would have been extremely reluctant to have severed his relation with the Society, even though he insisted after 1935 that he would never make a decision for it. Nevertheless his advice was sought on a variety of difficult and complex matters until the time of his death. Wrigley urged him again and again to reduce his efforts, but to no avail.

Other duties called him away from Hopkins. In 1938 he attended the International Geographical Congress in Amsterdam, and in April 1939 he visited the University of Puerto Rico as chairman of the commission appointed by the United States to investigate the possibilities of development of that university in the Pan American field. During 1939 Bowman was appointed chairman of the Commission on the Structure of Maryland State Government. He was elected to the directorate of the American Telephone and Telegraph Company, to the Board of Visitors to the Naval Academy, and to the Air University at Maxwell Field.

Following the 1938 International Geographical Congress in Amsterdam, Bowman spent a week in Germany talking with German geographers and assessing the chances of a war. He was aware that an outbreak of war would have immediate repercussions for Hopkins. He doubted "whether anyone will now venture to say confidently that there will or will not be war.... There are too many 'ifs'."[12]

He concluded that war could break out at a moment's notice on any one of a number of issues. When the United States did enter the war the University responded with additional offerings in the technological and engineering sector, and an expanded Reserve Officers Training Corps. Faculty teaching loads were increased and, beginning in 1942-43, an accelerated program of three sixteen-week terms per year was adopted. Education gave way to training, and technology began to dominate Hopkins. The School of engineering gave courses to individuals who would be staffing industrial plants, and opened its laboratories six days a week.

The physicists undertook top secret work for the government, as did the chemists, medical scientists, and others. Hopkins physicists developed a nondestructive test for determining the proper seating of rotating bands on shells, and played a leading role in the development of the "radio proximity fuse," which greatly increased the effectiveness of antiaircraft fire. Chemists studied the use of infrared rays as a detection device. Both chemists and physicists advanced work on certain materials to be used in the building of the atomic bomb. Hopkins was involved in approximately a hundred research projects, spent $15,000,000 in scientific research for government agencies, and at times employed up to two thousand workers on these problems. Additionally some 4,500 Hopkins graduate students and faculty members served in the United States armed forces; 122 gave their lives. Of the Hopkins war effort Bowman wrote:

> we have not been able to consider education in detached terms or
> as a thing in course of evolution from past designs; nor are we

able broadly to revise educational programs to accord with social changes that war so quickly imposes. What colleges and universities now supply need not be called education at all. It is rather the fullest possible use of plant and funds, knowledge and ideas, students and faculty, to meet the requirements of a war of inhuman intensity.[13]

Bowman spent two, and frequently three, days a week in Washington, as special advisor to the successive Secretaries of State Hull and Stettinius. He was a member of the Stettinius London mission in 1944, a member of the American delegation to the Dumbarton Oaks Conference, and advisor to the secretary of state at the 1945 San Francisco Conference which established the United Nations. Bowman's service to the government in these war years, the subject of the next chapter, was intricately interwoven with his work at Hopkins.

Meanwhile an opportunity had arisen to introduce geography into college and university offerings. Bowman had discussed the role of geography in the Army Specialized Training Program with Colonel Herman Beukema, director of the Army Specialized Training Division, and with Secretary of War Stimson. He has also discussed the subject with numerous other officials in the Pentagon. He wrote a confidential note to Gladys Wrigley:

> I have been in Washington two days, as a member of a committee of nine, setting up the curricula to be taken in large doses and in quick succession by the 150,000 who will be sent to the colleges for specialized training. Our two-day session was intense, and I want to tell you one day what I did with the section on geography![14]

Bowman's advice to Beukema to establish a program for the creation of an appropriate geographic literature and sufficient geographic teaching may have been decisive in adding the subject matter of geography to the Army Specialized Training Program.[15] If Hopkins wished to work with the army program, a geography offering had to provided at once. Bowman was elated. Karl Pelzer, officially with the Page School of International Relations at Hopkins, and essentially an intellectual valet to the beleaguered Bowman since 1936, was put in charge of the geographic work in the Army Training Program. Pelzer taught geography to distinguished professors in other disciplines and to graduate students, who then offered geography to the Army recruits. The emphasis was on Western Europe. Large numbers of army recruits passed through this fundamental geographic training, which was demonstrably valuable.

Bowman seized the opportunity to start a geography department in 1942-43. Pelzer suggested to Bowman that he hire George Carter, whom Pelzer had known in California; Carter was hired. Next came Andrew Clark and Jean Gottmann (then with the Institute for Advanced Study at Princeton). Bowman interviewed Gilbert White as a potential chairman of the department, but White was not available. Bowman also discussed positions in the department with Henry H. Bruman, G. M. McBride, Armstrong Price, Athelstan F. Spilhaus, Robert P. Sharp, Robert G. Stone, Richard J. Russell, Lloyd Brown, and John Kerr Rose.[16] He made a special attempt to secure Carl Sauer as a professor, but Sauer declined the opportunity.[17] John Leighly also refused a professorship,[18] and Bowman's attempt to secure Frank Debenham of Cambridge for one year came to nought. Nevertheless, before Bowman died on 6 January 1950, the geography department had additionally acquired the services of Robert L. Pendleton (soils), Ernest F. Penrose (economics), D. H. K. Lee (physiological climatology), C. W. Thornthwaite (climatology), and Lloyd A. Brown (history of cartography). Faculty in other departments taught related courses.

In his "Annual Report of the President" for 1943, Bowman made clear the need for geography at Hopkins, in the United States, and in the world. His statement was reprinted in *Science* and *School and Society,* and in the *Proceedings of the Association of American Colleges.* He referred to

> At least a hundred college heads [who] have enquired as to our plans for geography in the post-war years. . . . War and its related problems of peace-time organization for equity and freedom have at last taught the American people that modern geography is not children's geography to be finished in the seventh grade. That "imaginative grasp of space" which science shares with poetry seemed somehow to have been impossible to attain until our Army, Navy and Air Forces had taken their stations and begun their operations in almost every part of the world. For a full

generation we seemed unable in our thinking to synchronize time and space in a spreading network of technologies, trade, and international relations. . . .[19]

Bowman made the case for geography on the campus in terms of the national interest. While the faculty may not have been completely enthusiastic, the new department already offered more than a dozen courses, with other classes taught in the College for Teachers.[20]

Bowman appointed George Carter chairman of the department, but maintained a very close supervision of matters. The two exchanged memoranda regularly and once a week Carter reported to Bowman in the latter's office. Bowman talked to Carter of "the history of American Geography and reminisced about the great and lesser men of the field,"[21] while Carter kept Bowman informed about younger geographers and developments in the field. The two men worked well together, and both labored hard in the development of the department.

In order to retain all its staff members after the war, Bowman sought an endowment for the department. He felt it hardly possible to secure professors eminent in their field without being able to offer them permanent employ. To secure financial support Bowman felt obliged to develop a philosophy and statement of purpose for the department. In "A Department of Geography at Hopkins," he estimated the space needed and the architectural style and cost of a building modelled after Cambridge University and the Institut de Géographie at the Sorbonne, and said there was "a chance through geography (the geography of diseases and the geography of air transport are two striking and immediate responsibilities) to make a contribution to national welfare and security that is beyond anything we could have hoped to do in the pre-war years."[22] He shared his worries with Alfred H. Meyer.

What the curriculum makers do to the subject may be fatal to it, despite the indispensable contribution which it makes to education. My own feeling is that geography should be a separate department and establish whatever affiliations it desires. The relations with geology and biology in this institution will be close but the relations with the social sciences will be closer. At Hopkins we do not favor rigid definitions and classifications to so called "subjects." Our attempt is to fuse and interconnect and thus break down the boundaries that become so permanent in

practically every educational institution. As one man put it, we
try to avoid "hardening of the categories."[23]

As a fund-raising device, he wrote a tract called "Geography as an
Urgent University Need" in December 1944, and revised it in January
1947.[24] He sent it to university presidents considering the creation of a
department of geography, to members of the Board of Trustees, and to
wealthy individuals and business corporations. In the article he urged
an intelligent conservation of resources, and commented that the
United States was replacing Great Britain as a world power. After
summarizing British imperial history, Bowman said that the Cambridge
University department of geography "has rendered altogether
extraordinary services in the training of specialists serving British
interests. Both it and the nearby Scott Polar Research Institute are
filled with staffs in the service of the Admiralty and the War Office."[25]
He was not so complimentary toward geography in the United States,
saying that "with the single exception of California [University]
leaders have not been produced in proportion to expenditures. . . . High
concentration upon graduate training, as a primary feature of policy, is
now the outstanding need. . . ."[26] This statement, coupled with his
article "Science and Social Effects: Three Failures,"[27] was essentially
Bowman's rationale for the development of the Hopkins geography
department.

He arranged to have eminent geographers such as H. J. Fleure, Hans
W. Ahlmann, and C. B. Fawcett address the graduate students and
faculty, or the Hopkins and Baltimore community as a whole. Hopkins
provided a venue for negotiation between the Association of American
Geographers and the American Society for Professional Geographers
when the two bodies held different beliefs concerning membership in
the Association. And Bowman and Carter tried to host the annual
meeting of the Association of American Geographers. Bowman
continually sought to improve the quality of geographical classes, and
encouraged a variety of individuals to participate in the course and
seminar offerings. Even in his retirement he participated in the
seminars, which he insisted were the heart of the Hopkins program. In
November 1949 he wrote:

Yesterday we had a humdinger of a seminar in geography.
Lattimore spoke on the territory between Mongolia and the

Arctic in eastern Siberia. Stefansson, the Arctic explorer, came down for the occasion and so, too, did Sir Hubert Wilkins, the Australian who has done work in both the Arctic and Antarctic. They are old friends of mine....[28]

At the age of seventy he was still alert to opportunity. When Carlos Monge, a physician and director of the Institute of Andean Biology at the University of San Marcos, Peru, wrote a manuscript concerning acclimatization in the Andes, Bowman wrote the foreword to it, arranged for an English translation of the book, and had it published by The Johns Hopkins University Press in 1948 for distribution by the American Geographical Society. And when, in the previous year, Stephen S. Visher had completed work on a manuscript entitled "Scientists Starred 1903-1943 in American Men of Science," Bowman quickly recommended the study to his university press. Bowman had been "starred" as a geologist (geographers were not starred) in *American Men of Science* in 1920, and had unsuccessfully attempted to secure recognition for geographers in that notable book.

But it was the matter of intellectual descent that fascinated him. He feared mediocrity was flooding the country and had already entered the world of scholarship. He could not see the equal of Gilbert, Shaler, and Davis in the 1940s, and that spurred him to strive for a department of geography that would be outstanding in its field. Bowman wished to model the physical plant of his department of geography upon that of Cambridge University, which he admired very much. In fact, he paid Frank Debenham, chairman of the Cambridge department, to have plans to scale drawn of his facility, even including bookcases and map racks. And while Bowman was in England in the spring of 1944 on the Stettinius mission, he urged John Lee Pratt (one of the wealthiest members of the Hopkins Board of Trustees, and a fellow member of the Stettinius mission) to join him in a visit to the Cambridge department. Pratt obliged and, too, was impressed.

Bowman sought an endowment for geography at Hopkins in order to secure the finest talent available. He began the search for funds in the spring of 1944 and by autumn the first gifts were received. At first he sought one million dollars, but by 1947 had decided he needed two million. Shortly thereafter he tried to establish a School of Political Geography and proposed a twelve million dollar endowment for that purpose. Through numerous private conversations, a variety of memoranda, and a series of letters providing details of the many ways in which geography would facilitate growth, conserve resources and preserve the place of the United States in a rapidly changing world, he won the confidence of two of the wealthiest members of the Board of Trustees, John Pratt and Donaldson Brown. Other trustees followed suit. S. Page Nelson wrote Bowman:

> Until recently I had no real conception of the depths and extent of "University" geography. My understanding has been considerably improved from what you have said at meetings, in your memorandum of January 16, and in your book *The New World*. It goes without saying that establishment of a chair of geography at Johns Hopkins is desirable.[29]

Carlyle Barton, president of the Board of Trustees, had worked closely with Bowman for several years and by 1945 was in favor of proclaiming an "Isaiah Bowman School of Geography." Bowman urged suspension of such a title while he lived, but constantly reminded Barton of geographical significance in a changing world.[30] Pratt and Brown secured the interest of industry, and by November 1945 $500,000 had been raised towards the endowment. One million dollars had been secured by 1947. Pratt, Brown, and Bowman approached the Overseas Policy Group of General Motors, the Gulf Corporation, the Alfred P. Sloan Foundation, and Lammot du Pont. In February 1947, Bowman wrote to Donaldson Brown:

> It seems to me that the key idea in requesting support for the School of Geography is this: we cannot leave analyses of the world to our government. Large amounts of work are being done in different bureaus and some of it is objective and beyond reproach. Much of it is interpreted by policy makers, who take defensive positions and make everything seem all right. The most powerful nation in the world may go very far wrong if it does not have what I call private analysis. Modern geography offers a form of approach and a depth of analysis that we cannot afford to neglect. We must know more about the rest of the world and we must learn it quickly. Only critical and honest studies will be a sufficient guide.[31]

Bowman was prepared to have the geography department make studies of individual countries to benefit industry, which would then fund the university to undertake its research, securing more accurate work at a lesser price. Bowman had examined the regional studies of Brazil prepared by General Motors, and was convinced that the Hopkins geography department could do better. "I propose an extension of similar but more analytical studies to include every country in the world."[32] Under Bowman's sponsorship, E. F. Penrose, "Dr. Douglas Lee [and] Professor Pendleton ... agreed ... that the larger part of the difficulties of many countries of the Third World experienced as decolonization proceeded were connected to an important extent with the nature of the tropical environment in relation to the technological conditions of the age."[33]

Bowman anticipated that this educational program "would produce the occasional statesman," and would

> advance our knowledge of human development in the tropics ... we are obliged under present world conditions to be interested in them, to deal with them and to a certain extent live in them. We have to be expert as to tropical climates, tropical medicine, and tropical economic conditions and development ... no one in the Department of State at the present time has had basic training of this sort. The tradition has been to deal superficially with all such groups of problems ... I can see no way out of this difficulty except to form a school that joins a more intimate knowledge of the earth and its people with the comprehensive questions of foreign policy.[34]

Bowman urged study in what he termed "political composition," a composite judgement made by the trader and the geographer after analysis of resources, social and political organizations, and human abilities. This type of research, of practical value to industry, excited Bowman to write "that Johns Hopkins might make a unique contribution to American Geography."[35] He did succeed in obtaining a building for the department, to be known as the Julia Rogers House. The geography faculty and students, selected in the most careful manner, led to fine intellectual opportunity. Bowman proudly wrote, "No other department in the world gives its members the time and the opportunity now provided here for distinguished contributions to geographic science."[36]

During 1947 Bowman was taken ill with influenza on at least two occasions. His physician, Dr. Thomas Brown, spent much time with him, urging him to reduce his work load and increase his leisure time. Bowman reluctantly concluded that he should retire from the presidency of Hopkins. He was urged to retain the office until an appropriate successor could be installed. When Detlev W. Bronk became the sixth president of The Johns Hopkins University on 1 January 1949, Bowman retired. He had come to realize that his life itself was at stake, and he wanted to write a series of books on his international experiences. The press of his presidential work and other responsibilities was pitted against the pent-up desire to share his experience of the affairs of nations. By constitution and training committed to work hard and long hours, he did confess that anyone who maintained the schedule he did and lived to the age of seventy was a biological miracle.

He gave more thought to his family, his planned books, and began politely to refuse invitations to talk, join, or have conferred upon him yet more honors. One of his last acts as president of Hopkins was to have the trustees approve the establishment of an Advisory Committee for Geography. This nine-member advisory body was a substitute for his continual advice and encouragement to Chairman George Carter.

Yet with Bowman's retirement, his plans for the substantial funding of the department of geography began to founder. Trustee support, private donations, and corporate interest began to wane. When Donaldson Brown, one of the most active supporters of Bowman's geographical scheme, wrote to President Bronk that his contribution to geography need not now be considered restricted to that cause and that he was prepared to suggest a similar change to Mr. du Pont, it became abundantly clear that support had been for Bowman, not for geography.[37] When Owen Lattimore, who taught courses in the geography department, was accused by Senator Joseph McCarthy of being a Communist, and George Carter became one of Lattimore's adversaries, all that Bowman had hoped for was lost. A contemporary of Lattimore, E. Francis Penrose, recalled: "Work was interrupted, Johns Hopkins was made the object of public attacks by witch-hunt organizations, and the effects were disastrous for the development of the Department."[38] Jean Gottmann, who resigned his position in the department in 1948 to return to Paris, remembered:

> Early in 1949 the Lattimore affair blew up and bitterly divided the Department of Geography and the whole Hopkins campus ... that matter became a national and international affair ... the first accusation against Lattimore by Senator McCarthy started the episode known as "McCarthyism" in American history. It was based on some photographic work allegedly done in the dark room of the Bowman School of Geography. The Department was still a rather young, not fully established element at the Hopkins. It suffered from this situation.[39]

The Isaiah Bowman School of Geography, so named in 1948, was later reduced to the Isaiah Bowman Department of Geography, then Bowman's name was removed from the abbreviated title. Despite the conferral of the first doctorate on Edward C. Higbee and the subsequent success of other students, during the twelve months of his retirement, Bowman had reason to feel disappointed with the lack of progress on the matter of the endowment for the Isaiah Bowman School of Geography. He realized that the new president did not have geography high on his list of priorities.

Also disappointing to Bowman, and possibly damaging to the cause of geography at Hopkins, was the turn of events at Harvard. Bowman and Harvard's President James B. Conant had corresponded on the nature and worth of geography, especially since 1947. In the following year Bowman had been appointed to the Harvard Board of Overseers. Bowman urged the creation of a department of geography separate from geology, presented Conant with a copy of *Geography in Relation to the Social Sciences*, and provided a detailed description of geography at Hopkins.[40] When, early in 1948, Conant proclaimed "that geography is not a university subject," Bowman was very disappointed.[41]

In any assessment of Bowman's presidency it would be hard to overemphasize his political contribution. His concern and commitment to the international problem had become intense with the outbreak of war, and matters at the University seemed less significant to him than they had prior to 1941. He came to rely more heavily on the provost, P. Stewart Macaulay, and a young dean he appointed, Wilson Schaffer.

There was nevertheless a multiplicity of matters requiring his decision. Perhaps this was what produced in Bowman an urgency based on his sense of the shortness of life. Medical evidence suggests he may also have had an overactive thyroid condition. He simply could not tolerate the wasting of time. To some he appeared curt, intolerant, even authoritarian. Usually at faculty meetings he placed his large pocket watch on the table, set a time limit on discussions, and asked if anyone had been dissatisfied with his management of the previous meeting. This display of authority intimidated many faculty members.

There were other individual incidents which cost him popularity. Early in the war he established a Jewish quota, and although this was done with the consent of the Jewish community it led to a veiled charge of anti-Semitism. It was with the "liberals" on campus that the "conservative" Bowman seemed to clash most frequently.

> Bowman's unpopularity was due to a complex of things . . . Isaiah had been a bit of a liberal, but a long way back. He became more and more of a conservative and an active anti-communist. The faculty was solidly liberal and generally felt that a communist on the campus was a bit of intellectual decoration. Bowman managed to oust one or two of the excessively Liberal characters, and a Communist or two. He managed it well, using one excuse or other but the faculty was perfectly aware of the real reasons and hated him for it. One Liberal had called the Supreme Court "those nine old bastards" in class. On complaint, Bowman called the man in and faced him with it and when the man got mad and said that he'd resign, Mr. Bowman said "I accept!" The faculty felt that Bowman baited him and then trapped him. All hearsay for me, but it exemplifies the kind of talk that fed the feeling.[42]

His working position was to secure the trust and confidence of the trustees and to selectively accept or ignore the faculty. When the Hopkins chapter of the American Association of University Professors wrote to Charles Garland, president of the Board of Trustees, in 1948 concerning the nature of a university, the power of the faculty, and the selection of a president to replace Bowman, Bowman also wrote to Garland. His letter reduced the A.A.U.P. claims and warned of "cases of sad deterioration of academic standards," a presidential selection procedure which "is cumbersome and time consuming," and opined "on the basis of long experience as a member of different faculties and as president of this institution, that faculty members in general are unsophisticated persons. Their knowledge of human nature ... is academic. Their views on the duties of a president and on the rights and freedoms of faculty members are not infrequently naive."[43]

Bowman was able to remark of the faculty that they were a grand company of scholars, but he did not respect their collective ability to manage, even in part, the affairs of the university. He did not try hard to conceal this belief, but simply made important decisions himself after consorting with certain of the trustees. He was probably a good president for Hopkins, especially in a period of financial difficulty, though not a widely popular president. Perhaps he simply did not have much time to invest in the appearance of sharing governance with the faculty. Yet he interested himself in the publications of Hopkins scholars. When faculty members sent him recently published books or articles, Bowman acknowledged the courtesy with commentary or questions. He was an outspoken admirer of the scholarly work of several of his faculty members.

It was at this time in Bowman's life that he began to reflect most earnestly upon the influence by example of great teachers, those whom he had known or of whom he had heard or read, and those on his own faculty. He was eager to acquire the very best faculty members available—the scholars, not people versed in methods, techniques, and other variant themes of pedagogy. He personally sought such individuals in many disciplines, securing endorsement of their capacities through members of his formidable circle of acquaintances. Able to offer a university program in quest of intellectual excellence, he attracted some very talented teachers to the campus. In turn he felt an obligation to these new faculty members. When in 1946 President Truman invited, then urged, Bowman to accept membership on the projected five-member Atomic Energy Commission, Bowman declined.[44] The president had Secretary of the Navy Forrestal telephone several members of the Hopkins Board of Trustees, who in turn spoke with Bowman, but the latter wrote in a memorandum:

> I gave them all the same answer: At least a dozen young men of high position on our faculty asked me in continuing their appointments here or in accepting them, whether I intended to stay with the University or go into public affairs. I assured them

without qualification that I was staying at the University. To break my word with them would be fatal to their morale.[45]

He increasingly valued morale. He visited the staff of the Applied Physics Laboratory on social evenings, occasionally visited other department gatherings, and gave personal encouragement whenever he felt it would help. When John C. French, retired librarian of Hopkins, wrote a history of the first seventy years of the institution, Bowman contributed data and interpretation of his regime and career.[46] Hamilton Owens's *Baltimore Sun* review of French's book prompted Bowman to write a two-thousand word memorandum at variance with Owen's opinion, which was then placed with his private papers.[47] Bowman wrote that Owens failed to understand Gilman's intent as Hopkins's first president. Again and again Bowman returned to Gilman's writings in interpreting points of view regarding Hopkins policy.

Bowman had become very interested in the mechanics of administering a university and wrote several memoranda on the subject. He organized and encouraged appropriate committees, individual departmental goals, and a careful sifting of the best ideas which should then be taken by the president to the trustees. The trustees should be educated to the matter in hand and encouraged to support the matter with all the very considerable power at their disposal. Bowman's predecessor Ames had allowed trustees to produce notions which he had attempted to impose downwards through administration and faculty. Bowman reversed the trustee role, a difficult exercise which he managed with aplomb. Writing of individual trustees who had brought their own ideas on University policy to meetings, Bowmen commented:

> You will recall how much of this was done in the early part of my administration and how vigorously I had to protest to Mr. Willard and a few other members of the Board that they come to the Board meetings to make speeches and that I thought only one speech should be made at a Board meeting and that by the president of the University. Only when the Board is fully occupied with seasoned ideas and arguments brought before them by the president, are they fulfilling their highest responsiblity.

In fact Bowman and the Board accomplished much. He frequently wrote to individual trustees of particular matters that might interest them. He created the vision and the opportunity for University advancement, and expected the trustees to help secure the funds needed for implementation. Since the intellectual growth of the University and service to a larger public were clearly demonstrable in the Bowman years, the trustees accepted Bowman's leadership. A record of this University growth is most accurately revealed in the "Annual Report of the President," upon which Bowman spent considerable thought and time. The "Report" was read widely; by 1948 it was being circulated to twenty-one thousand alumni. Numerous university administrators beyond Hopkins read it, as did foundation officials.

From the outset of his presidency Bowman had determined to adopt a policy of helpful suport to the local community and society at large, for "if the operations and policy of the University are not tied to the society of which it is part, it will suffer the penalties of aloofness."[49] Upon his arrival in Baltimore, Bowman plunged into a series of public appearances and addresses which introduced him and reintroduced Hopkins. In a campaign which he mounted to secure funds in 1936, in a period of five months he made thirty addresses in Baltimore to as many different groups. Throughout his presidency at Hopkins he gave formal talks in Baltimore on approximately two hundred and fifty occasions. He quickly won for himself a position of influence: in 1937 he was appointed a member of the Board of Trustees of the Peabody Institute, and in 1938 he was appointed a member of the Board of School Commissioners from which in 1944 he was obliged to resign because of the pressure of work in the Department of State. Within a week of his election as governor of Maryland, Herbert O'Conor invited Bowman to chair the committee on the "Structure of the Maryland State Government" to reorganize the state's governmental machinery. Bowman accomplished this, and submitted a report by 31 December 1938, whose recommendations were closely followed. Daniel Willard, president of the Hopkins Board of Trustees, approved of the report and of Bowman's participation though he wished "more space had been given to the oyster industry, or perhaps it would be more correct to say the disappearing oyster industry, which certainly was a matter of very great importance in the State when I first came to Baltimore forty years ago."[50]

Shortly thereafter Bowman published an article in which he described "three failures in at least one of which forecast has been fully verified."[51] In this article which was accorded wide circulation and which urged a closing of the gap between findings and actions, he revealed the collapse of the Maryland oyster industry. It was a bold disclosure, the "failure" being so close to home, but the article pleased Daniel Willard and other trustees.

This local activity, appreciated and useful though it was, did not compare in significance with the work he did for the federal government. This included his labor on the refugee question, which had become ever more intense since 1938, and a government good-will mission to Colombia, Ecuador and Peru in 1941. By 1942 he was working two and three days a week in the State Department; by 1943 he had been appointed special advisor to President Roosevelt and to the secretary of state. In 1944 he was a member of the London Mission led by Stettinius, and later that same year he was made a member of the American delegation to the Dumbarton Oaks Conference. In 1945 he was official advisor to the American delegation to the United Nations Conference on International Organization. He declined still other political activities. Something of his contribution to the nation is recorded in the following chapter. That he could manage such commitments in addition to his duties at Hopkins is a revelation of the inner strengths of the man.

Chapter Ten

Politics and Political Geography

Bowman had developed a pronounced interest in international affairs during his work for the Inquiry and the American Commission to Negotiate Peace at Paris. It was at Paris that some of the members of the British and American delegations had agreed that their governments did not have a research division always ready to recommend courses of action, whether in peace or war. Scholars of the two delegations proposed that both governments establish such an intellectual apparatus. James Shotwell, then in London, wrote to Bowman:

> The idea is to have two centres—one in London, the other in New York, for the study of international politics, and that they will jointly bring out an annual volume or set of volumes containing studies of the big international problems of the year. The initial volume is on the Peace Conference. . . .[1]

A joint British-American organization was sought, but eventually two separate organizations were created: the British (now the Royal) Institute of International Affairs in London, and the Council on Foreign Relations in New York City.[2] Bowman was a founder of the Council, a member of its Board of Directors, and a member of the Editorial Advisory Board of its periodical *Foreign Affairs*.

163

The plan of having a journal and making it the best in the world and the related plan of setting up a research program that should be expressed in a series of volumes of the highest quality represented the judgement of Gay and myself ... it was a clear case of two men having almost exactly the same ideas regarding future development and having them at the same time in the same organization. At the meeting of the Board of Directors at which we presented our views we found immediate and generous offer of funds. These funds guaranteed *Foreign Affairs* for five years but left the matter of research and the publication of specific volumes to a later time.... Eventually and through the single-handed work of Gay, who never ceased to push for the execution of this part of the Council's program, money was obtained to set up a department in something like adequate form.[3]

Bowman's association with the Council on Foreign Relations kept him in touch with others interested in international affairs. In particular, it brought him into a lifelong association with Hamilton Fish Armstrong, longtime editor of *Foreign Affairs*. And it kept Bowman conversant with academic work on the subject. Bowman suggested authors, evaluated articles for the editor, and proposed improvements.

During the 1920s *The New World* became a source book for those interested in international affairs. Bowman gave numerous addresses and interviews in that decade concerning international affairs. He had come to the important realization that the study of geography had a role to play in settling the affairs of nations. His interest in the emerging genre, "political geography," was inevitable; his concern with the writings of the German geographers was intense. When Alexander Supan published *Leitlinien der allgemeinen politischen Geographie: Naturlehre des Staates* in 1922, Bowman "read his book very carefully, spending nearly two weeks upon it,"[4] and published a review of the book.

The trouble with Supan's philosophy lies in his almost instinctive search for a "system" wherein should be rationalized the facts comprised in political geography.... It is characteristic of the German school of political geography that its logic so often rests upon mere classification, and the descent is not far from this to *obiter dicta* and the worship of ritual and mummery ... and the book ends on a bitter note that refers particularly to the loss of the German colonies as a violation of any possible economic system. He inquires meaningfully, Cannot Slavs and Germans unite as a counterpoise to Anglo-Saxons, Latins, and Japanese?[5]

Later Bowman reviewed four more German political geography books[6] and found them all alike in elevating a "preconceived system of political geography and making all facts conform thereto."[7] It was significant to Bowman that the authors represented the point of view of a defeated power. Troubled by the growing use of propagandistic maps, mnemonic schemes, and other devices which achieved neither learning nor science, he commented, "Political geography is still merely a term, not a science."[8] Bowman perceived a national scheme in the writings of German political geographers, and began to wonder if a national purpose was not being wrought. Karl Haushofer had founded the "Work Group" for *Zeitschrift für Geopolitik* in 1924. *Macht und Erde*, a trilogy of books completed in 1934 and in large part the product of this group, was, according to Otto Maull, prepared as the German answer to Bowman's *The New World*.[9] Bowman believed that he and the German geopoliticians were opposed in philosophy. While he sought rational solutions based on circumstance, he felt the German geopoliticians wished to resolve problems or create change according to a preconceived plan already established in a national (German) interest.

Deeply disturbed by the rapid growth in Germany of the pseudo science of geopolitics and alarmed by its territorial theories and implications as displayed in widest panorama in the Zeitschrift fur Geopolitik, I attacked the school and its work in a group review in 1927. . . . Maull's "Politische Geographie" was especially selected for condemnaton in my review.[10]

To Jean Brunhes he wrote:

The world is not made according to a system and its political forms are not made according to a system . . . of the sort that the political geographers of Germany are so fond of talking about. . . . Here we have in the field of political geography an echo or counterpart of the controversy that raged in the middle ages

between the Realists and the Nominalists, the former believing
that the church was an entity apart from its members and the
latter believing that it was constituted by its members. So do the
philosophers in political geography in Germany talk today when
they think of the state as an organism apart from the individuals
composing it, when they talk about the rights of that organism, its
normal development, what it demands, the space it must have,
etc., etc. All these things may fit the situation of Germany but
they certainly do not fit the world.[11]

When Brunhes was preparing a French translation of *The New World*
Bowman suggested it might be "particularly useful to point out that
philosophies based upon the state as an entity and functioning as an
organism, such as flourish in German textbooks, are consciously left to
one side as unreal and fantastic."[12]

German opposition to *The New World* came in a review by Fritz
Klute.[13] Less immediate opposition, but in philosophical contrast to
The New World, Bowman felt, were Karl Haushofer's works. Bowman
had read Sir Halford John Mackinder carefully and regarded him as the
most important of the British geographers. He felt that Mackinder's
"heartland" notion had validity, that Haushofer had seized upon this,
and that "this philosophy ... has been adopted by Hitler.... He has
one object and that is to push his boundaries farther and farther until
he obtains a sufficient number of salt-water bases to make his final
thrust at England."[14]

Bowman corresponded with Nicholas J. Spykman, Robert Strausz-
Hupé and Hans W. Weigert. Later he reviewed Spykman's *America's
Strategy in World Politics*[15] and was inspired by Strausz-Hupé's
Geopolitics to write another article,[16] denouncing the word and the
meaning "geopolitic." By the 1940s Bowman's writings in the field of
political geography had a distinctive flavor. He wrote from his very
considerable knowledge of political reality, injecting geographical
(especially territorial) ideas which made his writing so useful:
"Politics amounts to little if used as flavoring in a geographical
description, whereas in my opinion geography amounts to a good deal
when used as flavoring in politics."[17] Many of his writings of the war
years were read by political figures.

This interest in political geography and international affairs kept
Bowman working closely with the Council on Foreign Relations. In

March 1929 he represented the Council at a "Conference of the Institutions for the Scientific Study of International Affairs" held at Chatham House, London, home of the Royal Institute of International Affairs. At that conference Bowman reported on the work of the Council and other institutions in the United States interested in international affairs. In a "Confidential Memorandum for Members" Bowman urged the creation of a similar institutional facility in the United States "so that editor and scholar can lay their hands immediately upon the essential things that they require for their work."[18]

The following year Bowman wrote a booklet entitled *International Relations* for the American Library Association "Reading with a Purpose" Series. It was a brief introduction to "the outlines of a new system of diplomacy" which was adumbrated in the Four-Power Treaty of 1922 relating to the Pacific, the Kellog-Briand Pact of 1929, the League of Nations and the Locarno Treaties. Bowman opined that these instruments "instead of being a call to arms are a call to the Conference Table." He wished to see men "pledged in advance to approach consultation in a spirit of good-will." Not convinced that the world had been made safe, he wrote that "the dragon of war is not slain; he is wounded only."[19] The book enjoyed substantial endorsement and a wide distribution. James T. Shotwell, then director of the Carnegie Endowment for International Peace, called the study "just about the finest thing that has been said about international relations. It is so compact, so just and sane, and yet so charged with suggestion for reform and reminder of responsibilities."[20]

The book represented much of Bowman's hitherto unpublished thought concerning the relations between nations. He intimated there his distrust of human nature, nations, and power:

> Energy still rules the world, not vision. We keep our dreams alive and we work toward them. That is one side of our nature. The other side consists of practical sense which says that refusal to fight under the American system is only to invite ourselves to fight under another system.[21]

It was this thinking that encouraged him to believe in a military draft, a belief which stengthened as the years passed so that after World War II he spoke in behalf of universal military training on numerous occasions. Notable were his addresses to the Senate Committee on Armed Services on 23 March 1948, and "Do We Need Universal Military Training?" delivered before the National Security Committee in Washington on 24 October 1947.

With the outbreak of World War II the Council on Foreign Relations formed a "Group on Territorial Questions" which began holding meetings in New York based upon printed "preliminary memoranda." Bowman was "Rapporteur" for a series on American interests. The group included Bowman, Philip E. Mosely, Hamilton Fish Armstrong, John C. Cooper, Jr., Bruce C. Hopper, Owen Lattimore, and William L. Westermann. After discussing a subject, they printed their findings, which were of considerable value to the State Department.

The value of these intellectual seminars was demonstrated on 5 August 1940 when Bowman found himself sitting opposite Secretary of Agriculture Henry Wallace on the train from New York to Baltimore.

> In the course of an extended conversation on the international situation he spoke of the President's reference at a recent Cabinet meeting to my views on Greenland and other European possessions in the Western Hemisphere. I replied that this was a friendly thing for the President to do but assumed it was only complimentary. He said it was more than that, for the President had based his judgment upon a memorandum he had with him, which bore my name and from which he quoted. Then he added details and points of view which were identical with those that we had included in memoranda prepared especially by the Council on Foreign Relations for the Department of State in the current series. I was agreeably surprised at the fulness and accuracy of his first-hand report of the material itself. . . . Nothing was said, nor did he enquire, about the circumstances under which the memoranda had been prepared. I merely said to him that I had not known that even Secretary Hull had read "the material that had been sent," much less the President. . . . It is of some importance, we think, that the invasion of Denmark was anticipated by a month by our committee, and when the crisis arose the committee's memorandum was ready for instant use by the Department of State and the President.[22]

These studies were read carefully by the State Department. Their value became obvious, and on 9 February 1942, Sumner Welles sent Bowman a letter marked "strictly confidential":

> The President has decided that vigorous and intensive work needs to be done now in preparation for this country's effective participation in the solution of the vast and complicated problems of international relations . . . after the final defeat of the forces of aggression. He has, therefore, directed that there be created in the Department of State an Advisory Committee on Post-War Foreign Policy, under the chairmanship of the Secretary of State, and the vice chairmanship of the Under Secretary of State to be charged with the conduct of the necessary studies and with the preparation of recommendations to be submitted to him. The Committee will work in the interrelated fields of political, territorial, and economic reconstruction and of general security.
>
> With the approval of the President and at the request of the Secretary, I take great pleasure in inviting you to become a member of this Committee. . . .[23]

On 12 February 1942, the Advisory Committee met for the first time in Under Secretary Welles's office.[24] Bowman was one of fourteen persons originally appointed to this committee, whose existence was kept secret. His colleagues were Cordell Hull, chairman; Sumner Welles, vice chairman; Norman Ii. Davis; Myron C. Taylor, Dean Acheson (assistant secretary of state); Hamilton Fish Armstrong (editor of *Foreign Affairs*); Adolf A. Berle, Jr. (assistant secretary of state); Benjamin V. Cohen (general counsel, National Power Policy Committee); Herbert Feis (State Department advisor on economic relations); Glen H. Hackworth (legal advisor); Harry C. Hawkins (chief of the Division of Commercial Policy); Mrs. Anne McCormick (editorial staff, the *New York Times*); and Leo Pasvolsky (special assistant to the secretary of state and chief of the Division of Special Research). Eventually the Committee had forty-five members grouped into subcommittees. Bowman chaired the one which dealt with territorial problems.

I continued in that post for three years. In that time we were concerned about two things, first, to bring our studies along as rapidly as possible so as to be ready for peace-making and, second, to bring the public understanding of international problems along at the same pace.[25]

Bowman always prepared most intently for meetings of the Committee. Sumner Welles felt that it would be "impossible to avoid emphasizing the contribution made by Dr. Bowman, because of his exceptional gift for making available to others the unique knowledge of geographic questions which he possesses."[26] Benjamin V. Cohen wrote:

> Whenever Professor Bowman spoke he impressed me with his great knowlege, particularly his knowledge of the history of territorial disputes and the difficulties of adjusting them after successive wars.... While he was effective and persuasive in committee discussion, I was under the impression his greatest contribution during this period was in collaborating with the State Department people in preparing their reports and studies, particularly on territorial disputes and adjustments that would confront the peace conferences at the end of the war.[27]

In October 1943 Secretary of State Cordell Hull flew to Moscow, the first flight he had ever made in his seventy-two years, to win Soviet support for a postwar organization of nations. Shortly after Hull's return Bowman noted that the secretary "has expressed great appreciation for the work of the Research Division and my part in it. He said that the documentation that had been prepared was indispensable at Moscow. He wishes the work continued and speeded up."[28] At Hull's request on 9 December 1943, an informal Political Agenda Group was organized for discussions solely of international organization. Bowman was asked to lead this group, which swiftly prepared a memorandum initialled by Hull and sent to President Roosevelt on 29 December 1943.

Early in 1944 Bowman's tasks became so numerous that he opted to discontinue meetings of the Territorial Committee in the Department. "After that came Dumbarton Oaks and San Francisco. It was therefore necessary to orient the whole territorial complex of questions in the direction of a United Nations Organization. So far as I know, this work has not yet been done in the State Department."[29] Bowman was encouraged to write an extended piece on the complexity of territorial matters which he showed to Stettinius, and which was later published.[30] Frequently during the war Bowman was appealed to for immediate opinions, as there was no one else in government with his breadth of knowledge concerning the earth's surface and its political divisions.

Bowman's previous contributions led to his participation in the Stettinius Mission to London (1944), in the Dumbarton Oaks Conference (1944), and the San Francisco Conference (1945). Cordell Hull later referred to Bowman as vice-chairman of the special London mission.[31] In 1940 Bernard Baruch had suggested to Bowman that he organize an Inquiry similar to that of 1917-18. Baruch offered to contribute $100,000 initially and provide further support as needed, but Bowman declined. He felt that such an undertaking was the responsibility of the government. He doubted "that the donor could keep his hands off the work. I have passed the point where mere money is very persuasive. Servitudes are inevitably associated with money. Better be free than bound."[32] All the same, Bowman felt that the idea of a second Inquiry was good:

> I wish that free money were available. We spent $250,000 on the Inquiry in 1918, and about that sum ought to be available now. Government cannot touch the problem because it is afraid of public reaction, and officials are too busy to think about the "order" that is to follow war. They overlook a primary obligation, namely, that the victor is responsible for his victory.[33]

Instead, the government operated on a more ad hoc basis, calling on Bowman at the shortest notice for advice to be acted upon immediately. Bowman wrote to Larry Hafstad, executive secretary of the Research and Development Board:

> We could give many instances of lack of geographical knowledge for which the armed services appealed in desperate haste in the course of the war. I undertook one such high-pressure ten-day job in locating possible air fields at a critical island-hopping stage in the Pacific, and the request came from the Chief of Staff of the Far Eastern Air Forces . . . the results . . . were of critical value for

about one month, whereupon my material became obsolete through the high level reconnaissance photography that the Air Force was able to carry out immediately it was able to get near enough.[34]

But it was Bowman's regular help that won for him high position in the government as he and four others,

> including the Secretary of State, went rather regularly to consult with President Roosevelt on leading issues in foreign policy, and once each week five of us met with the Secretary of State for a comprehensive review of policy. These and other meetings [were] held regularly with Senators and Congressmen to explain the evolution of our policy and to discuss desirable objectives. . . .[35]

On 24 February 1944, Under Secretary of State Edward Stettinius invited Bowman to be a member of a mission to visit London for political discussions with the British government. Additionally, Cordell Hull asked Bowman to assume one of two newly created posts of assistant secretary of state "to give all my time to the non-economic aspects of treaty making. . . . As I understand it, the trip to England is to precede appointment as Assistant Secretary of State."[36] A few days later, Bowman decided to join the London mission, but to decline the assistant secretaryship.

On 10 March Bowman, John L. Pratt, Wallace Murray, H. Freeman Matthews, and Robert Lynch held their first meeting with Stettinius. One week later Louis Hector was added to the group. Stettinius stated that "discussions would be informal and exploratory," and that they "would exchange views fully and frankly, but would make no commitments or agreements."[37] The group met for the second time on 17 March, and again the main topic of conversation was subject matter for discussion with the British. It was "agreed that we should be willing to exchange views with the British on anything which they might want to talk about. We would not close the door on the British on any particular subjects by saying that we have no authority to discuss them."[38] That same day the group visited Secretary of State Cordell Hull, who then arranged for them to meet with President Roosevelt. With both Hull and Roosevelt Bowman spoke about colonies and colonial trusteeship. Stettinius had already come to rely on Bowman's

very good sense of timing and judgement, for Bowman reported that
"on receiving Stettinius' repeated signal to barge in as agreed and ask
for instructions, I inquired if the President wanted to instruct us about
French Colonial policy...."[39] And again on the matter of issues to be
discussed, "Stettinius was anxious ... that I should raise this question
and came over and whispered to me his request that I ask it...."[40]
After further meetings with Stettinius and Hull, Bowman gave Leo
Pasvolsky the results of the conference:

> L. P. was excited and enthusiastic about my report and
> immediately gave me PWC-59 dated March 10, 1944, and PWC-
> 58, March 10, 1944, two secret documents that he thought
> represented the essence of World Organization documentation
> that we ought to have with us as background material to prepare
> us for talks with the British.[41]

On 30 March the group boarded the *Queen Elizabeth* at New York.
Conferences were held on board throughout the voyage, and in London
work began at once. Members of the American mission each talked
with different members of the British government.

> Mr. Stettinius would deal in the main with Mr. Eden, Mr.
> Cadogan and Mr. Law. He explained that Dr. Bowman would deal
> in the first instance with Nigel Donald who is in charge of post
> war planning in the Foreign Office. Mr. Pratt should immediately
> talk with Mr. Penrose in the Embassy and with Mr. Philip
> Reed....[42]

Bowman had intense sessions with the leading members of the British
government concerning "Surrender Terms," "World Organization,"
"the role of the Royal Institute of International Affairs and the
Council on Foreign Relations," and "The Colonial Question."
     Of the greatest significance, however, was a meeting of several
members of the mission with Winston Churchill on 15 April at
Chequers. Stettinius arranged for Bowman to represent the mission in
extended confidential conversation with Churchill. Matters discussed
privately included the division of Germany, land compensation for
flooded Holland, the future of India, the colonial question, the seat of a
World Organization (Churchill suggested Marrakesh), Communism,

and Palestine. The most important part of the conversation, and central to the propose of the entire mission, was the matter of world organization at the close of hostilities. The British prime minister was anxious to retain a regional organization.

In describing the world organization that he had in view, he referred to 'the tripod upon which peace depends.' Taking the sheet of paper on which a seating list had been prepared by Mrs. Churchill, he drew a tripod with a head on which stood the three powers and China. He said that he did not refer to China and the three great powers as "The Four Great Powers." He could not bring himself to do that. What China is and what she may become are two different things. . . . He referred to Chinese as 'the pigtails' . . . the head of his 'tripod of world peace' is the Supreme Council. . . . Then he drew three circles below the Supreme Council to indicate *the regional councils and their subsidiary position and authority*. The object of these councils is to have regional affairs settled regionally and thus avoid having every nation poking its finger into every other nation's business the world around.[43]

Unknown to Churchill was the fact that his own position on the subject of regional versus central authority had been the subject of formal analysis and discussion in the Territorial Committee of the State Department only months earlier. Apparently the mission, and particularly Bowman, did much to shift Churchill's thinking on this subject, for Sir Alexander Cadogan of the British government wrote to Bowman: "I can't exaggerate the change of atmosphere that has taken place in the Government with respect to world organization as a result of the Stettinius Mission."[44]

Later, on 18 May, Mr. Bucknell of the London embassy sent a telegram to the secretary and under secretary of state. Bowman wrote of the matter:

> What we said to Eden and the Foreign Office confirmed their own views on the importance of a World Organization as opposed to a regional organization. Until our visit it was not possible for them to oppose the Prime Minister successfully.[45]

Stettinius felt that much of the credit for this change in the British position was due to Bowman and gave the telegram to him for his personal files, for he well knew Bowman's penchant for collecting such memorabilia.

On the return journey to the United States Bowman persuaded the pilot to fly over the Grand Atlas, and a part of the Sahara. This much was a great satisfaction to Bowman who had long wished to view the Great Desert, but the sortie was viewed with concern by his travelling companions.

On 21 August 1944 a critical conference was held at Dumbarton Oaks, the former home of Mr. and Mrs. Robert Woods Bliss in Georgetown, and given by them to Harvard University in 1940. The purpose of these meetings was to establish the pattern, variable in detail but not in general plan, of international organization for the postwar world. Bowman was formally designated a member of the nonpartisan group to aid the under secretary of state in conversations with the United Kingdom and the Soviet Union and, subsequently, with groups representing the United Kingdom and the Republic of

China.[46] Cordell Hull, with the approval of the president, had already designated Bowman a special adviser to the secretary of state on postwar problems and plans.[47] Conversations lasted into October and substantial accord was reached. Bowman's work at the conference largely consisted of advising Stettinius.

> The attached paper . . . is the result of a request from Stettinius to me that I attempt to find a formula to get around the difficulty in which we now are directly involved of keeping Russian adherence to the plan for world organization without yielding to all of their demands that a State party to a dispute shall be allowed to vote in its own case. The Secretary has pressed . . . for a formula.[48]

At the same time, Bowman was involved in

> a long and ominous fight this week over the word "technical" which was introduced into the draft Charter by the Russians and the British. . . . With Stettinius and all the rest of the American group present I attacked the word "educational" for which I had been arguing if the word "technical" also went out. . . .

The next day Stettinius called me out and told me that he had won the British and Russians to our position and that the word "technical" had disappeared.

> He said that it had been a hard fight but he had gone into it with enthusiasm because I had scared him the previous day with my argument and made him feel that we would arouse great antagonism toward the Charter if we permitted the word to stand.[49]

Bowman subsequently accepted the words "social and humanitarian" for the word "educational" and for which the British and Russians wished to substitute the phrase "humanitarian principles." On this, as on numerous other occasions, Stettinius trusted Bowman's judgement implicitly. Ultimately, after the establishment of principles in committee, one person had to be responsible for decisions on details. Stettinius selected Bowman as that one individual.

Other than this duty, Bowman's main concern was the future of

Germany. During the conference Secretary Stimson invited Bowman to his office, and asked him questions to which Bowman made immediate reply. The resultant eight-page memorandum on the arguments for and against the unification of Germany was read by the president, and Bowman also argued the case directly with Roosevelt. Bowman wished to see a united Germany at the end of the war; the president wished to dismember Germany. The two men had no fewer than three private sessions on the subject, but Roosevelt was not moved by Bowman's argumentation. Bowman did urge H. F. Armstrong to secure an article from Mackinder on the danger of a strong Soviet Union and a divided Germany[50] which resulted in Mackinder's "The Round World and the Winning of the Peace." Bowman had that article clipped from the July 1943 issue of *Foreign Affairs* and sent it to the President, but he "was not converted and we left the matter as a difference in judgment."[51]

During September 1944, Bowman was one of five members of a State Department Committee which debated where to locate the permanent United Nations organization. Numerous locales suggested in earlier meetings of the Territorial Committee included Como and Maggiore, Geneva, Marrakesh, Vienna, Rio de Janeiro, Vancouver Island, Oporto, Brussels, Oslo, Luxembourg, the Azores, and the Hawaiian Islands. Bowman concluded "that Luxembourg is the best European site with Vienna a second best.... Better than either is a location in the eastern part of the United States in a climatic belt where an excellent year round site can be selected."[52] Pinehurst, North Carolina, was thought to represent the United States most adequately. The same committee sought a name for the proposed international organization. Suggestions included: The United Nations, The Union of Nations, The Association of States, The Neighborhood of Nations, The States General, The Congregation of Nations, The Congress of Nations, The Chamber of Nations, The Commonwealth of Nations, The Community of Nations, and The Society of Nations. The same committee proposed names for the basic instrument: Charter, Constitution, Compact, The Fundamental Agreement, Covenant. And it also recommended names—which were later adopted en masse—of the principal organs of the body, and titles for the principal officers. This committee did a great deal of valuable work in helping with the problematic details of the Charter. Its conclusions were given immediately to Stettinius at Dumbarton Oaks.

By 15 September documents representing approaches to a final agreement on the charter of the world organization had been completed. Bowman was deeply satisfied to have helped in the preparation of such a document. Of it he wrote in a private memorandum:

> The stiff and formal language of such a Charter does not make dramatic reading *unless* one is able to see back of each line the immense power of the three nations who have joined in agreement upon the line. The simplest kind of a statement, made by three great powers such as the United States, United Kingdom and U.S.S.R., rolls like thunder across the page of history. It is the fact of unity not the scope of the Charter itself. But no apologies need be made for the scope of the Charter. If we can agree upon this we have accomplished 90 per cent of the vast humane purposes which have animated the powers in approaching the task of World Organization.[53]

On numerous occasions Bowman argued for the retention of phrases to which the Russians had objected. He also pressed successfully for United States publication of the Dumbarton Oaks document. No sooner was accord reached than Stettinius began to urge public broadcast of this information. With the example of Woodrow Wilson and the League of Nations still close, the government felt that the public should be educated about the meaning of Dumbarton Oaks. To Arthur Sweetser, Office of War Information, Bowman wrote, "I agree with you most heartily on the need for a wider understanding of the Dumbarton Oaks proposals. This is the truly great job demanded at the present time."[54] To this end Bowman spoke to numerous influential groups, including the Advertising Club of Baltimore, the National Council of Chief State School Officers, the Association of American Colleges, and the National College of Preachers. He worked on State Department business with such intensity that for weeks at a time he became only an occasional visitor to The Johns Hopkins University where he was president. Of his daily round he wrote to Charles K. Webster, then of the Research Department in the London Foreign Office:

> I have just returned from talking to an audience of about 500

leading business men in Baltimore on the Dumbarton Oaks Proposals. I have another group to dinner at my house tonight to deal with the same subject. . . . I am planning to give a dozen such talks here and in nearby cities. The purpose of these statements is to show you that we are now engaged in the second part of our Dumbarton Oaks undertaking—the public debate of the Proposals and criticisms of them. Teams of speakers are being sent about the country and we hope public interest in our reports will rise now that the election is behind us. Not for many years have we had so clear a mandate from the people that we must be about the business of framing a World Organization for Peace and Security.[55]

When Felix Morley, president of Haverford College in Pennsylvania and contributing editor to *Human Events*, had published in that magazine an article entitled "At Dumbarton Oaks" which Bowman thought was harmful in its impact upon the public, he wrote an unusually terse letter to Morley complaining that the "world is getting to be a hell of a place if on the basis of misstatements, cynical conclusions are circulated that have the effect of turning the public against an effort to create a world organization for security and peace almost before the task of negotiation has been started."[56] An exchange of correspondence ensued in which Bowman enumerated his criticisms of Morley's article. He realized how important it was that the people understand the significance of the Dumbarton Oaks conversations.

I lived though the period of tension at Paris in 1919 and we all felt, as did the correspondents, that a fundamental mistake was made by President Wilson in his relations with the press and public opinion in America. The record shows that Secretary Hull has constantly remembered this mistake and has tried by every means in his power and to the last ounce of his strength to keep Congressional leaders, the public, and any and all who come to see him fully informed concerning the non-partisan character of the business and the public stake in the outcome.[57]

Bowman declined an invitation from the Council on Foreign Relations to write a book on the Dumbarton Oaks Conference.[58] But during 1944 and 1945 he did write about the theme and principles of the conference in "Peace a Condition of Living," "Peace—The Business of Every Citizen," and two further articles both entitled "The Dumbarton Oaks Proposals."

The third and final in this triad of conferences to which Bowman was invited as an adviser in the quest for a world organization opened on 25 April 1945, at San Francisco. Bowman received a formal invitation from Stettinius "to become an official adviser to the Delegation of the United States to the United Nations Conference on International Organization." Stettinius termed Bowman's "experience and the advice and counsel you will be able to give . . . of great value to the Delegation."[59] Once again Bowman placed the matter of an extended absence from Hopkins before the trustees, and once again the trustees encouraged his participation.

Before departing from Washington for California, Stettinius requested help specifically from Bowman on the major introductory address which he was to deliver at San Francisco. At San Francisco Bowman, Hamilton F. Armstrong, and John F. Dulles were the three principal advisers. Again Bowman was busy advising Stettinius on a multiplicity of matters, and working long hours each day. He did not at all like the "extras":

> They are a superflous body consisting of well doers, snoopers, gossipers in considerable number, mixed up with persons of serious purpose. It is extraordinary to what degree each day reveals superfluous people who came to San Francisco—they are camp followers of the enterprise who apparently want to take home some local color, with which to impress their friends and neighbors.[60]

When negotiations were in session he would sit

> at Van's suggestion, approved by Connally, between the two Senators and canvas their opinion. When they agree I signal Ed with a nod. If there is disagreement I see Stassen or Dulles or Dunn and try to get unanimity. Ed says "Keep your eye on me all the while because I can't commit the delegation unless I get your affirmative signal."[61]

Of the Conference proceedings Bowman wrote:

> Since everybody is interested in the answer and not how the
> answer is derived I am afraid I can tell you little about the
> Conference beyond what you read in the newspapers. On the
> technical side I shall have many stories to tell later.... It is
> extraordinary how constantly we search for words and arrange-
> ments of words that will shade meanings to the point where an
> agreement is possible among the Big Five especially. Then there
> are the differences in meaning from language to language; even in
> the case of words that we think we understand in another
> language, there is no end to the process.... More difficult still are
> the general lines of policy to be determined. An act now will have
> unexpected repercussions ten years and thirty years from now
> since we cannot forecast events with even approximate accuracy.
> ... Since other delegations may have different views on these
> matters we sometimes get into the state of the philosopher
> searching in a dark room for a black cat that isn't there. If the
> technical side of the business troubles us, the statesmanship side
> of the business worries us. And well it should: the dead are
> peering through the windows.[62]

On 22 May a Drafting Committee was established consisting of
Pasvolsky, Armstrong, Dunn, Hackworth, Dulles, and Bowman. This
committee was to review text that came largely from the Coordinating
Committee and the Jurist Committee. Additionally, a Style Committee
comprised of two British representatives and H. F. Armstrong and
Bowman was established to give good literary form to the Charter.

At the end of May, the United States delegation requested Bowman
to prepare a report to the president on the Conference. Bowman
organized a team of nearly thirty authors and editors and selected
seven to serve as an editorial board meeting daily for an hour and a
half.

The first manuscript was received on June 9 and was sent to the
printer on June 11. The last of the composition was done a few

minutes before President Truman completed his speech at the
Opera House, closing the Conference, about 5:05 P.M., June 26.
By June 29 the page proofs were corrected and by July 2 the entire
edition of 1,500 copies was printed and transported by aeroplane
from San Francisco to Washington, D.C.[63]

When Bowman received one of the original fifteen hundred copies, he
sent it immediately to the Hopkins librarian requesting "special care in
binding" for "in a few years it will be so rare that the present copy
ought not to be put on the shelves in the ordinary way."[64]

After the Conference Stettinius held confidential talks with
Bowman concerning the timing of his resignation. Stettinius had been
secretary of state under Roosevelt. Now that Harry Truman was
president, he wished to appoint James Byrnes to that post, and had
proposed that Stettinius be appointed United States representative to
the United Nations. The appointments had to be made before the
president left for the Three Power Conference planned for late July.
Stettinius had total faith in Bowman's ability and integrity and asked
him to handle the matter of his transition from the post of secretary of
state to another appointment. He even requested Bowman to persuade
his wife over the telephone to accept his swiftly taken decision.[65]

Bowman at once drafted a memorandum concerning the new office
which Stettinius was to occupy, and discussed the matter with
President Truman. Shortly afterward Stettinius wrote to Bowman "to
thank you again from the bottom of my heart for all you did. . . . As
usual you were a wise counsellor and a true friend at a difficult and
important moment."[66] Months later Bowman wrote Stettinius's letter
of resignation from his post at the United Nations,[67] then was asked to
further advise Stettinius on his career. When Stettinius wrote a book
about his political experiences he asked Bowman to read it critically.
Bowman offered numerous substantive criticisms, but historian
Walter Johnson who ghostwrote the book insisted on his own style and
accepted little outside revision.[68]

Bowman's position within the government had radically changed
with the death of Roosevelt. Prior to that time he had been readily
accessible to government officials. Cordell Hull had sought his advice
concerning the manuscript "Peace and War: United States Foreign
Policy, 1931-1941." Hull requested Bowman to "prepare some
comments on the work itself and on ways of making it most useful to

our fellow-citizens."[69] In July 1944 when Hull was considering resigning as secretary of state following conflict with Sumner Welles, Hull asked Bowman's advice again.[70] On 18 May 1944, Vice-President Wallace called on Bowman to discuss his trip to China. "He seemed much interested in my account of the possible use which Russia might make of Communism in North China in the event that Russia joins us in the war on Japan after defeating Germany."[71] And on 1 July 1944, Governor O'Conor of Maryland visited Bowman and requested a statement on United States foreign policy which he could deliver before a forthcoming conference at Washington.[72]

These and other government officials (especially Sumner Welles and Edward Stettinius) had called on him frequently, as had President Roosevelt. Bowman had not been able to admire some of Roosevelt's personal characteristics, but he had respected Roosevelt's knowledge, delegation of authority, choice of personnel, and method of handling political situations. Roosevelt had asked Bowman for advice on the refugee problem, and for a definition of the Western Hemisphere for security reasons, which had prompted a six-page statement on the subject.[73] At Roosevelt's request, Bowman had travelled to South America in August 1941 to investigate the Peru-Ecuador dispute, returning with recommendations for solution.[74] The president had also consulted Bowman on such matters as the significance of long-range weather forecasting to the military, the issue of a united or a divided Germany at the conclusion of the war, and world organization. Roosevelt had sent Secretary Stimson to ask Bowman to conduct the biological warfare unit in the War Department with "any amount of money I wanted and $10,000,000 to start with. Bundy, Stimson's aide, took me to lunch at the Metropolitan Club and presented the matter there."[75] Bowman declined the offer.

From the spring of 1944 until his death, Roosevelt was more withdrawn from government officials' view. Bowman attributed the diminution of presidential capacity in these months to the awful responsibility that he bore and his poor health.

It is against this background that I wish to throw two episodes that shed light on the tragic role that President Roosevelt played as the war and the impending peace plans grew beyond the capacity of any one mind. The first episode concerned Manchuria. "There Mr. President you will be required to take a position directly contrary to Soviet aims," I advised him. With a puzzled expression he asked why I was so deeply distrustful of the Soviet leaders. I answered that the whole of Russian history spoke eloquently on that point and the history of Manchuria in particular.... He replied that I was overlooking . . . "the treaty with China." I had shot my last bolt and it had missed. Against every indication of history and every sign of Soviet aggression President Roosevelt was trusting to a paper signed years before. It seemed incredible.

The reason was disclosed in the second episode. On the day that Secretary Hull signed the agreement with the Soviet government to join the other powers in exploring the possibilities of a cooperative peace, President Roosevelt sent for me and for forty minutes he spoke to me privately.... He seemed to have reached out for a sympathetic listener with whom in confidence he could share his joy and to whom he could express his hopes. "Cordell has also arranged to have a meeting with Stalin at Teheran. This is really a secret, remember. I want to sit down with that fellow. I think we can do business together. I have always wanted to meet him but I never could get him to agree. I think we shall get on very well." He then turned to a wide range of topics almost the world around, touching the high points of each one with firm assurance. I raised questions as he went along and he was responsive and keen. In retrospect it seems to me to have been the high point of intellectual exhilaration for him. His mind was racing over the grand design. His listener did not interrupt for the head of the most powerful government in the world was persuading the most powerful minds among contemporaries, Churchill and Stalin, forecasting world-shaking events, shaping a peaceful world—in imagination and as if with the broad strokes of a master painter working on a vast mural torn out of a piece of sky.

A very wise and wide observer and a warm friend of President Roosevelt soon afterward provided the chilly antidote. "It will take Stalin about five minutes to size up Mr. Roosevelt." . . . I asked the President who were to be his political advisers. For this meeting, he replied, a small first meeting, I shall need no great staff. We shall agree on a few over-all principles and map out the military strategy of final victory. This is improvisation.[76]

Occasionally during what Bowman considered to be Roosevelt's months of decline, he sent the president a note or a memorandum, usually through the medium of his friend Stettinius. One especially noteworthy communication urged greater speed "in plans for world organization . . . [to] stem the present growing tendency on the part of Britain and Russia to take unilateral action. It would be the greatest fear-remover the world could devise. . . ."[77]

It was this proximity to the president which enabled Bowman to feel that he was close to the seat of power. When Roosevelt died and Truman became president, Bowman increased his distance from the immediate political scene. He did not seem very appreciative of President Truman's capacity. But he kept his own council on that subject, and in 1946 Truman invited, then urged, him to accept membership in the Atomic Energy Commission.[78] Bowman declined, informing the president his "interest was in foreign affairs rather than in the creation of more power."[79]

Bowman did accept one invitation from Truman relating to the Atomic Energy Commission.[80] By 1949 David Lilienthal, chairman of the Atomic Energy Commission, and Senator Brien McMahon, chairman of the Joint Congressional Committee on Atomic Energy, had both suggested lifting the veil of secrecy that hung over information concerning the atomic bomb. In the wake of some popular articles on this theme a top secret committee was formed: James B. Conant as chairman; Isaiah Bowman; Erwin D. Canham; John Foster Dulles; Dwight D. Eisenhower; C. H. Greenewalt; and Frank B. Jewett. Messages were carried only by Army courier, and reference on all occasions was made to "our fishing trip." The investigation of the committee was widened to include "the atomic bomb, weapons of biological, chemical and radiological warfare."[81] The committee met in different venues from April until September of 1949, when Conant reported to Karl T. Compton that the committee had been divided in its opinion.[82] On the issue of the atomic bomb, the majority felt it desirable not to release a statement to the public.

In the postwar years Bowman participated in the work of the Economic Cooperation Administration (E.C.A.), for which his career had prepared him so well. When President Truman announced his Point Four Program, Bowman's research concerning the world's pioneer fringes, his thrust toward a specialization in tropical research at the Hopkins geography department, and his participation in the refugee feasibility studies all made him a logical choice for office. He was appointed a consultant to the E.C.A., then organized and chaired its Advisory Committee on Overseas Territories. But Bowman gave only a modest amount of time to this work, having decided to devote himself as much as possible to a series of books concerning foreign policy and international affairs.

Bowman sought $38,000, which he estimated was the "cost of assistants required for a study over a three-year period of national policy in relation to international affairs."[83] He submitted the request for money to Joseph W. Barker of the Research Corporation in New York City, but his project was not funded. He tried elsewhere, equally without success. It was a surprising and grave disappointment to him to find little support for this purpose. After some months he did find that the Carnegie Foundation was willing to help in a limited way, but by then his friend John L. Pratt of the Hopkins trustees decided to arrange suitable working accommodation, and the cost of at least a secretary for five years.[84] It was a grand gesture and one that encouraged Bowman. But he died before any of this manuscript reached completion. At his death he had only written about two hundred pages of his planned work, tentatively entitled "The Inquiry in Relation to Research in the State Department in World War II."

Chapter Eleven

The Geography of Isaiah Bowman:
Some Thought and Reflection

Bowman's early years were spent on his father's farm in eastern Michigan, an area not long since on the moving frontier and in his youth still characterized by frontier mores. Hard work was not only regarded as virtuous—it was necessary. Isaiah Bowman lived directly on the land, not divorced from it by the intercession of machine. He felt heat, cold, drought, abundance, and insufficiency. Perhaps his future was influenced by the place of frequent discussions of humanity on earth in church, or in the schoolroom, or with the retired sea captain living nearby who taught Bowman geometry in the 1890s. Or perhaps it was influenced by Bowman's mother, who encouraged him at a critical juncture. Whatever the source, Bowman was possessed of a desire to see more of the world and understand man's place in it. He decided

> to study geography professionally, to the dismay of my father who could not believe that a career could be based upon subject specialization. He was thinking of the law and medicine as great professional fields, but why should I study geography? I told him that I had observed an almost universal discontent with one's lot in the world. . . . I told my father, I had decided to study the thing

I liked best, and take the consequences, believing that happiness at least would come from studying what one greatly wished to study.[1]

His studies led him to Harlan H. Barrows at the Ferris Institute in Michigan, and then to Mark Jefferson, the first widely educated man that Bowman had met.[2] John K. Wright has proposed that Jefferson revealed to Bowman the role of the imagination in geographic thinking.[3] At least as important was the severity of Jefferson's mental discipline.

Jefferson sent Bowman to William Morris Davis at Harvard, who was then at the height of his pedagogic powers. "Davis' influence was most marked. His seminar in physiography was the most critical and stimulating scientific exercise that I have had, next to Geometry."[4] Davis taught Bowman physiography, then alerted him to the necessity of studying life response, or "ontography." Much of Bowman's career prior to 1935 may be regarded as the product of his desire to elaborate the position of physiography and ontography and to integrate them meaningfully in the regional synthesis. In the first notebook which Bowman maintained at Harvard in February 1903 (which he deposited in the American Geographical Society's archives), one notes: "two divisions of the subject of geography ... physiography, the study of forms. The Physical Environment of the Earth's inhabitants ... ontography. Organic conditions which are the responses of the inhabitants to their physical environment." And one finds there are references to regional geography and environmentalism.

The months of studying with both Jefferson and Davis provided Bowman with an acutely honed sense of the need for a geographic discipline and an individually developed critical faculty. Jefferson had taught Bowman the importance of thinking clearly. Davis had taught Bowman something of the very structure of thought and had revealed himself as a master logician.

W. M. Davis put it this way: if thinking is important then conscious thinking is still more important, since otherwise thought may easily run astray, especially when practised by an untrained or temperamentally uncritical mind. I am expressing the substance of Davis' thought, not quoting him. ... Davis ... has a good deal to say about thought processes in their application to geographical subjects, but . . . his application is far wider . . . his book "The Coral Reef Problem" . . . is worth reading if only for one phrase, "the inexhaustible inaccuracy of his Grace's imagination," on page 75.[5]

Bowman's contribution to Andean physiography has been noted in chapter 3. But he made other significant physiographic contributions. Two of the more notable cases involve the Red River Dispute and the difference of opinion which emerged between W. M. Davis and Albrecht and Walther Penck.

In June 1921, the Department of Justice requested Bowman to offer an opinion concerning ownership of an instrumentally unmapped section of the Red River between Oklahoma and Texas. When oil wells began to yield on the valley floor the matter of land ownership had become important, and a boundary suit between the two states had been brought before the Supreme Court. Bowman spent two weeks in the field, frequently with temperatures over 100°F., "travelling from the top of the high plains eastward from the 'Breaks' and out across the broken and then less broken plains down to the Arkansas border."[6] He wrote an opinion, withstood cross-examination of this physiographic testimony, then administered a riposte long remembered. The cross-examining attorney listened to Bowman's physiographic testimony involving prediction of natural events, then inquired whether the witness considered himself a prophet. "Major," Bowman replied, "because my name is Isaiah."[7]

The study demonstrated the utility of physiographic science. Bowman wrote an article on the subject,[8] and exploited his study in a chapter entitled "Measurement in Geography," published in his own *Geography in Relation to the Social Sciences.*[9] In 1943 his testimony was cited in the case, "Kansas v. Missouri."[10]

A second notable contribution which Bowman made toward elaboration of a fuller physiographic science came when Walther and Albrecht Penck differed with William Morris Davis on the philosophical postulates of that science. The difference of opinion arose over Davis's "explanatory description of land forms" and more particularly his "cycle of erosion." A squabble could have developed had not Bowman intervened. He corresponded with Davis and the Pencks, urging them to place the matter on the basis of science and not individual or national prejudice. He wrote his own opinions for *The Geographical*

Review.[11] Bowman felt that Walther Penck's work contained creative ideas, and he urged an English translation of Penck's *Die Morphologische Analyse.* He wrote to Douglas W. Johnson requesting support for the idea of the translation;[12] Johnson obliged.[13] But no translation was published until 1953.[14] Bowman's correspondence is much quoted in "A Fragment on the Penck(s)-Davis Conflict," by Geoffrey J. Martin.[15] It is of interest to note that thirty-five years after Bowman's first two publications, "A Typical Case of Stream-Capture in Michigan," and "Deflection of the Mississippi," both won attention in Armin K. Lobeck's compendious study of geomorphology.[16]

The personal example of Davis and Jefferson had also been of the greatest significance to Bowman. Bowman wrote frequently of Davis that he had taught by example. Two other men who influenced Bowman were Grove K. Gilbert and Thomas C. Chamberlin. Many years after the death of these men Bowman wrote, "I had the inestimable advantage of knowing both Gilbert and Chamberlin when I was a young man. To talk with them for only a few hours was to gain a sense of bigness, impartiality, judicial temper, and fairness, that subsequent years could not rub out."[17]

At Yale in 1905 Bowman offered "South America," one of the first regional geography courses to be taught in the United States. Here Bowman placed Jefferson's "man" on Davis's physiographic platform in the regional context. To Jefferson he wrote, "I have tried the 'man-first' idea in my course in South America, starting with your population map. . . ."[18] He did the same with his course on North America.

This point of view prevailed in Bowman's *South America: A Geography Reader.* Meanwhile Ellsworth Huntington's *Asia: A Geography Reader* had been published in 1912, and Mr. W. O. Wiley urged Bowman to extend the series. By 1921 Bowman had arranged for J. W. Gregory to write the volume on Africa, O. D. von Engeln to write on North America, and Marcel Aurousseau to write on Australia and the Pacific Islands. He then tried to persuade Albert Demangeon to write the volume on Europe.[19] Von Engeln's manuscript was not considered suitable, whereupon Bowman invited J. Paul Goode and then Lawrence Martin to write the volume on North America, but neither accepted. The series might well have given a substantial thrust to geographic education in the grade schools and to regional geography.

In 1907 when fifty-five members of the Association of American Geographers reported the variety of geography in which they were most interested, Bowman was the only one who answered "regional geography."[20] He was aware of the work of Herbertson, La Blache, and Hettner, which was undoubtedly of significance to his concept of region. In the 1914 publication of the results of the George B. Roorbach survey to which twenty-five geographers replied, nine respondents listed regional geography among the three most needed lines of investigation, though it is probable that the nine included scholars who considered areal physiography as part of regional geography. On that occasion Bowman wrote, "What is most needed is intensive field work in well selected regions. This means repeated return of the investigator to his chosen region...."[21]

Bowman's three expeditions to South America in 1907, 1911, and 1913 led to a variety of regionally inspired articles and two books which remain among the finest examples of regional scholarship in the history of American geography, *The Andes of Southern Peru* (1916) and *Desert Trails of Atacama* (1924). *The New World* and *The Pioneer Fringe* were also books for which Bowman drew on the regional inspiration. Chapter 5 of his *Geography in Relation to the Social Sciences* entitled "Regional Geography" was the fullest expression which he permitted himself concerning this genre. Part of the chapter was revised and published as "Regional Concepts and Their Application,"[22] and part of it reemerged in his presidential address before the International Geographical Congress in Warsaw, 1934.[23]

In the thirteen papers which Bowman delivered before the annual meetings of the Association of American Geographers he not infrequently returned to the theme of regional geography. Two papers warrant note: "Hogarth's 'The Nearer East' in Regional Geography" (1905), and "The Regional Geography of Long Island" (1909). He reviewed Hogarth's book, injecting something of his own thought concerning regional geography, in an abstract published in 1906.[24] He frequently asserted that the regional synthesis of life should be the geographer's first concern. In an editorial he reflected:

It is the purpose of geographical science to show man how he can use and possess this earth of his.... Man does not live history or geography or chemistry; he lives life and this is made up of cross sections of experience of infinite variety.... It is antiquarian, particularistic, microscopic, to look for a college and school subject in life. Subjects are the devices of the schoolmaster and college administrator.[25]

It was in similar vein that he wrote to Mark Jefferson, "Damn those boundary fellows who think the Lord created 'subjects.'"[26] And he remarked to W. M. Davis, "Advances are made by those people who have great interest in the subject and who pay more attention to the subject than they do the exact position of a given piece of investigation with respect to an artifical frontier."[27]

He was supportive of others' work in the regional cause. When J. Russell Smith's *North America* appeared in 1925 Bowman wrote, "Professor Smith has given us just the book that university geographical departments have needed for twenty years—a regional geography that describes and explains the real people of North America in a style that frequently displays the irresistible quality of genius."[28]

Bowman was thrilled with the volumes of *La Géographie Universelle*, the collective regional expression of the disciples of Vidal de La Blache. As each work appeared he read it with enthusiasm. To Emmanuel de Martonne he wrote:

> You are doing an extremely fine piece of work in the *Géographie Universelle. . . .* The combination of economic and political elements evokes only admiration. It is in my judgement a most effective synthesis and presents the realities of regional life in a way that a narrowly technical description could never do. It is in that direction that I am tending constantly in my own work. . . . Of course that is apparent in the *New World* and thus you may believe with what interest and approval I follow your work and that of your associates in the great series that you have undertaken.[29]

And Bowman wrote his onetime Harvard classmate Henri Baulig that "your two precious volumes on North America . . . are superb! The style of the text, the organization of the material, and the exquisitely drawn maps and diagrams form a whole which will make a deep impression upon American geography."[30]

When W. L. G. Joerg derived inspiration from Henri Baulig's *North America,* Bowman encouraged him to write a history of regional treatments in the geography of North America. Bowman contributed two long letters, pointed conversation, and encouragement to Joerg, who then wrote, "The Geography of North America: A History of its Regional Exposition."[31] It was a significant contribution to a scant literature. Bowman corresponded with Lucien Gallois in 1930 and 1931 about translating and publishing in English the twenty-two volumes of *Géographie Universelle*, twelve of which had by then been published.[32] He invited several publishers to send representatives to view the volumes, but all shrank from the commitment necessary to publish such a large work during the economic depression. Bowman could not restrain his enthusiasm for the project, and wrote to Scribner's "As for the quality of the volumes, there has never been in existence anything approaching them in completeness of contents, thoroughness of scholarship and excellence of illustration."[33] They were never translated as a series.

From William Morris Davis, Bowman had learned to seek life responses to the physical environment. He became familiar with the varieties of early twentieth century environmental determinism. When in 1907 Ellsworth Huntington joined the Yale faculty, Bowman was attracted by Huntington's notion of climatic change within historic time. At Davis's urging Bowman undertook an investigation which resulted in "Man and Climatic Change in South America."[34] Although Bowman retained an intellectual interest in climatic change and climatic influence and wrote of the matter intermittently, he became skeptical of this posture.

Perhaps Bowman's first considered published work to challenge the legitimacy of "influences" as the moving force in geography came in 1906, when an abstract of his paper "Hogarth's 'The Nearer East' in Regional Geography" appeared. In this article Bowman noted that Hogarth's concept of region was not dissimilar to that of A. J. Herbertson, whose "Natural Geographical Regions" had just appeared in *The Geographical Journal*,[35] and that Hogarth provided "a treatment differing from that of the anthropogeographer...."[36] Bowman's concept of region encouraged him to avoid the life-response theme as the main thrust and direction of his work. And, too, he had learned something of environmentalist restraint from Jefferson who had treated early forms of determinism with reserve, and who had substituted "anthropography" for "anthropogeography."[37] Bowman's attitude was rare in early twentieth century American geography. He perceived American geography in terms of an epic conquest and subjugation of the land by man rather than collisions and conflicts of peoples. A population, in its majority European, found combat in a settlement process with a physical environment and not with each other.

Yet determinism does appear in Bowman's earlier work, especially before 1919. In 1916 he wrote, "The strong climatic and topographic contrasts and the varied human life which the region contains are of geographic interest chiefly because they present so many and such clear cases of environmental control within short distances."[38] And the title of chapter 7 of that same book, "The Geographic Basis of Revolutions and of Human Character in the Peruvian Andes," also embraces determinism. But the work as a whole exhibited environmentalist restraint, as was noted in a review by Theodore Roosevelt.

> Especially wise is Mr. Bowman's refusal to follow those of his fellow geographers who, dazzled by the discovery of the profound effect of geographical conditions upon human nature, promptly proceed to explain all the immense complexus of the forces of social causation as simply due to geographical causes.... Geography has a profound effect upon character, but character is never a product of geography alone.[39]

Part of Bowman's maturity of disciplinal posture was the product of interdisciplinary exchange. Jean Gottman has suggested that Bowman was one of a group of young scholars to derive inspiration and functional science from the Yale physicist Josiah W. Gibbs, who developed the law of phases.[40] Bowman used similar methods to elaborate principles regarding demographic elements, an audacious conception of a thermodynamic social construct. Frequently between 1912 and 1914, Bowman and Ellsworth Huntington met informally with anthropologists in New York City. Bowman also sought opportunity for exchange with historians like J. T. Adams, C. A. Beard, C. L. Becker, and F. J. Turner. In the 1910s he held at least two weekend house parties solely for historians, for he had come to believe that geographers were neglecting the historical dimension. By 1919 Bowman had repudiated the looser forms of determinism then rampant in American geography. Perhaps that was in part due to his affiliation with the Inquiry and American Commission to Negotiate Peace. Here were Titans changing the shapes and extent of nations. The power and influence of governments was so immediate, so direct, and so close to Bowman that the physical environment came to seem much more remote to him in the rooms of the Quai D'Orsai than it had astride a mule in the Atacama. From Paris he wrote of Ellen Semple's work:

> I thought very well of it at one time but as a matter of fact and speaking quite frankly, the Semple bubble—if I may so put it—is forever punctured so far as I am concerned. This is quite confidential. I do not believe in that type of geography. It is vague, generalized, and mostly wrong ... my appreciation of Herbertson's work is increasing with every contact that I have with his ideas, and in just that proportion my appreciation of Miss Semple's work is diminishing. . . .[41]

And he wrote to his friend James Truslow Adams:

> In 1905 I began to teach geography at Yale and there was a lot of determinism in it. I got steadily away from it. The closer to the facts I got the less importance I attached to geographical environment. The other side of the picture is that there are many authentic cases of geographical control. . . . But that Society as a whole is guided predominantly by any one of these things is to me sheer rubbish. To me the evidence seems overwhelming.[42]

Bowman had developed the notion of a conditional conquest of nature by man, not always strictly observed but prevalent in his writing. It was not an acceptance of determination by nature but an awareness of humans' helplessness in a marginal environment. His philosophy accommodated the notion of limitation imposed by the environment, and recognized human possibilities in the exploitation of that environment. Much quoted is Bowman's aphorism, "He [man] cannot move mountains without floating a bond issue."[43] Bowman provided many examples of the way in which environmental circumstances change as technology changes. This led writers to call him a "possibilist." In the sense that Bowman viewed as suspect the more extreme dogmatism of environmentalism, he and Carl Sauer are joined by George Tatham as a part of the development of "possibilism" in the United States.[44] But Bowman did not march with the possibilist movement; analytical physiography, conjoined with human distribution and activity, rendered in a regional setting provided him with a literary disposition that did not stress determinisms.

Bowman's mature reflection upon the state of the discipline only occasionally emerged in correspondence or the printed word. His most complete statement concerning what he felt to be the essence of geography appeared in *Geography in Relation to the Social Sciences.* [45] A first statement on the general theme of that book was prepared and delivered at the Hanover, New Hampshire, conference of the Social Science Research Council in 1929. Bowman came under severe attack by other disciplinarians. It is interesting to note the circumstances.

In the summer of 1929, the Social Science Research Council had sponsored a meeting to discuss the role and work of the Commission on the Social Studies in the Schools. The subject of geography was not well treated there. One of the protagonists on that occasion was Edmund E. Day of the Rockefeller Foundation; another was Bowman. The two disagreed sharply on the worth of geography. They decided to discuss the nature of geography by correspondence throughout the coming winter, but this correspondence had not begun when Carlton Hayes, president of the Middle States History Teachers Association, invited Bowman to give an address on geography and its relation to the social sciences on 30 November 1929 at Atlantic City.

Bowman obliged, and sent a copy of this address to Day. Bowman was of course well aware that Rockefeller financial support for future geographical projects depended upon the outcome of this correspondence. Day had contended "that geography has no technique applicable to a study of humanity" and that "the American Geographical Society was not the place where a well-rounded investigation of New England ought to be made."[46] Bowman had such a study in mind. In the wake of a daunting letter by Day, Bowman determined to write an extended statement on the study of geography,[47] and spoke on this very theme at Hanover, 1 September 1930. The Commission on the Social Studies in the Schools appointed by the American Historical Association invited Bowman to represent geography and subsequently to write a book on the relation of that branch of science to the social studies.

The result, *Geography in Relation to the Social Sciences,* was read widely, and will perhaps be read after all his other books have lost much of their usefulness. Eva G. R. Taylor called the book "a sane and balanced exposition that should go far to correct the view that geography can be neglected with impunity."[48] Gladys Wrigley, who edited the work, described "it as a universal introduction to the study of geography—for professional and layman alike. It enlarges on the synthesizing function of geography which puts an emphasis on things as a whole, a function vastly important in a complex and varied world, ever changing at differential rates."[49]

Much of the book had been written in 1931, the same year in which he had been obliged to give the presidential address to the Association of American Geographers. He wrote to the secretary of the Association, Darrell H. Davis:

> Instead of giving the usual presidential address I should like to have something in the nature of a short paper . . . that I should like to circulate well in advance of the meeting. . . . It is a paper I gave at Hanover, before the Social Science Research Council, on geography as a Social Science. The conclusion was that it is not a social science but that it has contributions to make to social studies. This doesn't sound very exciting, but I know that the problem is troubling the geographers of the country a good deal both from the theoretical standpoint and from the practical standpoint of university organization.[50]

Some weeks later Bowman again wrote to Davis explaining that he had acquired fifty mimeographed copies of his Hanover address. He had planned to send these to interested members of the Association of American Geographers in order to secure as many comments on it as possible.

> If we could take a previously prepared case and let all interested persons have a whack at it—dissent as well as approve—we might get a better rounded statement of wider acceptance. This could then occupy a whole number of the Annals and be distributed to the "higher command" among college educators. . . .[51]

In a later letter Bowman added, "It is furthest from my thought to standardize our concepts or definitions and secure complete unanimity of opinion. I have but little respect for definitions except as tools to be used for the moment."[52] But Bowman decided to return to the pioneer fringe thesis, on which he was also working, for his presidential address, and leave discussion of the nature of geography to his book on the subject.

In early September of 1931 Bowman left for the International Geographical Congress in Paris, where he was elected president of the International Geographical Union. From Paris he planned to travel to China as one of the U.S. representatives to the Pan-Pacific Scientific Congress, returning to New York by 15 December, only days before a scheduled meeting in Ypsilanti, Michigan. He had also planned "a stop at Harbin, where I had a rendezvous with a half dozen experts to discuss colonization in northern Manchuria."[53] That trip was cancelled at the last moment, and Bowman returned to the American Geographical Society, whose funds had dwindled in the Great Depression. When Bowman assumed the chairmanship of the National Research Council in Washington in 1933, and accepted responsibiilty as vice chairman and director of the Science Advisory Board, he had bade farewell to a creative scholarship. And when he journeyed to Baltimore to become president of The Johns Hopkins University on 1 July 1935, he knew that he would have little time for geography.

Yet his combination of administrative ability, intellectual capacity, articulation, and judgement had brought him to high position in American geography. Elective membership in geographical societies, honorary degrees, and medals came to him in considerable numbers. Early in his career these thrilled him—he was especially pleased to receive the Bonaparte-Wyse Medal of the Paris Geographical Society in 1917—but later he tired of the process and urged that each award should be given to a younger person whom it might inspire. Although he "had to accept six or eight L.L.D's, I had the courage to decline 15 others. Honors become epidemic!"[54] Numerous other attentions were thrust upon him. In 1928 at London and Cambridge, England, Bowman attended his first International Geographical Congress. Unbeknown to him he had been selected president of the Historical Geography section of the Congress, was listed as a candidate for "The Commission on Types of Rural Habitation," and was appointed one of the vice-presidents of the International Geographical Union. On the occasion of the next such Congress, held in Paris in 1931, he spoke at the opening ceremony in behalf of the U.S. delegation, presented a paper relating to the American Geographical Society pioneer studies undertaking,[55] then was elected president of the Union. He presided at the Warsaw Congress of 1934, and attended the 1938 Amsterdam

Congress as an honored guest. This participation brought him further international attention as geographer and not inconsiderable academic acclaim at home.

The largest problem which Bowman faced as president of the Union was the exclusion of German geographers from participation in the congresses and Union activity. It was a matter that had divided the world of geography. Following the Paris conference Bowman had spent several days in Paris talking with the French geographers. Then he travelled to Poland to talk with the Polish geographers, and to Germany to reason with the German geographers. He worked with diligence and diplomacy to return the Germans to the Union. Upon his return to New York he resumed negotiation of the matter in correspondence, especially with Herbert J. Fleure and Emmanuel de Martonne.[56] He had already urged de Martonne that he not be appointed president of the Union, for as he wrote Fleure, "I was afraid we would get into a difficult situation in view of my determination to treat the Germans fairly and even generously. No one can be generous unless the victors are generous. . . ."[57]

The 1934 meeting was to be held in Poland, and Bowman had been deeply involved in the work of the Polish boundary commission at the Paris Peace Conference. The Germans were aware of this, and they viewed Bowman's *The New World* as a book by (if not for) the victors. But Bowman was elected president, and his friend Eugenius Romer, an ardent Polish nationalist, was eminent in congressional arrangements. However, at least in part because of Bowman's negotiations and urging of the German geographers, and support especially by Ruhl and Troll, a delegation of forty German geographers attended the Warsaw Congress. That was the first German geographical participation since the First World War.

The rapprochement with the German geographers was perhaps especially difficult for Bowman. Not only had he become for German geographers the Allied geographer who had helped supervise the reduction of Germany, but he had also supported and advanced the schema of Davisian physiography against the challenge posed by Walther and Albrecht Penck. These circumstances did not endear him to German geographers, and with his work at Paris, *The New World*, his friendship with and acclaim by French geographers, his Warsaw accomplishment was a feat as large as it was little heralded.

His acclaim, too, had led to another interesting departure from the

purely scholarly world. Early in 1935, shortly before Bowman was due
to leave the Geographical Society for Hopkins, he was asked by Marie
Peary Stafford, daughter of Admiral Robert E. Peary, to explain why
the Society had not given her father a medal for his polar achievement
in 1909. The question of whether Peary had reached the North Pole in
1909 was still controversial and vexing twenty-six years later.

Bowman's position was that "there was only one record of facts that
we desired .. the notebooks of Peary himself, the originals, the
day-by-day log of his journey from Cape Columbia to the Pole, and
back."[58] He proposed to Mrs. Peary and her daughter Marie "that if the
family would turn over to us every bit of evidence which they possess
bearing on the polar controversy ... the Society was ready to examine
the records in the greatest detail and issue a statement, provided that
the Society should be free to publish its findings, regardless of their
nature."[59] Not until 30 July 1935, when Bowman had already assumed
the presidency of The Johns Hopkins University, did he begin a
detailed study of Admiral Peary's records in the Admiral's house on
Eagle Island, Maine. Bowman met with Mrs. Peary and her daughter on
numerous occasions, had the Admiral's notes and diaries copied, then
established a large "spread" plotting all relevant data upon it, showing
the daily advance of Peary to the Pole. He secured the aid of Harry
Raymond of the Dudley Observatory in Albany, New York, and
invested a considerable amount of his own time in the investigation. It
was an exciting adjudication, privately conceived, and privately
undertaken. Bowman informally concluded that "Peary was a sloppy
recorder, but the sincerity and truth of his statements one can hardly
question after looking at the whole record."[60] It was the first time that
anyone outside the family had been allowed to study the Admiral's
papers. Bowman observed:

> If Peary reached the Pole, his critical marches were longer than
> he or anyone else has accomplished in similar circumstances
> before or since ... his previous record as a geographical observer
> was not unimpeachable. Given an unusually favourable combination
> of wind, drift, and ice conditions his final dash is not impossible.
> But it is perfectly reasonable to conclude, on a cool examination
> of his records and of the human probabilities involved, that Peary
> did not get within fifty miles of the Pole.[61]

Bowman did make one public commitment relative to Peary: in 1938 he wrote "The Peary Memorial at Jockey Gap, Fryburg, Maine: An Appreciation."[62]

Bowman had become a very influential person, one who shared the affairs of the day with university presidents, scientists, businessmen, and a host of organizations, including the state and federal governments. He did not publish another book in geographical vein, though *Limits of Land Settlement: A Report on Present-day Possibilities* (1937) was prepared under his direction and included preface, introduction, and a chapter which he had written. He also published *A Design for Scholarship* (1936) and *The Graduate School in American Democracy* (1939), both of which revealed something of his new course. Other than these books he published in 1935-50 eighty articles, four chapters and five forewords to different books, and two memorials. Additionally, he prepared a substantial number of unpublished addresses. Still a geographer at heart, he attempted new syntheses of the mind such as "Geography in the Creative Experiment" (*Geographical Review* 28 [1938]:1-19), "Science and Social Pioneering" (*Science* 90 [1939]:289-98), "Science and Social Effects: Three Failures" (*The Scientific Monthly* 50 [1940]:289-98), "Impact of Geography on National Power" (address presented at The National War College, 30 September 1946), and "The Geographical Situation of the United States in Relation to World Policies" (*Geographical Journal* 112 [1948]:129-45).

Bowman talked and wrote of the quintessence of geography "as one group among many groups of forces that have involved man in a vast and possibly timeless creative experiment ... out of this play of forces—by no means either infinite or hopelessly complex—man is progressively creating and experimenting, and the chief experiment is himself. He is changing himself as well as his world as he goes along. . . ."[63] He well realized the large sweep of knowledge which a geographer must have. He was concerned that the younger geographers in the United States did not read enough, and did not possess a power of language equal to that of the geographers of an earlier day. He worried that geography as a profession would consequently lose standing. He told Leo Waibel, "You are right about the deficiencies in the training of young geographers. As a class geographers don't know enough."[64] To Gladys Wrigley he wrote:

The young geographers got busy with the idea of measurement and the misfortune to American geography during the past twenty years has been their preoccupation with the measurement of trivialities in many instances. I hold to the view, no doubt old-fashioned, that ideas move the world and that ideas have been the foundation of every advance of importance in intellectual evolution. Techniques in a way take care of themselves. Geography has run to a kindergarten technique to serve purposes not yet defined by those who develop them ... I do not say these things with an air of despair for each science goes through the same stage. I say them only to express my dissatisfaction with definite measurements for indefinite purposes.[65]

He was not happy with the direction which geography in the United States had begun to assume in the twenties. Measurements, techniques, too great concern with apparatus, seemed to Bowman to dominate. Disappearing were the large themes, the moving visions, that made geography grand. He did not see figures of the stature of Davis, Gilbert, or Shaler appearing, and he was alarmed to note an unhappy separation of physical and human geography in geographers' writings which resulted in simplistic explanations. He summed up his feelings to Preston James:

Ideas make the world go round. Everyone is on the lookout for them. Instead of merely gathering together some descriptive material, why not make your descriptive material act as servant to your ideas? There is lots of room for discovery and it is the results of discovery that we want most. By discovery I do not mean the results of a journey into unexplored regions. It may be only a journey into your backyard, such as Darwin made when he studied the earthworms and wrote a classic about them.[66]

This quest for the large view of things led him to establish the Department of Geography at Hopkins. He hoped the department's carefully chosen staff would be "a group of really first-class brains who should lead the world to study objectively the scientific background of some great problems of the day."[67] Bowman was critical of large departments of geography in established universities which had "developed a subject doctrine that spells narrowness and self-sufficiency to an alarming degree.... Only a willing and vigorous policy of interdepartmental training can offset such a tendency."[68] Yet the department which Bowman created faltered, perhaps not due to "faults in the original scheme but to personal factors."[69] Perhaps significantly the failure of the scheme was not demonstrated during Bowman's presidential regime. And, too, the present Johns Hopkins Department of Geography and Environmental Engineering has evolved from Bowman's creation of the 1940s.

Bowman was critically wary of those who paraded pedagogic method. For him, the good teacher was one who knew the field, and "the best public school education is provided by men and women whose inspiration comes from the mastery of subject matter."[70] But it was research that thrilled him and fascinated him, research which he saw as "not merely the way of life of a modern highbrow; it is an ancient calling, as the book of Proverbs bears witness: it is 'the honour of Kings ... to search out a matter....' "[71] He became increasingly aware of the need for people with knowledge to gain experience with the social forces of the day. He urged that science had a vital role to play in life itself, and that it should not be set aside from the mainstream. Science was for Bowman a part of humanism.

> It would be easy to compile a list of beneficial effects following upon the application of science to social problems.... But might it not prove equally useful, now and then, to analyze instances of social failures which were definitely forecast if the related science were neglected? I propose to describe three failures in at least one of which forecast has been fully verified. They relate to the hitherto unsolved problems of peace-making, the decline of the oyster industry of Maryland and the destruction, with tragic human consequences, of certain tropical soils....[72]

He urged recognition of the fact that science "does not close the gap between findings and actions" and urged education as the only medium which would reduce that gap in a democratic society.[73] Perhaps this larger view of matters was a result of his assumption of a university presidency, but the warfare which had commenced in Europe in 1939 prompted his urging a more rational world order.

Although in the last ten years of his life he produced numerous essays concerning science and social betterment, he turned his attention chiefly to war and postwar matters.

Not optimistic about the future of mankind, he wondered if world peace could last. In his notes he frequently mentioned "clashes of will," "conflicting governmental aims," "language problems," and "low grade populations" as problems confronting the postwar world. Since 1938 he had witnessed the reluctance of governments to accept refugees. He had seen the repudiation of the League of Nations, and a later emerging skepticism regarding the United Nations, by the people of his own country. And grave doubts had begun to assail him concerning the way in which leaders were selected and the motivations of those seeking leadership roles. As a corrective he frequently attempted to intrude the intellectual point of view in the councils of power, and to his credit he made that point of view respected and respectable. Cordell Hull wrote:

> during the years President Bowman labored with the President and officials of the State Department to promote conditions of peace and suitable draft of the world peace organization, there was no one upon whom President Roosevelt and I leaned more heavily. I know of no person better and more fully equipped for this difficult and all important work than President Bowman. He performed his task at all times with masterly skill and ability.[74]

Secretary of State Dean Acheson called Bowman "one of the architects of the United Nations."[75]

But Gladys Wrigley wrote, "It was a misfortune for geography when Isaiah Bowman assumed his larger responsibilities in 1935."[76] A further loss came with his retirement, interrupted by his labors for the Economic Cooperation Administration, and soon to be cut short by death. In retirement he had thought of republishing at least *Desert Trails of Atacama*. From time to time he had considered producing a "New World" which would have been to World War II what *The New World* was to the First World War. And he had a series of little books in mind, some of which were written in essay form and delivered as addresses to civic audiences. In part these essays which asked such questions as "Who are you?" "What do you do?" were autobiographical in nature, yet Bowman saw in them the quality of field work.

His larger plan for retirement was to offer the world his rich experience in international affairs. At an early stage in his life Bowman had begun to keep notes or a diary, and at times both. This had become a habit with him by the time of the Inquiry and Paris Peace Conference, and it was a system of reference which was to prove most valuable. Frequently, if a matter seemed to command special attention, he would write a "memorandum" on the subject, usually typed, signed, and dated. In this way he accumulated a formidable record of events both national and international, seen from his vantage point. His intent was to convert this mass of data into a series of meaningful publications. But his time was continuously interrupted.

> There is just nothing to this retirement business. What I overlooked in thinking of leisure was the fact that outside interests had come to occupy so large a part of my time. I have written not a single line of my Rutgers address, to be given on April 6, and to be submitted by April 1. The ECA load increases. Stettinius wants the manuscript of his book read; Grew sends me a batch of his material to be read; a State Department book arrives in thick bundles of manuscript. All shout for speed.[77]

His first large manuscript began to assume form in October 1949, and by November he was at work on the first chapter of the book, "Where the Forces Strive."[78] He had asked Gladys Wrigley if she would edit the manuscript as it proceeded, and she had agreed. In sending her the first chapter he attempted a description of the book as it had developed in his mind:

> I ... therefore propose to take certain major themes. One of them ECA, another is the concept and experience with world organizations for peace (League of Nations, United Nations), a third might be the meaning of forms of international collaboration now generally accepted; still another might be the diversities of the world that confront us as difficulties in trying to get international agreements. Another is international law.
>
> I do not propose to deal with each of these themes in a cut and dried manner, giving out loads of information systematically assembled. There are plenty of books that have done that. Instead, I would like to write a book in somewhat the style of this

first chapter, with examples in almost every paragraph and a sprinkling of pointed quotations. The book is meant to be read![79]

By 29 November he had started a chapter on "Settlement and Migration," and was planning another on the E.C.A. "One day we can make a start on the Mohammedan World. But the first chapter must be a vital element in the whole business and is almost infinitely difficult to write."[80] On 18 December he "started on Latin America on the general principle of beginning a number of chapters so as to alternate between the more abstract writing of a first chapter and the specific treatment of particular regions or tropics."[81] And on 3 January he wrote Wrigley that he had "tried another introduction to the book" during the holidays.[82] Three days later Bowman died. Wrigley examined the manuscript and surviving sheets of notes to see if the whole could be satisfactorily edited, but there was too much still undone for her to be able to complete the book.

John K. Wright supposed that Bowman's success was attributable to "five personal endowments": an enthusiastic imaginative curiosity, self-discipline, self-reliance, articulateness, and vitality.[83] To that list might be added native ability. Bowman could administer and simultaneously practice scholarship. In administering he was very successful because he was efficient, and his efficiency was based on his ability to secure the best people for the work at hand. He knew incapacity or inefficiency when he saw it, and would speak his mind promptly, leaving in his trail not a few enemies. But he did conserve much time in this fashion, and time he declared was the most precious of all assets. A shrewd judge of people, he was not unable to change his mind about them. In the twenties Bowman and Sauer were not en rapport, but later Bowman developed the highest regard for Sauer's work. Perhaps their early difference of opinion stemmed in part from Sauer's published and spoken disbelief in political geography during the twenties,[84] the very decade in which Bowman's book *The New World: Problems in Political Geography* was published in four editions. But by 1939, as chairman of the Association of American Geographers nominating committee, Bowman could "propose that Sauer should be invited to serve as president . . . Sauer should have been selected long ago and, in my opinion, it is a mistake to overlook an obvious choice, such overlooking being the result as a rule of some individual's prejudice."[85]

His judgement of projects was also excellent. The three themes he selected for research in his twenty years at the American Geographical Society—the Hispanic American program, polar research, and pioneer settlement studies—became an integral part of geography as it was fashioned in the United States. Nothing less than the large project, largely conceived and well executed, was his goal. And, too, his own contribution was substantial. Some of Bowman's best work may have been the product of the early physiographic studies of his Yale years. *Forest Physiography*, "the first comprehensive account of the relief, climate, soils, and vegetation of the United States," was assayed by Robert Beckinsale as "a masterly summary."[86] In 1912 A. J. Herbertson called it "one of the most valuable contributions to the descriptive physical geography of the United States. It summarizes the innumerable special studies which are the despair of the European. . . ."[87] Reprinted as late as 1930, *Forest Physiography* led to a number of articles and books by such scholars as Nevin M. Fenneman, Mark Jefferson, W.L.G. Joerg, and François E. Matthes.

Bowman's South America field trips led to some work of lasting geomorphological worth. His research included contributions to the studies of the influence of highland climate on landscape and life, the complex nature of the Andean Cordillera, glaciation within the tropics, and especially processes involved in the formation of cirques. Additionally, according to Beckinsale, "he showed a true realisation of the need for quantification. . . . The results are often crude but the effect is striking and the concept, for the time, markedly modern." Bowman's regional diagram constituted an original contribution to the field.[88] A. G. Ogilvie supported Bowman's contention that "despite the absence of stratigraphic evidence for long periods, a geological history of the Andes could be written from the interpretation of the surface."[89]

His contribution toward a better understanding of the frontier, pioneer fringe, rural settlement, and a "science of settlement," much scattered, was an attempt at disciplinal order. The studies were put to remarkable practical use during the war years and afterwards. L. Dudley Stamp found Bowman's researches of benefit to his own British Land Utilization Survey. The two men enjoyed extended conversation in late 1933, owing in considerable part to Bowman's support of Stamp for the financial assistance which enabled him to visit North America. Aside from reviewing *The Pioneer Fringe*, Stamp retained a copy of the book as "almost a primer," and later endorsed

"Isaiah Bowman's famous study on *The Pioneer Fringe.*"[90] Jean
Gottman viewed Bowman's conception of the pioneer fringe as one of
the larger advances to human geography in the first half of the
twentieth century, possibly initiating the idea of cycles of population
similar to cycles of erosion.[91] Charles Aiken considered *The Pioneer
Fringe* Bowman's best-known work, and suggested that Bowman was
one of a very few geographers to inject something of agrarianism into
American geography.[92]

Bowman's own scholarly contribution has been useful as an
educational force. *The New World* was the first book in the United
States to be adopted as a text in political geography courses. His
organization of the translation and editing of Brunhes's *Human
Geography* brought French geographic thinking into the minds and
classrooms of geographers across the United States, and parts of the
British Empire. Laurence M. Gould, president of Carleton College in
Minnesota (better known for the Byrd polar penetrations), wrote
Bowman:

> It happens that I find myself teaching a course in the Geography
> of North America this semester. My knowledge of that subject I
> find to be very deficient. . . . What with Bowman's "New World,"
> his "Pioneer Fringe" and his "Forest Physiography" I am giving
> a Bowman course in geography. I am bodily stealing lecture after
> lecture from you.[93]

Numerous people have written of an intellectual debt which they
felt they owed to Bowman. James T. Adams wrote to Bowman,
"Frankly I think I owe more to you in my life than to any other
man. . . ."[94] Earl P. Hanson has referred to Bowman as "one of the
creators of modern geography."[95] Thor Heyerdahl mentioned Bowman's
"kindness towards a perfect stranger like me when I first met him . . .
he went to great trouble to give me references to scientific literature
and helping me to borrow books from libraries. . . . Isaiah Bowman will
always be remembered by me as one of the few but truly outstanding
scientific personalities willing to listen to a young man with rather
revolutionary ideas. . . ."[96] Owen Lattimore wrote, "He was the first in
America to 'recognise' me professionally. He backed me in spite of my
lack of formal education, for the award of foundation grants."[97] Robert
A. Millikan was "simply overwhelmed by [Bowman's] kindness . . . if

we make a success I owe it to [him] more than anyone else."[98] Finn
Ronne acknowledged Bowman as first among those "who were willing
to place considerable confidence" in him.[99] Charles Seymour wrote,
"My sense of personal obligation to Isaiah Bowman is vivid; for I was
one of the hundreds whose life and interests were touched and inspired
by his influence and friendship. No one could share in that experience
without feeling impelled toward higher ideals of scholarship and
toward more intense effort of mind and body."[100]

While it would be presumptous to write of a disciple record, there
were those whom he tutored at Yale, those at the Society whom he had
selected for employment and then fashioned in the image of his
research design, and those whom he otherwise "discovered." When
Stephen Visher wrote to Bowman, "AAG pupil members listed as
especially influenced by you are McBride, Miller, Platt (Raye R.),
Wrigley and Wright. Should others be included...?"[101] Bowman
added the name of Elizabeth T. Platt.[102] Each of these talented
individuals enriched the ranks of geographers. Gladys Wrigley and
George M. McBride were the outstanding students whom he
encouraged and tutored while at Yale. John K. Wright and Raye R.
Platt might well not have entered the field of geography had it not been
for the opportunity Bowman provided at the Society, for neither
wanted to teach.

It is difficult to characterize the geography and geographic
contribution of Isaiah Bowman. His thoughts evolved parallel to the
emergence of intellectual discipline and institutional organization in
American geography. To both of these developments he contributed
much. He always felt that American thought, of which geography was a
part, was influenced by the wilderness-conquest experience of a
people in creation of a distinctive way of life.

Bowman contributed a series of books and articles—an additive
literature—to American geography, rather than a literature cumulative
in its effect. He did not seize hold of a theme, and expand and expound
on it for a lifetime. Instead he published on a wide variety of subjects
and themes, working always from a deep personal interest and
involvement. Each one of his books became, as Bowman would say, "a
brick," which helped build and develop the geographer's field. Several
of his books were the product of a need and so assumed a contemporary
significance which they might not otherwise have enjoyed. But that
they have retained their place in noted geographical literature

bespeaks their incisive and profound accomplishment. A lifetime so spent is rather well summed in a letter which Bowman wrote only two weeks before his death, "I like geography."[103]

His capacity for intellectual toil, his desire to reveal and share geography with others, and a life spent helping both individuals and organizations, were productive of a formidable array of published works and a host of less visible and now largely forgotten assistances, which were indeed a significant part of American geography in the making.

Abbreviations

AAG   Association of American Geographers (deposit with the
          Smithsonian Institution, Washington, D.C.)
AGS   American Geographical Society, New York, New York
Bowman   Isaiah Bowman
EMU   Eastern Michigan University, Ypsilanti, Michigan
FDR   Franklin Delano Roosevelt Collection, Hyde Park, New
          York
GJM   Geoffrey J. Martin, Easton, Connecticut
HU   Harvard University, Cambridge, Massachusetts
JHU   The Johns Hopkins University, Baltimore, Maryland
NA   National Archives, Washington, D.C.
RGB   Robert G. Bowman, Lincoln, Nebraska
RGS   Royal Geographical Society, London, England
UC   University of Chicago, Chicago, Illinois
YU   Yale University, New Haven, Connecticut

211

Notes

Notes to Preface

1. Bowman to Robert D. Williamson, 1 March 1944. JHU
2. Bowman, "Memorandum," February 1949. RGB

Notes to Chapter 1

1. *Chronik der Familie Buman aus dem Durcenmoos.* See also: W. R.Cutter and W. F. Adams, *Genealogical and Personal Memoirs* (New York: 1910), pp.382–83.
2. Howard H. M. Bowman to Bowman, 20 March 1936. JHU
3. Bowman to John C. French, 5 January 1946. JHU
4. Ibid.
5. Ibid.
6. Bowman to James Lee Love, 17 November 1939. RGB
7. "The Faith We Celebrate," *Teachers College Record* 46 (1944):151–56.
8. Bowman to Edwin G. Baetjer, 10 November 1942. JHU
9. Bowman to John C. French, 5 January 1946. JHU
10. Ibid.
11. Bowman to James Lee Love, 17 November 1939. RGB

12. "What Do You Do?" *The Barnwell Bulletin* 15 (1937):30–31.
13. Bowman to John C. French, 5 January 1946. JHU
14. "Why We Believe," *University of Virginia Alumni News* 25 (1937):154.
15. John Munson, "Isaiah Bowman: Obituary," *Eastern Michigan State College Newsletter*, February 1950, p. 2.
16. Bowman to James Lee Love, 7 November 1939. RGB
17. *Science* n.s. 20 (1904):273–77.
18. *Journal of Geology* 12 (1904):326-34.
19. Bowman to Robert G. Bowman, 25 October 1933. RGB
20. Bowman to James Lee Love, 7 November 1939. RGB
21. Ibid.
22. Bowman, "Criticism and the Seminar," 1948. JHU. See also: Bowman to Abel Wolman, 18 February 1948. JHU
23. Bowman to Mark Jefferson, 9 November 1902. EMU
24. Bowman to Mark Jefferson, 2 January 1903. EMU
25. Bowman to Mark Jefferson, 6 March 1903. EMU
26. Bowman to Mark Jefferson, 13 May 1903. EMU
27. Ibid.
28. "A Sense of Reality" (Proceedings, Southern University Conference, Memphis, Tennessee, 21–22 October 1940), pp. 55–70.
29. *Science* n.s. 20 (1904):273–77.
30. A. C. Veatch, C. S. Slichter, I. Bowman, W. O. Crosby, and R. E. Horton, *U.S. Geological Survey. Professional Paper. No. 44* (1906).
31. Bowman to Mark Jefferson, 13 June 1903. EMU
32. Bowman to Mark Jefferson, undated letter of 1904. EMU
33. Bowman to John C. French, 5 January 1946. JHU
34. Bowman to Mark Jefferson, 16 October 1904. EMU
35. Ibid.
36. Bowman to Mark Jefferson, 30 November 1904. EMU
37. Bowman to Mark Jefferson, undated letter of autumn, 1904. EMU
38. Bowman to Mark Jefferson, undated letter of autumn, 1904. EMU
39. Bowman to James Lee Love, 30 July 1946. RGB
40. Bowman to James Lee Love, 7 November 1939. RGB
41. Bowman and Robert L. Sackett, *U.S. Geological Survey. Water-Supply Paper. No. 113* (1905), pp. 36–48.
42. "Tom's Column," *The Johnson Drillers' Journal*, November-December 1973, p. 5.
43. Bowman to William Morris Davis, 1 February 1925. AGS

Notes to Chapter 2

1. H. E. Gregory to Anson Phelps Stokes, 25 July 1907. YU
2. *Doctors of Philosophy of Yale University with the Titles of Their Dissertations, 1861-1915* (Yale University: 1916), pp. 5–7.
3. *A Half Century of Geography—What Next?* (University of Chicago: 1955), p. 1.
4. For further data see the appropriate university catalogues for these years.
5. Bowman to James Lee Love, 30 July 1946. RGB
6. H. E. Gregory, comp., "Yale University, Department of Geology, History of Department 1802-1915." YU
7. William Morris Davis to Bowman, 18 March 1906. RGB

8. Bowman to Mark Jefferson, 6 October 1905. EMU
9. Bowman to Mark Jefferson, 2 February 1906. EMU
10. Bowman to Mark Jefferson, 1 August 1906. EMU
11. *Yale University Catalogue* 1906-7, p. 151.
12. *Yale University Catalogue* 1909-10, p. 386.
13. Bowman, *A Design for Scholarship* (Baltimore: 1936), p. 10
14. Ibid., p. 16.
15. Bowman to Alice Foster, 10 December 1936. JHU
16. *University of Virginia Alumni News* 25 (1937):156.
17. *A Sense of Reality* (Proceedings, Southern University Conference, Memphis, Tennessee, 21-22 October 1940), pp. 55-56.
18. Bowman to E. B. Wilson, 25 November 1932. AGS
19. Robert Rosenbluth to Geoffrey J. Martin, 28 October 1972. GJM
20. Hugh P. Brady to Geoffrey J. Martin, 3 May 1974. GJM
21. George Carrington to Geoffrey J. Martin, 4 May 1974. GJM
22. Roy Nash to Geoffrey J. Martin, 15 September 1974. GJM
23. Bowman to Anson Phelps Stokes, 13 April 1935. AGS
24. Bowman to Albert P. Brigham, 27 May 1910. AAG
25. Bowman to Charles C. Colby, 2 March 1921. AGS
26. Bowman, *Forest Physiography: Physiography of the United States and Principles of Soils in Relation to Forestry* (New York: 1911), p. viii.
27. E. W. Hilgard to Bowman, 7 December 1911. RGB
28. Bowman to Mark Jefferson, 19 March 1912. EMU
29. Bowman to Mark Jefferson, 1 August 1906. EMU
30. *Harvard College Class of 1905. Third Report* (Harvard: 1915), p. 56.
31. Charles Seymour, *Geography, Justice and Politics at the Paris Peace Conference of 1919* (New York: 1951), p. 1
32. H. E. Gregory, "Tribute to Professor Bowman," *The Yale Daily News*, 10 January 1915, p. 1.
33. Bowman, "Professor Rice as a Scientist," in *Tributes to Professor William North Rice* (Wesleyan Alumni Council: 1915), pp. 7-14.
34. Bowman to Mark Jefferson, 1908. EMU
35. Bowman to Rollin D. Salisbury, 24 February 1911. UC
36. Ibid.
37. Bowman, undated statement on the occasion of Jean Brunhes's death. AGS
38. Lawrence Martin to Bowman, 16 March 1914. AGS
39. "Geography at Yale University," *Journal of Geography* 7 (1908):61.
40. Bowman to Richard F. Flint, 8 April 1932. AGS
41. Bowman to William Morris Davis, 8 December 1925. AGS
42. Bowman filed his candidacy with the dean of the Yale Graduate School on 20 December 1905.
43. Charles Schuchert to Andrew Phillips, 19 May 1909. YU
44. The committee recommending Bowman for the degree of Doctor of Philosophy included Charles Schuchert, H. E. Gregory, and L. V. Pirsson.
45. Geoffrey J. Martin, *Ellsworth Huntington: His Life and Thought* (Hamden, Connecticut: 1973), p. 79.
46. Bowman to Rollin D. Salisbury, 24 February 1911. UC
47. For titles and abstracts see *The Annals of the Association of American Geographers* 1-4 (1911-14).
48. Gregory, "Yale University, Department of Geology."

49. H. E. Gregory to G. W. Littlehales, 13 December 1907. YU
50. Gregory, "Yale University, Department of Geology."
51. Bowman to Rollin D. Salisbury, 19 December 1914. UC
52. Joseph Barrell to Rollin D. Salisbury, 8 March 1915. UC

Notes to Chapter 3

1. Bowman, "Geography at Yale University," *Journal of Geography* 7 (1908):60. See
   also: Paul G. Merrow Gurley, "Geography of South America," an account of the
   lectures of Bowman, February-June 1909. YU
2. The Reverend J. A. Zahm also wrote under the names H. J. Mozans and J. A.
   Manso. Among his better known publications are *Along the Andes and Down the
   Amazon* (New York: 1911) and *The Quest of El Dorado* (New York: 1917).
3. Bowman to Mark Jefferson, 9 June 1907. EMU
4. "The Ever-New El Dorado," *New York Herald-Tribune*, 10 March 1947, p. 18.
5. *Bulletin of the American Geographical Society* 46 (1914):161.
6. Bowman, "Peruvian Physiography," undated. RGB
7. Bowman, "The Geography of the Central Andes" (Ph.D. dissertation, Yale
   University, 1909), preface.
8. *The Educational Bi-Monthly*, June 1911, pp. 1–21.
9. *Bulletin of the Geographical Society of Philadelphia* 7 (1909):74–93.
10. *Bulletin of the Geographical Society of Philadelphia* 7 (1909):159–84.
11. *Geographical Journal* 33 (1909):267–78.
12. *American Journal of Science* 28 (1909):197–217 and 373–402.
13. *Bulletin of the American Geographical Society* 41 (1909):142–54 and 193–211.
14. *Bulletin of the American Geographical Society* 42 (1910):1–43.
15. Bowman to Mark Jefferson, 31 January 1910. EMU
16. Atsushi Tsuyusaki to Bowman, 1 April 1929, and Bowman to Tsuyusaki, 28 May
    1929. AGS
17. Bowman to Mark Jefferson, 31 January 1910. EMU
18. Bowman to Mark Jefferson, 22 June 1911. EMU
19. Ibid.
20. Hiram Bingham to J. S. Keltie, 3 August 1911. RGS
21. "Yale Scientific Discoveries in Peru. Results of the Bingham Expedition,
    including the Location of a Number of Lost Megalithic and Inca Cities and the First
    Discovery in America of Actual Remains of Glacial Man," *Yale Alumni Weekly* 21
    (1912):465.
22. Bowman, *Yale Alumni Weekly* 22: (1912):103–4.
23. Bowman, "A Buried Wall at Cuzco and its Relation to the Question of a Pre-Inca
    Race," *American Journal of Science* 34 (1912):497–509.
24. Ibid.
25. *Bulletin of the American Geographical Society* 44 (1912):881-97.
26. *American Journal of Science* 33 (1912):306–25.
27. *Journal of Geography* 11 (1912):114–19.
28. *Sonder-Abdruck aus der Zeitschrift für Gletscherkunde, für Eiszeitforschung und
    Geschichte des Klimas* 7 (1913):119–27.
29. Abstract published in the *Annals of the Association of American Geographers* 2
    (1912):108.

30. Abstract published in the *Annals of the Association of American Geographers* 3 (1913):114.
31. John K. Wright, *Geography in the Making: The American Geographical Society 1851-1951* (New York: 1952), p. 185.
32. Bowman to J. S. Keltie, 24 March 1913. RGS
33. "Central Andes Expedition," *Bulletin of the American Geographical Society* 45 (1913):348-51.
34. Bowman, "Results of an Expedition to the Central Andes," *Bulletin of the American Geographical Society* 46 (1914):161.
35. Bowman, *Desert Trails of Atacama* (American Geographical Society Special Publication No. 5, 1924), pp. v and 362.
36. *Bulletin of the American Geographical Society* 45 (1913):750-53.
37. *Bulletin of the American Geographical Society* 46 (1914):161-83.
38. Bowman, "The Millionth Map of Hispanic America," *Science* 103 (1946):319.
39. *Harvard College Class of 1905. Third Report* (Harvard: 1915), p. 57.
40. Carlos Nicholson to Bowman, 30 November 1937. JHU
41. William Vogt to Bowman, 28 October 1942. JHU
42. Bowman, *The Andes of Southern Peru* (New York: 1916), p. 51.
43. *Annals of the American Academy of Political & Social Science* 73 (1917):233.
44. *The Nation* 105 (1917):203.
45. "Books Worth Reading," *New York Times Book Review*, 22 July 1917, p. 273.
46. *Boston Transcript*, 24 January 1917. p. 8.
47. *The Geographical Review* 3 (1917):317-22.
48. *The Geographical Journal* 50 (1917):225-26.
49. *The Geographical Journal* 51 (1918):62-63.
50. *The Geographical Journal* 51 (1918):63-64.
51. Jean Brunhes, *Human Geography: An Attempt at a Positive Classification; Principles and Examples*, trans. I. C. LeCompte, ed. I. Bowman and R. E. Dodge, (New York: 1920), pp. 453-98.
52. Arthur N. Strahler, *Physical Geography*, 2d ed. (New York: 1960), p. 508.
53. *A Basic Geographical Library: A Selected and Annotated Book List for American Colleges* (Commission on College Geography, Publication No. 2, Association of American Geographers, 1966), p. 94.
54. Bowman to George G. Chisholm, 21 December 1922. AGS
55. Bowman, *Desert Trails*, p. v.
56. *The Geographical Review* 14 (1924):137-38.
57. Albert Demangeon, "Pampa et Puna dans le Chili et l'Argentine," *Annales de Géographie* 33 (1924):567-74.
58. *The Geographical Teacher* 13 (1925):83.
59. Gladys M. Wrigley to Robert G. Bowman, 21 April 1950. RGB
60. Bowman to C. Halliwell Duell, 17 March 1949. RGB
61. Gladys M. Wrigley, "Isaiah Bowman," *The Geographical Review* 41 (1951):10.
62. Richard Light, "Atacama Revisited: Desert Trails Seen from the Air," *The Geographical Review* 36 (1946):525.
63. Ibid., p. 526.
64. William E. Rudolph, *Vanishing Trails of Atacama* (American Geographical Society Research Series No. 24, 1963).
65. Bowman to Mahonri Mackintosh Young, 6 January 1948. RGB
66. Much of what follows is taken from Robert P. Beckinsale, "The Geomorphological

Importance of the Writings of Isaiah Bowman," 8 February 1977, unpublished. GJM

67. A. K. Lobeck, *Geomorphology: An Introduction to the Study of Landscapes* (New York: 1939), p. 646.
68. F. E. Matthes, "Glacial Sculpture of the Bighorn Mountains, Wyoming," *20th Annual Report, U.S. Geological Survey* (Washington, D.C.: 1899–1900), pt. 2, pp. 167–90.
69. Bowman, *The Andes*, p. 289.
70. Ibid., p. 295.
71. Beckinsale, "The Geomorphological Importance," pp. 11–12.
72. Cited in Bowman, "Peruvian Physiography," pp. 8–9. JHU
73. Ibid.
74. Ibid.
75. Bowman, *Limits of Land Settlement* (New York: 1937), pp. 293–337.
76. Charles C. Colby, ed., *Geographical Aspects of International Relations* (Chicago: 1938), pp. 1–41.
77. "The Ever-New El Dorado," p. 18.
78. Carlos Monge, *Acclimatization in the Andes* (Baltimore: 1948), pp. vii–x.
79. *Volumen Jubilar*, XXV Aniversario, Sociedad Geologica del Peru, Parte II, 1949, Fasc 18.
80. Bowman to Gladys M. Wrigley, 26 March 1946. JHU

Notes to Chapter 4

1. Bowman to John K. Wright, 22 July 1949. JHU
2. Ibid.
3. Ibid.
4. Bowman to Gladys M. Wrigley, 19 February 1915. AGS
5. John K. Wright, *Geography in the Making: The American Geographical Society 1851–1951* (New York: 1952), p. 190.
6. Marcel Aurousseau to Geoffrey J. Martin, 26 March 1974. GJM
7. Bowman to Emmanuel de Martonne, 13 September 1934. AGS
8. Bowman to Carl C. Shippee, 18 February 1935. AGS
9. William Morris Davis to Bowman, 17 September 1919. AGS
10. Bowman to Carl C. Shippee, 18 February 1935. AGS
11. William Morris Davis to Bowman, 26 July 1919. AGS
12. William Morris Davis to Bowman, 17 September 1919. AGS
13. William Morris Davis to Bowman, 23 November 1919. AGS.
14. Bowman to James Lee Love, 7 November 1939. RGB
15. Bowman to John K. Wright, 3 June 1938. AGS
16. Bowman to John K. Wright, 22 July 1949. AGS
17. Bowman to J. Russell Smith, 7 August 1915. AGS
18. *Geographical Review* 1 (1916):1–2.
19. Gladys M. Wrigley, "Adventures in Serendipity," *Geographical Review* 42 (1952):511–42.
20. Bowman to Cyrus Townshend Brady, Jr., 9 January 1917. AGS
21. Bowman to Richard E. Dodge, 22 January 1918. AAG
22. Bowman to John Greenough, 2 February 1919. AGS
23. Mark Jefferson to Bowman, 2 February 1921. AGS

24. Jovan Cvijic to Bowman, 20 June 1918. AGS
25. William Morris Davis to Bowman, 23 November 1918. AGS
26. Wright, *Geography in the Making,* p. 261.
27. Hubert A. Bauer, "A World Map of Tides," *Geographical Review* 23 (1933):259-70.
28. Hugh H. Bennett, "Some Geographic Aspects of Cuban Soils," *Geographical Review* 18 (1928):62-82.
29. Hugh H. Bennett, "The Quantitative Study of Erosion Technique and Some Preliminary Results," *Geographical Review* 23 (1933):423-32.
30. C. Warren Thornthwaite, "The Climates of North America According to a New Classification," *Geographical Review* 21 (1931):633-55.
31. C. Warren Thornthwaite, "An Approach Toward a Rational Classification of Climate," *Geographical Review* 38 (1948):55-94.
32. Bowman to D. H. Davis, 31 January 1935. AGS
33. Robert C. Murphy to Geoffrey J. Martin, 7 March 1973. GJM
34. Bowman to Richard Hartshorne, 24 December 1936. JHU
35. Bowman to William Morris Davis, 31 July 1923. AGS
36. Mabel H. Ward to Geoffrey J. Martin, 27 December 1973. GJM
37. Marcel Aurousseau to Geoffrey J. Martin, 26 March 1974. GJM
38. Marcel Aurousseau to Geoffrey J. Martin, 27 March 1974. GJM
39. Mabel H. Ward to Geoffrey J. Martin, 27 December 1973. GJM
40. Lawrence Martin to Bowman, June 1915 (no day given). AGS
41. R. H. Whitbeck to Bowman, 24 June 1915. AGS
42. Bowman to R. H. Whitbeck, 12 July 1915. AGS
43. Bowman to G. J. Miller, 24 March 1920. AGS
44. Minutes of the Council, American Geographical Society, 18 March 1920. AGS
45. Bowman to E. B. Mathews, 16 March 1920. AGS
46. Bowman to Richard E. Dodge, 31 January 1920. AAG
47. Bowman to Kirtley F. Mather, 6 December 1926. AGS
48. Bowman to Alan G. Ogilvie, 10 April 1925. AGS
49. Marcel Aurousseau to Geoffrey J. Martin, 27 March 1974. GJM
50. Bowman to N. M. Fennemen, 6 May 1929. AGS
51. Bowman to Richard E. Dodge, 24 March 1920. AAG
52. Wright, *Geography in the Making*, p. 206.
53. Bowman to Alan G. Ogilvie, 23 April 1920. AGS
54. "New Map of Brazil on the Millionth Scale," *Geographical Review* 13 (1923):465-67.
55. Marcel Aurousseau to Geoffrey J. Martin, 27 March 1974. GJM
56. Bowman to Edwin G. Conklin, 7 June 1938. JHU
57. RGB
58. Bowman, "The Millionth Map of Hispanic America," *Science* 103 (1946):320.
59. RGB
60. Bowman to John K. Wright, 31 January 1949. JHU
61. Bowman to Hugh Robert Mill, 2 January 1929. AGS
62. W. L. G. Joerg, ed., *Problems of Polar Research* (New York: 1928), pp. 10 and 396.
63. "Antarctica," *Proceedings of the American Philosophical Society* 69 (1930):19-43.
64. Bowman to John K. Wright, 26 June 1947. JHU
65. Bowman to William Morris Davis, 9 June 1933. AGS
66. Bowman to C. H. Birdseye, 12 May 1926. AGS
67. Gerhardt Schott to Bowman, undated but probably 1932. AGS
68. Interview with Walter P. Bowman, 2 August 1977.

69. Interview with Mabel Ward, 12 August 1977.
70. Bowman to John K. Wright, 12 January 1940. JHU

Notes to Chapter 5

1. Bowman to Nordis Felland, 26 October 1947. AGS. For the definitive account of the Inquiry, see: Arthur Walworth, *America's Moment: 1918—American Diplomacy at the End of World War I* (New York: 1976).
2. Joseph Grew to Bowman, 9 October 1946. NA
3. Bowman, "Notes on the Inquiry," 30 November 1918. JHU. This source provides information for much of what follows.
4. Bowman, "Notes," p. 2.
5. "Statement made by Dr. Bowman concerning the reorganization of The Inquiry," 14 March 1932. JHU
6. Bowman, "The Geographical Program of the American Peace Delegation" (undated but probably 1919), p. 4. AGS
7. Ibid., p. 7.
8. Bowman to Charles Seymour, 24 May 1928. AGS
9. Bowman, "The Geographical Program," p. 7.
10. *The Geographical Review* 5 (1918):345-61.
11. *The Geographical Review* 5 (1918):470-82.
12. *The Geographical Review* 5 (1918):257-73.
13. *The Geographical Review* 6 (1918):19-36.
14. *The Geographical Review* 6 (1918):465-80.
15. *The Geographical Review* 6 (1918):421-35.
16. *The Geographical Review* 6 (1918):52-65.
17. *The Geographical Review* 6 (1918):156-71.
18. *The Geographical Review* 6 (1918):268-81.
19. *The Geographical Review* 6 (1918):341-53.
20. *The Geographical Review* 7 (1919):129-48.
21. Geoffrey J. Martin, *Mark Jefferson: Geographer* (Ypsilanti, Michigan: 1968), pp. 145-66.
22. Bowman, "Notes," pp. 4-7.
23. Bowman, "Memorandum," 14 November 1939. JHU
24. For the northwestern frontier, Charles H. Haskins (Harvard University); for Poland and Russia, Robert H. Lord (Harvard); for Austria-Hungary, Charles Seymour (Yale University); for Italian boundaries, William E. Lunt (Haverford College); for the Balkans, Clive Day (Yale); for western Asia, William L. Westermann (University of Wisconsin); for the Far East, Captain S. K. Hornbeck (U.S.A. military); for colonial problems, George L. Beer (formerly Columbia University); economic specialist, Allyn A. Young (Cornell University); librarian and specialist in history, James T. Shotwell (Columbia); chief cartographer, Mark Jefferson (State Normal College, Ypsilanti, Michigan).
25. Other members of the Inquiry associated with its mapping and cartographic section included: C. Besswerger, W. J. Blank, J. B. Braback, W. Breisemeister, M. Cawood, S. Davis, D. Johnson, C. B. Krisch, A. K. Lobeck, W. F. Mathews, H. Nagel, H. D. Ralphs, E. Semple, E. Taidor, R. Wiget, and C. Wittenberg.
26. Bowman to James Truslow Adams, 12 May 1922. AGS
27. Bowman to Gladys M. Wrigley, 9 October 1939. JHU

28. Bowman diary, 4 December 1918. RGB
29. Bowman, "Inquiry," 28 August 1939. JHU
30. Ibid.
31. Ibid.
32. Bowman, "Memorandum on Remarks by the President to Members of the Inquiry on December 10, 1918," p. 6. JHU
33. Bowman, "Inquiry," pp. 3-4.
34. Interview with Walter P. Bowman, 2 August 1977.
35. Bowman diary, 13 December 1918.RGB
36. Bowman diary, 14 December 1918. RGB
37. Bowman diary, 15 December 1918. RGB
38. Bowman diary, 22 December 1918. RGB
39. Bowman, "American Commission to Negotiate Peace," statement written to W. L. G. Joerg for inclusion in the National Archives, 16 February 1942, p. 2. NA
40. Bowman to Douglas Freeman, 22 September 1938. JHU
41. Bowman to Jean Brunhes, 17 September 1925. AGS
42. Bowman diary, 22 January 1919. RGB
43. Bowman diary, 31 January 1919. RGB
44. Ibid.
45. Bowman diary, 10 March 1919. RGB
46. Bowman diary, 19 March 1919. RGB
47. James T. Shotwell, *At the Paris Peace Conference* (New York: 1937), pp. 304-5.
48. Bowman diary, 29 April 1919. RGB
49. Bowman diary, 29 March 1919. RGB
50. Bowman diary, 3 April 1919. RGB
51. Bowman diary, 21 February 1919. RGB
52. Bowman diary, 30 and 31 March 1919. RGB
53. Bowman to John Greenough, 2 February 1919. AGS
54. Bowman to Cora Bowman, 27 November 1919. RGB
55. Bowman diary, 13 April 1919. RGB
56. Bowman to Charles Seymour, 24 September 1920. AGS
57. Bowman, "Memorandum," 27 August 1939. JHU
58. Shotwell, *Paris Peace Conference*, p. 317.
59. John K. Wright, *Geography in the Making: the American Geographical Society 1851-1951* (New York: 1952), p. 202.
60. Bowman to W. N. Ferris, 24 September 1920. AGS
61. Woodrow Wilson to Bowman, 6 September 1919. JHU
62. Bowman to John Greenough, 4 November 1919. AGS
63. Ibid.
64. Bowman to Cora Bowman, 19 October 1919. RGB
65. Bowman to Upton Sinclair, 2 October 1939. JHU
66. Bowman to Eduard Brückner, 25 February 1920. AGS

Notes to Chapter 6

1. Samuel Van Valkenburg, *Elements of Political Geography* (New York: 1939), dedicatory page.
2. J. Russell Smith, *Geography and Our Need of It* (Chicago: 1928), p. 42-43.
3. Bowman to J. Russell Smith, 7 January 1929. AGS

4. Richard Hartshorne, "Recent Developments in Political Geography," *American Political Science Review* 29 (1935):785.

5. Richard Hartshorne, *The Nature of Geography* (Lancaster, Pennsylvania: 1939), p. 248.

6. Bowman to James T. Shotwell, 28 January 1922. AGS

7. Bowman to Mark Jefferson, 20 December 1921. AGS

8. Ibid.

9. Hartshorne, *The Nature of Geography*, p. 248.

10. P. E. James and C. F. Jones, eds., *American Geography: Inventory and Prospect* (Syracuse, New York: 1954), p. 171.

11. E. C. Hayes, ed., *Recent Development in the Social Sciences* (New York: 1927), p. 207.

12. Bowman, *The New World* (New York: 1921), p. v.

13. Bowman to James T. Shotwell, 6 December 1921. AGS

14. Bowman to Jean Brunhes, 18 January 1922. RGB

15. Bowman to James Walter Goldthwait, 4 November 1927. AGS

16. Ellsworth Huntington to Bowman, 1 February 1922. AGS

17. Bowman to Jovan Cvijic, 6 June 1922. AGS

18. William Morris Davis to Bowman, 16 October 1921. AGS

19. Bowman, *The New World*, 4th ed. (Yonkers-on-Hudson, New York: 1928), p. iii.

20. Bowman to James T. Shotwell, 9 October 1928. AGS

21. James T. Shotwell to Bowman, 12 October 1928. AGS

22. Walter Fitzgerald to Bowman, 27 April 1944. JHU

23. Frank Debenham to Bowman, 9 January 1929. AGS

24. Nicholas J. Spykman to Bowman, 2 July 1937. JHU

25. Bowman to Nicholas J. Spykman, 21 July 1937. JHU

26. Bowman to Jean Brunhes, 22 October 1928. RGB

27. Bowman to J. Russell Smith, 20 December 1923. AGS

28. Bowman to Harlan H. Barrows, 8 October 1921. AGS

29. Rose B. Clark to Bowman, 9 May 1925. AGS

30. Bowman, "Memorandum," 26 February 1944. JHU

31. Bowman to Jean Brunhes, 11 April 1922. RGB

32. Fritz Klute, "Review of The New World," *Weltwirtschaftliches Archiv* 22 (1925):26.

33. Bowman to Jean Brunhes, 21 September 1925. RGB

34. Vilhjalmur Stefansson to F. A. Brockhaus, 15 October 1924. AGS

35. Bowman to Nordis Felland, 26 October 1947. JHU

36. Bowman to G. Halliwell Duell, 28 July 1948. JHU

37. Bowman to G. Halliwell Duell, 17 March 1949. JHU

38. W. Gordon East to Geoffrey J. Martin, 23 June 1976. GJM

Notes to Chapter 7

1. Bowman to Edward A. Filene, 8 May 1930. AGS. Much of the information here is taken from my interviews with Ethel Bowman on 20 June 1972 and Raye R. Platt on 3 August 1971.

2. Bowman, "Settlement by the Modern Pioneer," in *Geography in the Twentieth Century*, ed. T. Griffith Taylor (New York: 1951), p. 248.

3. Bowman to John K. Wright, 22 July 1949. JHU

4. P. E. James and C. F. Jones, eds., *American Geography: Inventory and Prospect* (Syracuse, New York: 1954), pp. 124-41.
5. David White to Bowman, 4 May 1925. AGS
6. David White to Bowman, 8 June 1925. AGS
7. Bowman to David White, 30 December 1925. AGS
8. Arnold B. Hall to Bowman, 17 February 1926. AGS
9. Vernor C. Finch to Bowman, 13 May 1926. AGS
10. Bowman to Vernor C. Finch, 28 June 1926. AGS
11. Robert E. Park to Bowman, 19 August 1926. AGS
12. Bowman, "The Scientific Study of Settlement," *Geographical Review* 16 (1926):647-53.
13. Bowman, "The Pioneer Fringe," *Foreign Affairs* 6 (1927):49-66.
14. Bowman to F. Merk, 10 September 1928. AGS
15. F. Merk to W. A. Mackintosh, 9 November 1928. AGS
16. Bowman to Chester I. Barnard, 8 March 1949. JHU
17. William F. Ogburn to Bowman, 30 January 1929. AGS
18. Bowman to William Morris Davis, 23 August 1930. AGS
19. Bowman to Mark Jefferson, 27 September 1932. AGS
20. Bowman, "Jordan Country," *Geographical Review* 21 (1931):22-55.
21. Gladys M. Wrigley, "Isaiah Bowman," *Geographical Review* 41 (1951):30.
22. Bowman, "Correlation of Sedimentary and Climatic Records," *Proceedings of the National Academy of Sciences* 19 (1933):376-86.
23. Bowman, "Pioneer Settlement," *Comptes Rendus du Congrès International de Géographie* 3 (1931):279-80.
24. Bowman, "Planning in Pioneer Settlement," *Annals of the Association of American Geographers* 22 (1932):93-107.
25. Ibid., p. 102.
26. Bowman, *The Pioneer Fringe* (New York: 1931), pp. v-vi.
27. Carl O. Sauer to Bowman, 8 September 1932. JHU
28. John K. Wright, *Geography in the Making: The American Geographical Society 1851-1951* (New York: 1952), p. 258.
29. L. Dudley Stamp, "The Pioneer Fringe," *The Geographical Journal* 80 (1932):84-86.
30. Bowman to Frederick J. Turner, 5 January 1932. AGS
31. Frederick J. Turner to Bowman, 12 January 1932. AGS
32. Frederick J. Turner to Bowman, 24 December 1931. AGS
33. Bowman to Frederick J. Turner, 5 January 1932. AGS
34. Bowman, "Settlement by the Modern Pioneer," in *Geography in the Twentieth Century*, ed. T. Griffith Taylor (New York: 1951), p. 248.
35. *Compendium of the Eleventh U.S. Census* (Washington, D.C.: 1890), p. xlviii.
36. Henry A. Wallace, "Wanted: A Master Conservation Plan," *New York Times Magazine*, 5 May 1940, p. 6.
37. Bowman to Henry A. Wallace, 6 May 1940. JHU
38. *The Historical World of Frederick Jackson Turner with Selections from his Correspondence*, narrative by Wilbur R. Jacobs (New Haven: 1968), pp. 169-70.
39. Bowman, *The Pioneer Fringe*, p. 18.
40. Frederick J. Turner, *The Significance of Sections in American History* (New York: 1932), introduction.
41. George A. Knadler, "Isaiah Bowman: Background of his Contribution to Thought" (Ed. D. diss., Indiana University, 1958), p. 117.

42. Bowman, "Frederick Jackson Turner," *Geographical Review* 22 (1932):499.

43. Roy F. Nichols, "The Development of Frederick Jackson Turner as a Historical Thinker," *Geographical Review* 34 (1944):510-11.

44. Bowman to Gladys M. Wrigley, 6 March 1944. JHU

45. Nichols, "The Development of Frederick Jackson Turner," p. 510.

46. Bowman, *A Design for Scholarship* (Baltimore: 1936), pp. 137-38.

47. Bowman, "Settlement," p. 248.

48. W. L. G. Joerg, ed., *Pioneer Settlement* (New York: 1932), p. v.

Notes to Chapter 8

1. Bowman to Franklin D. Roosevelt, 10 December 1931. JHU

2. *Limits of Land Settlement: A Report on Present Day Possibilities*, prepared under the direction of Bowman (New York: 1937).

3. Karl J. Pelzer to Geoffrey J. Martin, 2 August 1977. GJM

4. E. K. Cubin to Bowman, 6 January 1938. JHU

5. Franklin D. Roosevelt to Bowman, 14 October 1938. JHU

6. Bowman to Franklin D. Roosevelt, 15 October 1938. JHU

7. Bowman to Franklin D. Roosevelt, 31 October 1938. JHU

8. Franklin D. Roosevelt to Bowman, 2 November 1938. JHU

9. Bowman to Franklin D. Roosevelt, 4 November 1938. JHU

10. Bowman to Franklin D. Roosevelt, 10 December 1938. JHU

11. Karl J. Pelzer to Geoffrey J. Martin, 2 August 1977. GJM

12. Stanton Youngberg to Bowman, 7 April 1939. JHU

13. Bowman to Gladys M. Wrigley, 15 October 1938. JHU

14. Bowman to Franklin D. Roosevelt, 10 December 1938. JHU

15. Franklin D. Roosevelt to Bowman, 15 December 1938. JHU

16. Bowman, "Memorandum," 16 November 1938. JHU

17. Bowman to Lionel Curtis, 2 November 1939. JHU

18. Bowman to Franklin D. Roosevelt, 25 November 1938. JHU

19. See, for example, Bowman to Theodore C. Achilles, 26 December 1938. JHU

20. Bowman to James G. McDonald, 17 April 1941. JHU

21. Bowman to Charles Liebman, 19 January 1942. JHU

22. Bowman to Franklin D. Roosevelt, 22 May 1943. JHU

23. Bowman, "Memorandum," 10 August 1943. JHU

24. Bowman to William L. Langer, 2 January 1946. JHU

25. Malvina Thompson to Bowman, 18 December 1943. JHU

26. Bowman, "Memorandum," 7 January 1944. JHU

27. Rose L. Halprin to Eleanor Roosevelt, 26 November 1943. FDR

28. Bowman, "Memorandum," 7 January 1944, p. 2. JHU

29. Ibid., p. 3.

30. The following quotations are taken from Henry Field, "Isaiah Bowman," 25 November 1972. GJM

31. Ibid., pp. 4-5.

32. Henry Field to Geoffrey J. Martin, 25 November 1972. GJM

33. Field, "Isaiah Bowman," p. 6.

34. Henry Field and John F. Carter, "Interim Report on 'M' Project," 23 April 1945. NA

35. Ladislas Farago, "Refugees: The Solution as F.D.R. Saw It," *United Nations World* 1 (1947):15.
36. Field, "Isaiah Bowman," pp. 6-7.
37. Ibid., p. 8.
38. Henry Field to Geoffrey J. Martin, 19 May 1974. GJM
39. Bowman, "Memorandum," 2 March 1949. JHU
40. Bowman to Chester I. Barnard, 8 March 1949. JHU
41. Bowman to John L. Pratt, 30 December 1948. JHU
42. Bowman to Hugh H. Bennett, 18 February 1949. JHU
43. Bowman to John K. Wright, 2 March 1949. JHU

Notes to Chapter 9

1. Robert P. Sharkey, *Johns Hopkins, Centennial Portrait of a University* (Baltimore: 1975), p. 16.
2. Bowman, "Annual Report of the President," *The Johns Hopkins University Circular*, n.s., November 1936, no. 9, p. 4.
3. Bowman to Frank E. Williams, 22 December 1937. JHU
4. John K. Wright, "Daniel Coit Gilman: Geographer and Historian," *Geographical Review* 51 (1961):381-99.
5. Bowman, "Gilman, Creator of the American University: A Review," *The Evening Sun*, 5 November 1946.
6. William Bullock Clark, "Geology," *The Johns Hopkins University Circular* no. 1, 1906, pp. 42-44.
7. Bowman, *A Design for Scholarship* (Baltimore: 1936).
8. Bowman, "Annual Report of the President," *The Johns Hopkins University Circular*, n.s., November 1938, no. 9, p. 2.
9. Bowman, "Annual Report of the President," *The Johns Hopkins University Circular*, n.s., November 1937, no. 9, pp. 5-6.
10. Bowman, "Annual Report of the President," *The Johns Hopkins University Circular*, n.s., November 1939, no. 8, p. 1.
11. Daniel Willard to Bowman, 18 February 1938. JHU
12. Bowman to Daniel Willard, 7 August 1938. JHU
13. Bowman, "Annual Report of the President," *The Johns Hopkins University Circular*, n.s., November 1942, no. 8, p. 1.
14. Bowman to Gladys M. Wrigley, 4 February 1943. JHU
15. Bowman to Herman Beukema, 3 January 1943. JHU
16. Correspondence with each of these persons is in the archives of The Johns Hopkins University.
17. Carl O. Sauer to Bowman, 21 May 1944. JHU
18. John B. Leighly to Geoffrey J. Martin, 24 March 1976. GJM
19. Bowman, "Annual Report of the President," *The Johns Hopkins University Circular*, n.s., December 1943, no. 8, p. 15.
20. The Johns Hopkins University Catalogues for 1943 and 1944 include such courses as "Physical Geography—The Earth Condition of Human Society"; "Economic Geography—Use of Earth Resources in Different Regions of the World"; "Political and Social Organization of the Earth's Surface"; "Geography of the Far East"; "Geography of Southeastern Asia" (two semesters); "Geography of the Mediter-

ranean World"; "Geography of Western Europe"; "Geography of Northern and
Central Europe"; "Geography of the Soviet Union"; "Geography of Latin
America"; "The History of Cartography"; and "The Mapping of America from 1493
to 1800."

21. George F. Carter to Geoffrey J. Martin, 2 April 1973. GJM
22. Bowman, "A Department of Geography at Hopkins," 9 November 1944, pp. 3-4.
JHU
23. Bowman to Alfred H. Meyer, 11 March 1944. JHU
24. Bowman, "Geography as an Urgent University Need," 1944. JHU
25. Ibid., p. 2.
26. Ibid.
27. Bowman, "Science and Social Effects: Three Failures," *Scientific Monthly* 50
(1940):289-98.
28. Bowman to John L. Pratt, 11 November 1949. JHU
29. S. Page Nelson to Bowman, 23 February 1945. JHU
30. Bowman to Carlyle Barton, 5 January 1945. JHU
31. Bowman to Donaldson Brown, 18 February 1947. JHU
32. Bowman, "A Proposal," 29 January 1946. JHU
33. E. Francis Penrose to Geoffrey J. Martin, 22 March 1977. GJM
34. Bowman to Lammot du Pont, 9 July 1947. JHU
35. Bowman, "The Design of the Department of Geography," 16 December 1947, p. 2.
JHU
36. Ibid., p. 4.
37. Donaldson Brown to Detlev W. Bronk, 24 June 1949. JHU
38. E. Francis Penrose to Geoffrey J. Martin, 27 January 1977. GJM
39. Jean Gottmann to Geoffrey J. Martin, 18 November 1976. GJM
40. Bowman to James B. Conant, 26 November 1947, and 8 December 1947. JHU
41. Kirk Bryan to Bowman, 16 March 1948. JHU
42. George F. Carter to Geoffrey J. Martin, 2 April 1973. GJM
43. Bowman to Charles S. Garland, 4 June 1948. JHU
44. Bowman to Harry S. Truman, 12 September 1946. JHU
45. Bowman, "Memorandum," 25 September 1946. JHU
46. John C. French, *History of the University Founded by Johns Hopkins* (Baltimore:
1946), pp. 456-62.
47. Bowman, "Memorandum," 4 March 1947. JHU
48. Bowman to Carlyle Barton, 1 April 1948. JHU
49. Bowman to Carlyle Barton, 10 March 1948. JHU
50. Daniel Willard to Bowman, 12 January 1939. JHU
51. Bowman, "Science and Social Effects," p. 289.

Notes to Chapter Ten

1. James T. Shotwell to Bowman, 2 December 1919. AGS
2. Whitney H. Shepardson, *Early History of the Council on Foreign Relations* (New
York: 1960), pp. 1-3.
3. Bowman to James T. Shotwell, 16 May 1933. AGS
4. Bowman to Jean Brunhes, 21 September 1925. RGB
5. Bowman, "Alexander Supan. Leitlinien der allgemeinen politischen Geographie:
Naturlehre des Staates," *The Geographical Review* 14 (1924):665-66.

6. Bowman, "Some German Works on Political Geography," *The Geographical Review* 17 (1927):511-13. The works reviewed were: Otto Maul, *Politische Geographie* (Berlin: 1925); Walther Vogel, *Politische Geographie* (Berlin: 1922); Walther Vogel, *Das neue Europa und seine historisch-geographischen Grundlagen* (2d ed., Bonn: 1923); and Rudolf Reinhard, *Weltwirtschaftliche und politische Erdkunde* (Breslau: 1925).

7. Bowman to Jean Brunhes, 21 September 1925. RGB

8. Bowman, "Some German Works," p. 511.

9. Robert Strausz-Hupé, *Geopolitics: The Struggle for Space and Power* (New York: 1942), p. 52.

10. Bowman, "Geography vs. Geopolitics," *The Geographical Review* 32 (1942):646-58.

11. Bowman to Jean Brunhes, 21 September 1925. RGB

12. Ibid.

13. Fritz Klute, "Review of *The New World*," *Weltwirtschaftliches Archiv* 22 (1925):26.

14. Bowman to Lionel Curtis, 2 November 1939. JHU

15. Bowman, "Political Geography of Power," *The Geographical Review* 32 (1942):349-52.

16. Bowman, "Geography vs. Geopolitics."

17. Bowman to Gladys M. Wrigley, 30 October 1945. JHU

18. Bowman, "Confidential Memorandum for Members," 27 May 1929. AGS

19. Bowman, *International Relations* (Chicago: 1930), p. 10

20. James T. Shotwell to Bowman, 7 November 1930. AGS

21. Bowman to Elizabeth Stewart Waters, 18 September 1940. JHU

22. Bowman to Joseph H. Willits, 8 August 1940. JHU

23. Sumner Welles to Bowman, 9 February 1942. JHU

24. Cordell Hull, *The Memoirs of Cordell Hull* (New York: 1948), pp. 1632-34.

25. Bowman, *Citizen-Scientists* (Baltimore: 1946), p.3.

26. Sumner Welles, *Where Are We Heading?* (New York: 1946), p. 22.

27. Benjamin V. Cohen to Geoffrey J. Martin, 21 May 1976. GJM

28. Bowman, "Memorandum," 13 December 1943. JHU

29. Bowman to Hamilton Fish Armstrong, 19 November 1945. JHU

30. Bowman, "The Strategy of Territorial Decisions," *Foreign Affairs* 24 (1946):177-94.

31. Hull, *Memoirs*, p. 1428.

32. Bowman to E. B. Wilson, 19 April 1941. JHU

33. Ibid.

34. Bowman to L. P. Hafstad, 22 March 1948. RGB

35. Bowman to Joseph W. Barker, 3 May 1948. JHU

36. Bowman, "London Mission Memorandum," 24 and 25 February 1944, pp. 1 and 2. JHU

37. Diary of Louis Hector, 10 March 1944. RGB

38. Ibid.

39. Bowman, "Memorandum," 17 March 1944, p. 1. JHU

40. Ibid., p. 3.

41. Ibid., p. 4.

42. "Minutes of the Meeting of Stettinius' Mission to London," 1 April 1944, p. 3. JHU

43. Bowman, "Report by Isaiah Bowman on Chequers Conversation," 15 April 1944, pp. 4 and 5. JHU

44. Sir Alexander Cadogan to Bowman, 24 April 1944. JHU

45. Bowman, "Memorandum," 13 June 1944. JHU
46. Cordell Hull to Bowman, 19 August 1944. JHU
47. "Departmental Designation 46," 27 July 1944. JHU
48. Bowman, "Memorandum," 13 September 1944, introduction. JHU
49. Ibid., pp. 4 and 5.
50. Bowman to Lionel Curtis, 2 November 1939: "the strengthening of Russia may produce such disastrous effects . . . that it is neither idiotic nor fanciful to say that within ten years France and England may be fighting side by side with Germany in order to hold Russia in check." JHU
51. Bowman, "Memorandum," 13 January 1947. JHU
52. Bowman, "Location," 23 September 1944, p. 5. JHU
53. Bowman, "Memorandum," 15 September 1944. JHU
54. Bowman to Arthur Sweetser, 1 November 1944. JHU
55. Bowman to Charles K. Webster, 20 November 1944. JHU
56. Bowman to Felix Morley, 26 August 1944. JHU
57. Ibid.
58. Bowman to Edward R. Stettinius, 11 December 1944. JHU
59. Edward R. Stettinius to Bowman, 31 March 1945. JHU
60. Bowman, "Memorandum," 27 April 1945, p. 2. JHU
61. Bowman, "Memorandum," 6 May 1945, pp. 1–2. JHU
62. Bowman to his family, 21 May 1945. RGB
63. Bowman to Homer Halvorson, 4 August 1945. JHU
64. Ibid.
65. Bowman, "Memorandum," 29 June 1945. JHU
66. Edward R. Stettinius to Bowman, 3 July 1945. JHU
67. Edward R. Stettinius to Harry S. Truman, 23 May 1946. JHU
68. Walter Johnson to Geoffrey J. Martin, 15 July 1975. GJM
69. Cordell Hull to Bowman, 31 December 1942. JHU
70. Bowman to Cordell Hull, 10 July 1944. JHU
71. Bowman, "Memorandum," 18 May 1944. JHU
72. Bowman, "Memorandum," 5 July 1944. JHU
73. Bowman to Franklin D. Roosevelt, 19 May 1941. JHU
74. Bowman, "Talk with Arroyo Del Rio, President of Ecuador at his office, August 25, 1941." JHU
75. Bowman, "Biological Warfare," undated. JHU
76. Bowman, unpublished manuscript, written in 1949, pp. 209–11. RGB
77. Bowman, "Memorandum to the President," 5 January 1945. JHU
78. Bowman, "Memorandum," 25 September 1946, p. 4. JHU
79. Bowman to Arthur H. Vandenberg, 19 January 1949. JHU
80. Karl T. Compton to Bowman, 14 March 1949. JHU
81. Bowman, "Memorandum," 5 April 1949. JHU
82. James B. Conant to Karl T. Compton, 28 September 1949. JHU
83. Bowman to Joseph W. Barker, 17 April 1948 and 3 May 1948. JHU
84. John L. Pratt to Carlyle Barton, 9 November 1948. JHU

Notes to Chapter 11

1. Bowman to John C. French, 5 January 1946. JHU
2. Bowman, "Mark Jefferson," *The Geographical Review* 40 (1950):134–37.

3. John K. Wright and George F. Carter, "Isaiah Bowman, December 26, 1878–January 6, 1950," *National Academy of Sciences of the U.S.A., Biographical Memoirs* 33 (1959):41–42.

4. Bowman to James Lee Love, 7 November 1939. RGB

5. Bowman to E. B. Wilson, 25 November 1932. AGS

6. Bowman to William Morris Davis, 28 July 1921. AGS

7. Gladys M. Wrigley, "Isaiah Bowman," *The Geographical Review* 41 (1951):21.

8. Bowman, "An American Boundary Dispute: Decision of the Supreme Court of the United States with Respect to the Texas-Oklahoma Boundary," *The Geographical Review* 13 (1923):161–89.

9. Bowman, *Geography in Relation to the Social Sciences* (New York: 1934), pp. 51–53.

10. *Kansas v. Missouri*, 11 October 1943, p. 706. *United States Reports*, vol. 320.

11. Bowman, "The Analysis of Land Forms: Walther Penck on the Topographic Cycle," *The Geographical Review* 16 (1926):122–32.

12. Bowman to Douglas W. Johnson, 19 November 1925. AGS

13. Douglas W. Johnson to W. O. Wiley, 16 December 1925. AGS

14. Walther Penck, *Morphological Analysis of Land Forms*, trans. Hella Czech and Katharine Cumming Boswell (London: 1953).

15. Geoffrey J. Martin, "A Fragment on the Penck(s)-Davis Conflict," *Geography and Map Division: Special Libraries Association Bulletin* 98 (1974):11–27.

16. Armin K. Lobeck, *Geomorphology: An Introduction to the Study of Landscapes* (New York: 1939), pp. 200–201.

17. Bowman to George F. Carter, 10 July 1945. JHU

18. Geoffrey J. Martin, *Mark Jefferson: Geographer* (Ypsilanti, Michigan: 1968), p. 87.

19. Bowman to Albert Demangeon, 6 December 1921. AGS

20. Derwent Whittlesey et al., "The Regional Concept and the Regional Method," in *American Geography: Inventory and Prospect*, ed. P. E. James and C. F. Jones (Syracuse, New York: 1954), p. 24.

21. G.B. Roorbach, "The Trend of Modern Geography: A Symposium," *Bulletin of the American Geographical Society* 46 (1914):806.

22. Bowman, "Regional Concepts and Their Application," in *Zbiór Prac Poświecony Przez Towarzystwo Geograficzne We Lwowie Eugenjuszowi Romerowi*, ed. Henryk Arctowski (Lwow: 1934), pp. 25-46.

23. Bowman, "The Collected Papers of Isaiah Bowman," vol. 3, pp. 385-86. JHU

24. Bowman, "Hogarth's 'The Nearer East' in Regional Geography," *Bulletin of the American Geographical Society* 38 (1906):86-87.

25. Bowman, "Geography: Modern Style," *Outlook and Independent* 152 (1929):461.

26. Bowman to Mark Jefferson, 6 September 1936. JHU

27. Bowman to William Morris Davis, 31 October 1922. AGS

28. Bowman, "The Geography of North America," *The Geographical Review* 15 (1925):328.

29. Bowman to Emmanuel de Martonne, 10 January 1929. AGS

30. Bowman to Henri Baulig, 28 September 1936. JHU

31. W. L. G. Joerg, "The Geography of North America: A History of its Regional Exposition," *The Geographical Review* 26 (1936):640-63.

32. Bowman to Lucien Gallois, 13 July 1930 and 21 February 1931. AGS

33. Bowman to Charles Scribner's Sons, 31 January 1931. AGS

34. Bowman, "Man and Climatic Change in South America," *The Geographical Journal* 33 (1909):267-78.

35. A. J. Herbertson, "The Major Natural Regions: An Essay in Systematic

Geography," *The Geographical Journal* 25 (1905):300-310.

36. Bowman, "Hogarth's 'The Nearer East,'" p. 87

37. Martin, *Mark Jefferson*, p. 227.

38. Bowman, *The Andes of Southern Peru* (New York: 1916), p. vii.

39. Theodore Roosevelt, "The Andes of Southern Peru — A Review," *The Geographical Review* 3 (1917):321-22.

40. Jean Gottmann, "De la méthode d'analyse en géographie humaine," *Annales de géographie* 301 (1947):4-5.

41. Bowman to Gladys M. Wrigley, 15 March 1919. AGS

42. Bowman to James Truslow Adams, 2 August 1924. AGS

43. Bowman, *Geography in Relation to the Social Sciences* (New York: 1934), pp. 3-4.

44. George Tatham, "Environmentalism and Possibilism," in *Geography in the Twentieth Century*, ed. T. Griffith Taylor (New York: 1951), p. 151.

45. Bowman, *Geography in Relation to the Social Sciences*, pp. 4, 33, and 218.

46. Edmund E. Day to Bowman, 25 April 1930. AGS

47. Ibid.

48. Eva G. R. Taylor, "Geography in Relation to the Social Sciences," *The Geographical Journal* 84 (1934):459.

49. Wrigley, "Isaiah Bowman," p. 29.

50. Bowman to Darrell H. Davis, 23 January 1931. AGS

51. Bowman to Darrell H. Davis, 5 May 1931. AGS

52. Bowman to Darrell H. Davis, 14 May 1931. AGS

53. Bowman to J. Mackintosh Bell, 28 December 1931. AGS

54. Bowman to Hamilton F. Kean, 26 February 1938. JHU

55. Bowman, "Pioneer Settlement," *Comptes Rendus du Congrès International de Géographie* 3 (1931):279-80.

56. Bowman to Emmanuel de Martonne, 17 December 1930. AGS

57. Bowman to H. J. Fleure, 15 February 1932. AGS

58. Bowman, "Memorandum of a Visit to Mrs. Stafford (Marie Peary)," 5 February 1935. RGB

59. Bowman, "Memorandum," 5 February 1935. RGB

60. Bowman to Harry Raymond, 5 November 1935. RGB

61. Bowman, "Memorandum," 21 December 1935. RGB

62. Bowman, "The Peary Memorial at Jockey Gap, Fryburg, Maine: An Appreciation," August 1938. RGB

63. Bowman, "Geography in the Creative Experiment," *The Geographical Review* 28 (1938):2.

64. Bowman to Leo Waibel, 5 February 1945. AGS

65. Bowman to Gladys M. Wrigley, 12 October 1938. AGS

66. Bowman to Preston James, 12 December 1923. AGS

67. L. Dudley Stamp, "Discussion," *The Geographical Journal* 119 (1953):31.

68. Bowman, "Annual Report of the President," *The Johns Hopkins University Circular*, n. s., 1947, no. 8, p. 8.

69. E. F. Penrose to Geoffrey J. Martin, 21 December 1976. GJM

70. Bowman, *A Design for Scholarship* (Baltimore: 1936), p. 22.

71. Ibid., p. 12.

72. Bowman, "Science and Social Effects: Three Failures," *The Scientific Monthly* 50 (1940):289.

73. Ibid.

74. Cordell Hull to David W. Robinson, 12 January 1946. JHU

75. Dean Acheson, "Statement by Secretary of State Dean Acheson Regarding the Death of Isaiah Bowman," 6 January 1950. JHU
76. Wrigley, "Isaiah Bowman," p. 43.
77. Bowman to Gladys M. Wrigley, 19 March 1949. JHU
78. Bowman to Gladys M. Wrigley, 7 November 1949. JHU
79. Bowman to Gladys M. Wrigley, 11 November 1949. JHU
80. Bowman to Gladys M. Wrigley, 29 November 1949. JHU
81. Bowman to Gladys M. Wrigley, 19 December 1949. JHU
82. Bowman to Gladys M. Wrigley, 3 January 1950. JHU
83. Wright and Carter, "Isaiah Bowman," pp. 39-40.
84. Carl O. Sauer, "Recent Developments in Cultural Geography," in *Recent Developments in the Social Sciences*, ed. E. C. Hayes (New York: 1927), p. 207.
85. Bowman to Glenn T. Trewartha, 7 January 1939. JHU
86. Robert P. Beckinsale, "Geomorphological Importance of the Writings of Isaiah Bowman," 8 February 1977, unpublished, p. 1. GJM.
87. A. J. Herbertson, "Physical Geography of the United States," *The Geographical Journal* 40 (1912): 208-9.
88. Beckinsale, "Geomorphological Importance," p. 2.
89. A. G. Ogilvie, "Isaiah Bowman: An Appreciation," *The Geographical Journal* 115 (1950):226-30.
90. L. Dudley Stamp, *Land for Tomorrow: The Underdeveloped World* (Bloomington, Indiana: 1952), p. 176.
91. Jean Gottmann, "De la méthode d'analyse en géographie humaine," *Annales de Géographie* 301 (1947):3.
92. Charles S. Aiken, "Expressions of Agrarianism in American Geography: The Cases of Isaiah Bowman, J. Russell Smith and O. E. Baker," *The Professional Geographer* 27 (1975):19-29.
93. Laurence M. Gould to Bowman, 21 February 1933. RGB
94. James T. Adams to Bowman, 31 March 1919. AGS
95. Earl P. Hanson to Geoffrey J. Martin, 10 March 1973. GJM
96. Thor Heyerdahl to Geoffrey J. Martin, 26 February 1973. GJM
97. Owen Lattimore to Geoffrey J. Martin, 18 March 1973. GJM
98. Wrigley, "Isaiah Bowman," p. 53.
99. Finn Ronne, *Antarctic Conquest* (New York: 1949), p. xvii.
100. Charles Seymour, *Geography, Justice, and Politics at the Paris Peace Conference of 1919* (New York: 1951), p. 1.
101. Stephen S. Visher to Bowman, 10 October 1939. JHU
102. Bowman to Stephen S. Visher, 16 October 1939. JHU
103. Bowman to Gladys M. Wrigley, 9 December 1949. JHU

A Bibliographical Note

This book derives in large measure from archival sources. Correspondence and interviews with those still living have been especially helpful in providing additional information. Helpful, too, has been the published literature dealing in whole or in part with Isaiah Bowman.

Archival Sources:

The American Geographical Society holds considerable "Bowmania" for the years 1915-35. The deposit extends to approximately twenty-eight linear feet. The collection does not include all Bowman's correspondence and memoranda for this period. Other material, some of which has been made available to the writer, is secreted in the vaults of the Society.

The Johns Hopkins University is in possession of the larger part of all known "Bowmania." There are twenty-three linear feet of material in the unrestricted section of the Isaiah Bowman collection in "Special Collections" of the Milton S. Eisenhower Library, and twenty-five linear feet in the restricted section. This latter is the material which was sealed by the terms of Bowman's will until twenty-five years after his death, and which was opened formally on 6 January 1975. This deposit is available to scholars only as per the terms of Bowman's will.

Bowman material in the University Archives collection extends to six linear feet. Additionally there are numerous letters and memoranda to and from Bowman shelved with The Johns Hopkins University Presidents' Papers.

Most of these papers relate to the 1935-50 period. The exception is the restricted material relating to the Inquiry and the Paris Peace Conference.

Robert G. Bowman, Lincoln, Nebraska, retains a private collection of archival "Bowmania" extending to fourteen linear feet. This material is chiefly from 1935-50.

Lesser deposits of Bowman-related archival matter are to be found in the collections of the following institutions: Association of American Geographers, University of Chicago, Council on Foreign Relations, Ferris Institute, Harvard University, Huntington Library, National Archives, Paris Geographical Society, Royal Geographical Society, University of California-Berkeley, University of Cincinnati, Wesleyan University, and Yale University.

Contemporary Correspondence:

Correspondence exchanged between the author and a large number of individuals who knew Bowman at Yale, at the American Geographical Society, at The Johns Hopkins University, in government service, and elsewhere constitutes a valuable documentary source. This collection of letters (c. 1971-77) is in the possession of the author.

Published Sources:

Gladys M. Wrigley's moving essay entitled "Isaiah Bowman" (*Geographical Review* 41, [1951]: 7-65) reveals the man and much of his complex professional career as she had come to know it over thirty-seven years. Parts of John K. Wright's *Geography in the Making: The American Geographical Society, 1851-1951* (1952) provide valuable history and insights relative to Bowman. Especially well revealed in this book is Bowman's achievement as director of the American Geographical Society. Wright and George F. Carter wrote "Isaiah Bowman" (*National Academy of Sciences of the U.S.A., Biographical Memoirs* 33 [1959]: 39-54), with Wright assuming responsibility for the pre-1935 Bowman, and Carter for the post-1935 period. George A. Knadler contributed "Isaiah Bowman: Background of his Contributions to Thought" (Ed. D. diss., Indiana University, 1958) and James

M. Smythe wrote "Huntington and Bowman: A Comparative Study of Their Geographic Concepts" (M.A. thesis, University of Toronto, 1952). Both are ventures in intellectual history, though Knadler's work is more substantive and less speculative than that of Smythe.

Obituaries and memorials duplicate each other in considerable measure. Especial mention might be made of "Isaiah Bowman (1878-1950)" by Henri Baulig (*Annales de Géographie* 60 [1951]: 48-50); "Isaiah Bowman, 1878-1950" by George F. Carter (*Annals of the Association of American Geographers* 40 [1950]: 335-50; and "Isaiah Bowman: An Appreciation," by Alan G. Ogilvie (*Geographical Journal* 115 [1950]: 226-30.

Selected Memberships, Offices, Honors

1905   B.S., Harvard University
        Appointed instructor, Yale University, Geology Department
1906   Elected a member, Association of American Geographers
        Elected a member, National Geographic Society
1909   Ph.D., Yale University
        Appointed assistant professor, Yale University, Geology
          Department
        Associate editor, *Bulletin of the American Geographical Society*
1912   Marshal, American Geographical Society Transcontinental
          Excursion
        Second vice-president, Association of American Geographers
1914   Secretary, Association of American Geographers
        Corresponding member, Austrian Geographical Society
1915   Director, The American Geographical Society
        Elected a corresponding member, Hispanic Society of America
        Member, The Explorers Club
1916   Member, Board of Directors, National Council of Geography
          Teachers
        Member, Publication Committee of the Association of American
          Geographers

1917   Bonaparte-Wyse Gold Medal of the Geographical Society of
          Paris
        Councilor of the New York Academy of Sciences
1918   Chief territorial specialist with the American Commission to
          Negotiate Peace
1919   Chairman, Geography Committee, Geology and Geography
          Division, National Research Council
        Second vice-president, Association of American Geographers
1920   Member, Board of Governors, Yale Publication Association
        "Starred" as a geologist in *American Men of Science*
1921   Member, Board of Directors, Council on Foreign Relations
        Honorary M.A., Yale University
        Member, Editorial Advisory Board, *Foreign Affairs*
        Physiographer, United States Department of Justice in Red
          River Boundary Dispute
        Member, Board of Directors, Council of *Foreign Affairs*
1922   Member, National Parks Committee
        Vice-president and director, The Explorers Club
1923   Secretary, The Explorers Club
        Elected a member, American Philosophical Society
1924   Elected a member, Geological Society of America
        Vice-chairman, Division of Geology and Geography, National
          Research Council
        Secretary and chairman, Nominating Committee, The Explorers
          Club
1927   The Helen Culver Gold Medal of the Geographic Society of
          Chicago
        Member, advisory board (advisor in geography and related
          subjects) to the *Encyclopedia Britannica*
        Honorary M.Ed., Michigan State Normal College
1928   The Geographic Board, Ottawa, Canada, recognizes Bowman
          Bay in Baffin Island
        President and chairman, Board of Directors, Social Science
          Abstracts, Inc.
        Vice-president, International Geographical Union
        Chairman, Historical Geography Section, International Geo-
          graphical Congress, Cambridge (England).
        Corresponding member, Gesellschaft für Erdkunde zu Berlin

Livingstone Gold Medal of the Royal Scottish Geographical Society

1929   President and chairman of the Board, Social Science Abstracts, Inc.

Honorary member, Detroit Aviation Society

Chairman, American National Committee, International Geographical Union

Honorary founding member, Florence Nightingale Institute of Honorables

1930   Elected to the National Academy of Sciences

Member, Advisory Board, John Simon Guggenheim Memorial Foundation

Member, Commission on Direction, American Historical Association: Investigation of the Social Studies in the Schools

Corresponding member, State Russian Geographical Society

Honorary member, Royal Italian Geographical Society

1931   Elected a member, Board of Trustees, Woods Hole Oceanographic Institution

President, International Geographical Union

Bowman Island named in Antarctica

President, Association of American Geographers

Hon. Sc.D., Bowdoin College

1932   Chairman, National Research Council Committee on Pan American Institute of Geography and History

Member, American National Committee on International Intellectual Cooperation

Honorary member, Geographic Society of the University of Belgrade

Councilor, Association of American Geographers

Member, Finnish Geographical Society

Advisor on geography, "Century of Progress" International Exhibition at Chicago (1933)

Member, Advisory Committee on Policies and projects, Geological Society of America

Member, Commission of Inquiry into national policy in international economic relations

1933   Vice-chairman and director, Science Advisory Board

Diploma of Honorary Membership conferred by the Geographical Society of Berlin

Member, Spanish Geographical Society

Chairman, National Research Council

1935   President, The Johns Hopkins University

1935   Cvijic medal of the Geographic Society of Belgrade

Bryant medal of the Geographical Society of Philadelphia

Member, Committee on the International Map of the World

Hon. LL.D., Dartmouth College

Hon. LL.D., College of Charleston

Hon. LL.D., Dickinson College

Hon. LL.D., University of Pennsylvania

Councilor, American Geographical Society

1936   Honorary diploma, Verein für Geographie und Statistik, Frankfort

Hon. LL.D., University of Wisconsin

Hon. LL.D., Harvard University

Distinguished Service Award of the National Council of Geography Teachers

Elected a member, American Society of Naturalists

Appointed a member, National Research Council's Committee on Relationships with the War and Navy Departments

Member, Science Committee for Geography, The Explorers Club

1937   Appointed a member, Advisory Committee on Graduate Study and Research, the U.S. Office of Education

Hon. LL.D., Queens University, Canada

Hon. LL.D., University of Western Ontario

Henry Grier Bryant Gold Medal of the Geographic Society of Philadelphia

1938   One of the five foreign members of the jury charged with the selection of a recipient for the Prix Angrand

Member, Board of Directors, Teaching Film Custodians

Chairman, Committee on the Structure of the Maryland State Government

1939   Chairman, Committee to Nominate Officers, Association of American Geographers

Elected an honorary member, The Explorers Club

Member, Advisory Committee on the Maryland Geological
Economic Survey

Elected a member, Trustees of the Railroad Employers Benefit
Fund, Baltimore and Ohio Railroad

1940 Member, Maryland Council of Defense and Resources

Elected a member, College of Electors, Hall of Fame

Member Governor's (Maryland) Forestry Committee

Hon. LL.D., Washington College

Member, Maryland Council of Defense and Resources

Chairman, Territorial Committee, Council on Foreign Relations,
New York, with advisory relations to the Department of State
(1940-45)

Vice-president, National Academy of Sciences

Member, Permanent International Commission, China and
United States

1941 Member and vice chairman, Advisory Committee on the
A.S.T.P. Program, War Department, Washington, D.C.
(1941-43)

Chairman, Committee on Human Resources and Skills,
Council of Defense and Resources

Member, Maryland Board of Natural Resources

Hon. Sc.D., University of Cuzco, Peru

Hon. Sc. D., University of Arequipa, Peru

Awarded Patron's medal, Royal Geographical Society (London),
which was received in 1948.

1942 Member, (Maryland Governmental) Special Committee to
Undertake the Preparations of the Program of War
Emergency Legislation

Elected a member, Board of Directors, American Telephone
and Telegraph Co.

Chairman, Territorial Committee, Department of State; member, Political Committee and Policy Committee, Department
of State 1942-44

1943 President, American Association for the Advancement of
Science

Vice-chairman, Post-War Advisory Council, and chairman,
Territorial Committee, Department of State

Special advisor to the secretary of state and to President
Roosevelt

Copernican Award of the Kosciuszko Foundation

1944　Special advisor to the secretary of state (1944-45)

Member, London Mission, Department of State, April 1944

Member, American delegation, Dumbarton Oaks Conference, August-September 1944

Vice-chairman, Advisory Council on Post-war Foreign Policy

President, History of Science Society

1945　Member, General Committee, Franklin D. Roosevelt Memorial Foundation

Official advisor to the American delegation, United Nations Conference on International Organization and chairman of Advisory group, San Francisco Conference on United Nations Organization

David Livingstone Centenary Medal of the American Geographical Society

1946　Elected one of the honorary presidents, International Longfellow Society

Member, Advisory Committee, United Negro College Fund, Inc.

1947　Vice-chairman, National Security Committee

Elected a member, Finish Academy of Sciences

Elected an honorary member, Polish Geographical Society, Warsaw

Bowman Peninsula named in Antarctica

Hon. LL.D., Marietta College

Elected a member, Citizen's Emergency Committee for Universal Military Training

1948　Elected a member, China Public Advisory Board

Elected to the Board of Overseers, Harvard University

Appointed to the Commission on the Organization of the Executive Branch of the Government

Elected a member, Chesapeake-Potomac Study Commission

Elected chairman, Maryland Commission on Conservation of Natural Resources

Honorary Doctorate, Oxford University

Announcement of Isaiah Bowman School of Geography, The Johns Hopkins University

1949　Appointed head, Economic Cooperation Administration, New

Colonial Development Division

Explorers Club Medal, presented posthumously

LL.D., The Johns Hopkins University

1950   Isaiah Bowman Memorial Award created by Archer M. Huntington

1967   Dedication of the Isaiah Bowman Building of Social Sciences, University of Waterloo, Ontario, Canada

Isaiah Bowman: A Bibliography

"A Classification of Rivers Based on Water Supply." *Journal of Geography* 4 (1904):202–212.

"Deflection of the Mississippi." *Science,* 20 (1904):273–77.

"Pre-Pleistocene Deposits at Third Cliff, Massachusetts." (cited as a publication by Bowman but place of publication not known)

"A Typical Case of Stream Capture in Michigan." *Journal of Geology* 12 (1904):326–34.

"The Disposal of Strawboard and Oil-Well Wastes." In collaboration with Robert Lemuel Sackett, *Water-Supply and Irrigation Paper No. 113,* pp. 36–48. Washington, D.C.: Government Printing Office, 1905.

"Northward Extension of the Atlantic Preglacial Deposits." *American Journal of Science* 22 (1906):313–25.

Water Resources of the East St. Louis District. Assisted by Chester Albert Reeds. Urbana: University of Illinois, 1907.

"Geography at Yale University." *Journal of Geography* 7 (1908):59–61.

"Brazil's Failure to Control the Price of Coffee." *Bulletin of the American Geographical Society* 4 (1909):220–22.

"The Distribution of Population in Bolivia." *Bulletin of the Geographical Society of Philadelphia* 7 (1909):74–93.

"The Geology of the Cromwell Subdivision, Western Otago Division." *Bulletin of the American Geographical Society* 41 (1909):50–53.

"The Highland Dweller of Bolivia: An Anthropogeographic Interpretation." *Bulletin of the Geographical Society of Philadelphia* 7 (1909):159–84.

"Man and Climatic Change in South America." *Geographical Journal* 33 (1909):267–78.

"The Mississippi Channel Bottom and Gulf Level." *Science,* 29 (1909):418–19.

"The Physiography of the Central Andes: I, The Maritime Andes; II, The Eastern Andes." *American Journal of Science* 28 (1909): 197–217, 373–402.

Practical Exercises in Physical Geography. Journal of Geography 7 (1908–9):70–72

"Regional Population Groups of Atacama," *Bulletin of the American Geographical Society* 41 (1909):142–54, 193–211.

Geography of the Middle Illinois Valley. Bulletin of the American Geographical Society 42 (1910):690–92.

"Trade Routes in the Economic Geography of Bolivia." *Bulletin of the American Geographical Society* 42 (1910):1–43.

"The World's Great Rivers. The Amazon." *Journal of Geography* 9 (1910–11):36–38.

Forest Physiography; Physiography of the United States and Principles of Soils in Relation to Forestry. New York: J. Wiley & Sons, 1911.

"The Military Geography of Atacama." *The Educational Bi-Monthly,* June 1911, 1–21.

Well-Drilling Methods. Washington, D.C.: Government Printing Office, 1911.

"A Buried Wall at Cuzco and its Relation to the Question of a Pre-Inca Race." *American Journal of Science* 34 (1912):497–509.

"The Canon of the Urubamba." *Bulletin of the American Geographical Society* 44 (1912):881–97.

"The Geologic Relations of the Cuzco Remains." *American Journal of Science* 33 (1912):306–25.

"The Valley People of Eastern Bolivia." *Journal of Geography* 11 (1912):114–19.

"Asymmetrical Crest Lines and Abnormal Valley Profiles in the Central Andes." *Sonder-Abdruck aus der Zeitschrift für Gletscher-*

kunde, für Eiszeitforschung und Geschichte des Klimas. 7 (1913): 119-27.

"The Dwarf Forests of Southern California." *Bulletin of the American Geographical Society* 45 (1913):13-16.

"First Report of Professor Bowman's Expedition." *Bulletin of the American Geographical Society* 45 (1913):750-53.

"Geographical Aspects of the New Madeira-Mamoré Railroad."*Bulletin of the American Geographical Society* 45 (1913):275-81.

"Geographical Expedition of 1913 to the Central Andes. Results of Professor Bowman's Expedition to South America During the Last Summer." *Yale Alumni Weekly* 23 (1913):107-8.

"Results of an Expedition to the Central Andes."*Bulletin of the American Geographical Society* 46 (1914):161-83.

"Northern Patagonia. A Resumé of Mr. Bailey Willis's Surveys along the Forty-first Parallel." *Bulletin of the American Geographical Society* 47 (1915):348-57.

Professor Rice as a Scientist. The Wesleyan Alumni Council, 1915.

"Through The Brazilian Wilderness." Bulletin of the American Geographical Society* 47 (1915):216-17.

The Andes of Southern Peru: Geographical Reconnaissance along the Seventy-third Meridian. Published for the American Geographical Society of New York. New York: Henry Holt & Co., 1916.

"The Country of the Shepherds." (A chapter from *The Andes of Southern Peru.*) *Geographical Review* 1 (1916):419-42.

"Exploration of the Rio Ananas, Brazil."*Geographical Review* 1 (1916):50.

"Non-Existence of Peary Channel." *Geographical Review* 1 (1916): 448-52.

"Frontier Region of Mexico. Notes to Accompany a Map of the Frontier." *Geographical Review* 3 (1917):16-27.

"New Port on the West Coast of Peru," "The Effects of the War on the Chilean Nitrate Region," and "A New Determination of the Area of Peru."*Geographical Review* 4 (1917):219-20.

"The American Geographical Society's Contribution to the Peace Conference." *Geographical Review* 7 (1919):1-10.

"Die Italiener in der Schweiz: Ein Beitrag sur Fremdenfrage." *Geographical Review* 10 (1920):351.

"Special Studies of Natural Units. Second Example: Types of 'Islands'

of the High Mountains: The Central Andes. The Regional
Diagram, Irrigation, Nomadism." In *Human Geography,* edited
by Jean Brunhes, pp. 453–98. New York: Rand, McNally & Co.,
1920.

"Coal and Iron in the Political and Economic Geography of
Northeastern France and Western Germany." *Geographical
Review* 11 (1921):299–301.

"Coastal Belt of Peru." *Geographical Review* 11 (1921):297–98.

"Decline of Europe." *Geographical Review* 11 (1921):302–3.

"Geography in Human Terms: Jean Brunhes Gives a Dry Science a
Social Trend." *La France* 5 (1921):173 and 183.

"Italian-Yugo-Slav Boundary and the Free State of Fiume." *Geographical Review* 11 (1921):142–43.

"The Mesta: A Study in Spanish Economic History, 1273-1836." Geo-
graphical Review 11 (1921):453–54.

The New World: Problems in Political Geography. Yonkers-on-Hudson,
New York: World Book Co., 1921.

"Nouveau traite des Eaux Souterraines." Geographical Review 11
(1921):630–32.

"Boundaries of the Spanish Sahara and the Ifni Enclave." *Geographical Review* 12 (1922):651–52.

"Effect on Modern Policy of Political Situation in Near East." Lecture
delivered to the Class of 1923, Naval War College, 18 August
1922, Newport, Rhode Island. Mimeographed.

"Famine Belt of Russia." *Geographical Review* 12 (1922):489.

"The Friendly Arctic: The Story of Five Years in Polar Regions." Geo-
graphical Review 12 (1922):314–16.

Introduction to *Geography of the Central Andes,* by Alan G. Ogilvie.
New York: American Geographical Society, 1922.

"Modifications in the Western Boundary of Hungary." *Geographical
Review* 12 (1922):650–51.

"A Note on the Political Map of Turkey." *Foreign Affairs* 1
(1922):158–61.

"Overpopulation in Relation to Agriculture and Famine in Eastern
Europe." *Geographical Review* 12 (1922):489–91.

"Political Geography of Italian North Africa." *Geographical Review* 12
(1922):134–37.

"Recent Movements of Population." *Geographical Review* 12 (1922):
307–9.

"Spanish Emigration." *Geographical Review* 12 (1922):309-10.

"Steppe and Forest in the Settlement of Southern Russia." *Geographical Review* 12 (1922):491-92.

"An American Boundary Dispute. Decision of the Supreme Court of the United States with Respect to the Texas-Oklahoma Boundary." *Geographical Review* 13 (1923):161-89.

"Boundaries of Turkey According to the Treaty of Lausanne." *Geographical Review* 13 (1923):627-29.

"Geographical Elements in the Turkish Situation: A Note on the Political Map." *Geographical Review* 13 (1923):122-29.

"New Map of Brazil on the Millionth Scale." *Geographical Review* 13 (1923):465-67.

"New Relief Maps by the U.S. Geological Survey." *Geographical Review* 13 (1923):304.

"Routes to Desert Watering Places in the Southwest." *Geographical Review* 13 (1923):303-4.

Desert Trails of Atacama. New York: American Geographical Society, 1924.

"*Leitlinien der allgemeinen politischen Geographie: Naturlehre des Staates.*" *Geographical Review* 14 (1924):665-66.

"The Mohammedan World." *Geographical Review* 14 (1924):62-74.

The New World Supplement. Yonkers-on-Hudson, New York: World Book Co., 1924.

"A Note on Tangier and the Spanish Zones in Africa." *Foreign Affairs* 2 (1924):500-503.

"Progress in Red River Boundary Survey." *Geographical Review* 14 (1924):139.

The Situation of the United States. Yonkers-on-Hudson, New York: World Book Co., 1924.

"Texan Study in Range Economics." *Geographical Review* 14 (1924):639.

"*The Bird Islands of Peru.*" *Publisher's Weekly*, January 1925.

"Commercial Geography as a Science. Reflections on Some Recent Books." *Geographical Review* 15 (1925):285-94.

The Field of Geography. New York: Columbia University, 1925.

"Food Supply of New England." *Geographical Review* 15 (1925):478.

"Land Waste in Michigan." *Geographical Review* 15 (1925):478-79.

"Memorandum on Pioneer Belts." (Extracted from stenographic

record of extemporaneous statement.—National Research Council, 1925. JHU

"Monographies synthétiques de géographie humaine. Second exemple: 'Isles humaines' de la haute montagne dans les Andes Centrales (Pérou, Bolivie, Argentine et Chili). Hauts paturages et transhumance, oasis de culture et irrigation." In *La Géographie Humaine*, 3rd ed., edited by Jean Brunhes, pp. 619–59. Paris: Félix Alcan, 1925.

"North America: Its People and the Resources, Development and Prospects of the Continent as an Agricultural, Industrial, and Commercial Area." Geographical Review 15 (1925):328–29.

"The Real Rhodesia." Geographical Review 15 (1925):161–62.

"Settlement on the Border with Government Aid." *Geographical Review* 15 (1925):494–95.

"Traité de géographie physique." Geographical Review 15 (1925):336–37

"The Analysis of Land Forms: Walther Penck on the Topographic Cycle." *Geographical Review* 15 (1926):122–32.

"Argentine Geographical Studies." *Geographical Review* 16 (1926): 656–58.

"The Concentration of Population and the Distribution of Raw Materials." *Proceedings of the Academy of Political Science* 12 (1926):145–52.

"Geography and Boundaries at Mosul." *Geographical Review* 16 (1926):143–44.

"Polar Flights of Byrd and Amundsen." *Geographical Review* 16 (1926):662–64.

"Scientific Study of Settlement." *Geographical Review* 16 (1926): 647–53.

"Traité de géographie physique." *Geographical Review* 16 (1926): 686–87.

"The Transactions of the First World Power Conference." Geographical Review 16 (1926):504–5.

"Abstract of A.D. Lindsey: Review of *The Modern State* by R. M. MacIver." *Economic Journal*, March 1927, pp. 126–29.

"Across Arctic America." Saturday Review of Literature, 23 April 1927.

"The Boundaries of the Nejd. A Note on Special Conditions." *Geographical Review* 17 (1927):128–34.

"Concentración de población y la distribución de materias primas." *Boletin de la Union Panamericana*, March 1927, pp. 240–46.

The New World (translated into Chinese). Shanghai: Commercial Press, 1927. 2d ed. 1928.

"The Pioneer Fringe." *Foreign Affairs* 6 (1927):49–66.

"The International Geographical Congress." *Geographical Review* 18 (1928):661–67.

"Millionth Scale Map of Hispanic America." *Science* 68 (1928):367–69.

Le Monde Nouveau; Tableau Général de Géographie Politique Universelle Adapté de l'Anglais et mis au Courant des Derniers Événements Internationaux par Jean Brunhes. Avec la collaboration d'Annette et Henri Colin-Delavaud et de Mariel Jean-Brunhes (Mme. Raymond Delamarre). Paris: Payot, 1928.

The New World: Problems in Political Geography. 4th ed. Yonkers-on-Hudson, N.Y.: World Book Co., 1928.

"Proceedings of the Royal Scottish Geographical Society." (Minutes of the meeting of the Society recording the presentation of the Livingstone Gold Medal to Isaiah Bowman, 12 July 1928) *Scottish Geographical Magazine* 44 (1928):292–97.

"Byrd Flight Covers 35,000 Square Miles Open to U.S. Claim. Dr. Bowman Estimates Extent of Latest Aerial Exploration Outside British Domain." *New York Times,* 8 December 1929, pp. 1 and 3.

Dr. Bowman's Report on the London Conference (Conference of the Institutions for the Scientific Study of International Affairs, London, March 11–14, 1929). Confidential Memorandum for Members. New York: Council on Foreign Relations, 1929.

"Geography in Relation to the Social Sciences." Montpelier, Vermont: Capital City Press, 1929.

"Geography, Modern Style." *The Outlook,* 17 July 1929, p. 461.

"Modern Pioneering." *The Outlook,* 31 July 1929, p. 541.

"The Scientist." *Vilhjalmur Stefansson,* p. 7 New York: the Macmillan Co., 1929.

"What's the Use of Explorers?" *The Outlook,* 21 August 1929, p. 659.

"Antarctica." *Proceedings of the American Philosophical Society* 69 (1930):19–43.

"Antarctica." *The Scientific Monthly* 30 (1930):341–51.

Introduction to *The Work of the Byrd Antarctic Expedition 1928–1930,* by W. L. G. Joerg. New York: American Geographical Society, 1930.

"Polar Exploration." *Science* 72 (1930):439–49.

"The Political Geography of the Mohammedan World." *The Moslem World* 20 (1930):1–4.

"Reading with a Purpose." In *International Relations.* Chicago: American Library Association, 1930.

"The Work of Wilkins." *New York Times,* 23 March 1930, section 3, p. 4.

"The World and Its Peoples." Introduction to *Lands and Peoples.* Edited by H. Thompson. 7 vols. New York: Grolier Society, 1930.

"Inaugural Address." *Comptes Rendus du Congrès International de Géographie, Paris 1931.* Vol. 1, pp. 86–87. Paris: Librarie Armand Colin, 1931.

Introduction to *Directory of American Agencies.* New York: Council on Foreign Relations, 1931.

"Jordan Country." *Geographical Review* 21 (1931):22–55.

The Pioneer Fringe. New York: American Geographical Society, 1931.

"Pioneer Settlement." *Comptes Rendus du Congrès International de Géographie,* Paris 1931. Vol. 3, pp. 279–80. Paris: Librarie Armand Colin, 1931.

"The Pioneering Process." *Science* 75 (1932):521–28.

"Planning in Pioneer settlement." *Annals of the Association of American Geographers* 22 (1932):93–107.

"Correlation of Sedimentary and Climatic Records." *Proceedings of the National Academy of Science* 19 (1933):376–86.

"Geography and the Farm Problem." *Science News Letter,* 25 March 1933, pp. 182–83.

"Jehol: City of Emperors and *Across the Gobi Desert." The Yale Review,* spring 1933, pp. 624–26.

"Address by the chairman of the National Research Council." *Shore and Beach* 2 (1934):3–4.

"Applied Geography." *The Scientific Monthly* 38 (1934):173–76.

Geography in Relation to the Social Sciences. With *Geography in the Schools of Europe* by Rose B. Clark. New York: Charles Scribner's Sons, 1934.

"John Greenough. (1894–1934)." *Geographical Review* 24 (1934): 351–52.

"Regional Concepts and Their Application." In *Zbiór Prac Poświecony Przez Towarzystwo Geografiezne We Lwowie Eugenjuszowi Romerowi,* pp. 25–46. Edited by Henryk Arctowski. Lwów: 1934.

"William Morris Davis." *Geographical Review* 24 (1934):177–81.

"Address of the President of the International Geographical Congress." *Science*, 81 (1935):389-91.

"Appropriations for Grants-In-Aid by the National Research Council." *Science* 81 (1935):592-94.

"The Business of Diplomacy." 28 October 1935. JHU

"For Their Work Continueth." 18 September 1935. JHU

"The Fourteenth International Geographical Congress, Warsaw, 1934." *Geographical Review* 25 (1935):142-48.

"The Hopkins Guild." 7 November 1935. JHU

"Jeffersonian Freedom of Speech from the Standpoint of Science." *Science* 82 (1935):529-32.

"The Land of Your Possession" *Science* 82 (1935):285-93.

"Next Steps in American Universities." In *Proceedings, Constitution and By-Laws*, pp. 23-36. Atlanta: Southern University Conference, 1935.

"Opening Address by Isaiah Bowman, President." In *Comptes Rendus Du Congrès International de Géographie, Varsovie 1934*, vol. 1, pp. 99-103. Warsaw: The International Geographical Union, 1935.

"Our Expanding and Contracting 'Desert.'" *Geographical Review* 25 (1935):43-61.

"Perils of the Adolescent Idea." 21 November 1935. JHU

"The Promethean Gift." 23 April 1935. JHU

"Summary Statement of the Work of the National Research Council—1934-35." *Science* 82 (1935):337-42.

"This Your New and Admirable Skill." 2 November 1935. JHU

"To Administrative Committee of the Baltimore Public Schools." 8 October 1935. JHU

"Where Do You Live?" 16 December 1935. JHU

"Address on Presenting Medal of National Institute of Social Sciences to Nicholas Murray Butler." 6 May 1936. JHU

"The Andes of Southern Peru." 30 September 1936. JHU

"The Decisive Hour." 7 December 1936. JHU

A Design for Scholarship. Baltimore: The Johns Hopkins University Press, 1936.

"A Design for Scholarship." *School and Society* 43 (1936):377-86.

"The Framework of University Policy." 18 November 1936. JHU

"Geology in the Evolution of Culture." 7 December 1936. JHU

"Human Geography of the Central Andes." 3 April 1936. JHU

"The Human Geography of the Central Andes." 7 April 1936. JHU

"Influence of Vegetation on Land-Water Relationships." In, *Head-waters Control and Use*, pp. 76-96. Washington, D.C.: Upstream Engineering Conference, 1936.

"Interplay of Home and School." 18 December 1936. JHU

"Medical and Surgical Association Meeting—Remarks." 20 February 1936. JHU

"Messenger Lectures." 21 October 1936. JHU

"New York-New Jersey Alumni Associations—Remarks." 16 October 1936. JHU

"Political Geography." September 1936. JHU

"Remarks on Presenting Explorers' Medal to Lincoln Ellsworth." 12 June 1936. JHU

"Rebuilding the Public Domain." *Geographical Review* 26 (1936): 691-92.

"Sustaining Fund Address." 26 May 1936. JHU

"Trails and Camps of the Central Andes." 6 November 1936. JHU

"The University in Exile." 15 January 1936. JHU

"War and Human Nature." 15 February 1936. JHU

"Cooperation in Administration at Johns Hopkins." *American Association of University Professors Bulletin* 23 (1937):285-87.

"Financial Outlook for Institutions of Higher Education." In *Proceedings, Constitution and By-Laws*, pp. 66-69. Atlanta: Southern University Conference, 1937.

"Flood Control." 19 April 1937. JHU

"Forecasting What A Democracy Will Do." 12 May 1937. JHU

"The Future of University Research in Relation to Financial Support." *Journal of Proceedings and Addresses of the Association of American Universities*, November 1937, pp. 78-81.

"Geographical Factors." In *Conference on Canadian-American Affairs*, pp. 57-60, 69-70. Edited by R. G. Trotter, A. B. Corey and W. M. McLaren. Boston: Ginn & Co., 1937.

"Geography and the Creative Experiment." 22 October 1937. JHU

"Is There A Logic in International Situations?" 13 May 1937. JHU

Limits of Land Settlement; a Report on Present-day Possibilities. Prepared under the direction of Isaiah Bowman. New York: Council on Foreign Relations, 1937.

"Modern Pioneering." 8 April 1937 JHU

"Modern Pioneers." 12 July 1937. JHU

"A New Chapter in Pan-American Cartography." In *Mélanges de géographie et d'orientalisme offerts à* E. F. Gautier, Tours: Arrault et Cie., 1937. pp. 88-95.

"Pioneering, Modern Style." 22 September 1937. JHU

"Population Outlets in Overseas Territories." In *Geographic Aspects of International Relations*, pp. 1-41. Edited by Charles C. Colby. Chicago: University of Chicago Press, 1938.

"Putting Our Shields Together." 20 October 1937. JHU

"Queen's University Conference on Canadian-American Affairs." 9 April 1937. JHU

"Radio Welcome to Australian Debating Team on WBAL." 2 December 1937. JHU

"Remarks at Dinner Honoring J. L. Gamble." 30 March 1937. JHU

"Trends in Modern Education." *Southern Association Quarterly*, May 1937, pp. 1-9.

"What Do You Do?" *The Barnwell Bulletin*, December 1937, pp. 19-33.

"Wish Versus Reason in Politics." 18 May 1937. JHU

"Why We Believe." *University of Virginia Alumni News*, April 1937, pp. 154-56, 177-78, 180.

"Women's Club of Roland Park." 11 March 1937. JHU

"Address of Dr. Isaiah Bowman, President, Johns Hopkins University, before the Congress of American Industry and the Annual Convention of the National Association of Manufacturers." 8 December 1938. JHU

Los Andes del sur del Peru; reconocimiento geográfico a le largo del meridiano setenta y tres. Translated by Carlos Nicholson. Arequipa, Peru: Editorial La Colmena, 1938.

"Annual Report of the President." *The Johns Hopkins University Circular*, n.s., 1938, no. 4, pp. 1-11.

"Curricula and Methods of Study of Universities Today and Fifty Years Ago." 28 January 1938. JHU

"Discours du Prof. Dr. I. Bowman." In *Comptes Rendus du Congrès International de Géographie, Amsterdam, 1938*, vol. 1, pp. 12-13. Leiden: E. J. Brill, 1938.

"Education Through Discovery." *Association of American Colleges Bulletin* 24 (1938):464-68.

"Geography in the Creative Experiment." *Geographical Review* (1938):1-19.

"Inquiry vs. Advocacy." In *The Inauguration of Oliver C. Carmichael as Chancellor of Vanderbilt University and a Symposium on Higher Education in the South*, pp. 20-32. Nashville: Vanderbilt University, 1938.

"National Committee on the Cause and Cure of Wars." 2 January 1938. JHU

"Remarks upon accepting the Thomas S. Cullen portrait." 19 November 1938. JHU

"Report of the committee on the Structure of the Maryland State Government." 31 December 1938. JHU

"Research in Private Industry." 21 November 1938. JHU

"Some Aspects of Geography." 25 October 1938. JHU

"The University As A Cultural Workshop." 14 February 1938. JHU

"Who Are You?" 12 January 1938. JHU

"Graduate School." *School and Society* 49 (1939):28-30.

The Graduate School in American Democracy. Washington, D.C.: Government Printing Office, 1939.

"The Pursuit of Happiness." 6 June 1939. JHU

"Science and Social Pioneering." *Science* 90 (1939):309-19.

"What Do You Believe?" 2 June 1939. JHU

"What Do You Do?" 5 June 1939. JHU

"Who is Responsible for Peace?" 29 December 1939. JHU

"Enduring Purpose." *Washington College Bulletin* 18 (1940):10-16.

Foreword to *International Boundaries: A Study of Boundary Functions and Problems*, by S. Whittemore Boggs. New York: Columbia University Press, 1940.

"The Inquiry." In *Dictionary of American History*, p. 124. Edited by James T. Adams, New York: Scribner, 1940.

"John Huston Finley, 1863-1940." *Geographical Review* 30 (1940): 355-57.

"John Huston Finley, to Whom Tribute Is Due." *The Alumni Magazine*, The Johns Hopkins University, June 1940, pp. 118-19.

"Madame Sigrid Undset." *America*, 9 November 1940, pp. 119-120.

"Our Better Ordering and Preservation." *Science*, n.s. 93 (1941): 191-97.

"A Preface to a Community Fine Arts Program." 1940. JHU

Remembering the Beauty. (Sidney Lanier, February 3, 1842-September 7, 1881). Baltimore: The Johns Hopkins University Press, 1940.

"Science and Social Effects: Three Failures." *The Scientific Monthly* 50 (1940):289-98.

"A Sense of Reality." In *Proceedings, Constitution and By-Laws*, pp. 55-70. Atlanta: Southern University Conference, 1940.

What Do You Know? Baltimore: The Johns Hopkins University Press, 1940.

"When Energy Rules the World." 24 October 1940. JHU

"The Associated Harvard Clubs, 44th Annual Meeting, May 16-18, 1941 at Baltimore." *Proceedings and Reports*, pp. 59-60, 66-67, 70-71, 73.

"Basic Issues in National Defense from the Standpoint of Higher Education. Organizing Higher Education for National Defense." 1941. JHU

"La Cultura de America." *Letras* 19:275-84.

"La Cultura en America." *Revista Universitaria* 30, (1941):147-57.

Foreword to *Focus on Africa*, by Richard Upjohn Light. New York: American Geographical Society, 1941.

"The Future of Education and Military Defense." *The Educational Record* 22 (1941):428-35.

"Knowledge is Not Enough." *The Rice Institute Pamphlet* 28 (1941):134-52.

"El mapa al millonésimo de Hispano América. Una Empresa Cooperativa Inter Americana." *Revista Universitaria* 30 (1941): 187-204.

"Our Favored Land." *Scientific Monthly* 53 (1941):568.

"Peace and Power Politics 1941." *Baltimore Bulletin of Education* 18 (1941):171-80.

"Peace and Power Politics. 1941." *The Nation's Schools*, March 1941, pp. 49-50.

"Peace and Power Politics, 1941." *Proceedings*, National Education Association of the United States, 79 (1941):241-51.

"Tribute to Daniel Willard." *Baltimore* 25 (1941):15-17.

"Twelve Houses of Heaven." 16 June 1941. JHU

"Will Our Camps Build Citizen-Soldiers?" *Town Meeting* 6 (1941):1-30.

"Annual Report of the President." *The Johns Hopkins University Circular*, n.s., 1942, no. 8, pp. 1-12.

"Choose, Therefore." *The Johns Hopkins Nurses Alumni Magazine* 41 (1942):54–58.

"Dr. Bowman's Tribute to Mr. Willard." *Baltimore and Ohio Magazine*, January 1942, pp. 11-13.

"The Ecuador-Peru Boundary Dispute." *Foreign Affairs* 20 (1942): 757-761.

"Four Indispensable Qualities. The Tribute of Dr. Isaiah Bowman, President of the Johns Hopkins University." *Baltimore and Ohio Magazine*, August 1942, p. 36.

"Geography vs. Geopolitics." *Geographical Review* 32 (1942):646-58.

"Higher Education Faces the Future." *Association of American Colleges Bulletin* 28 (1942):44-50.

"El mapa al millonésimo de Hispano América." In *Una Empresa Cooperativa Inter Americano Boletin del Centro Geografico del Cusco*, pp. 15-32. Cusco: 1942.

"The Outlook for Education." *Science* 95 (1942):126-27.

"Political Geography of Power." *Geographical Review* 32 (1942): 349-52.

"Power and Peace: Excerpts from an article written for the *Geographical Review* by the president of Johns Hopkins University on Nicholas J. Spykman's book, *American Strategy in World Politics.*" *Baltimore Sun*, 3 April 1942.

Los senderos del desierto de Atacama. Santiago de Chile: Sociedad chilena de historia y geografia, 1942.

"What is an American?" 5 June 1942. JHU

"Address by Dr. Isaiah Bowman." In *Proceedings of the Consultation on Geodesy, Aeronautical Charts and Topographic Maps*, pp. 42-45. Washington, D.C.: 1943.

"Albert Lloyd Barrows 1883-1942." *Science*, n.s. 97 (1943):346-47.

"Annual Report of the President." *The Johns Hopkins University Circular*, n.s., 1943, no. 8, pp. 1-25.

"A Department of Geography." *Science* 98 (1943):564-66.

Science and Our Future. New York: Commission to Study the Organization of Peace, 1943.

"Science Shapes the Future." *A.A.A.S. Bulletin* 2 (1943):50-51.

"Science Shapes the Future." *Cranbrook Institute of Science Newsletter* 13 (1943):1-3.

"Annual Report of the President." *The Johns Hopkins University Circular*, n.s., 1944, no. 7, pp. 1-15.

"Commanding Our Wealth." *Science* 100 (1944):151-56.

"Dumbarton Oaks Proposals." 20 November 1944. JHU

"The Faith We Celebrate." *Teachers College Record* 46 (1944):151–56.

"On Becoming a Freeman." 3 July 1944. JHU

"Peace a Condition of Living." *Blueprints of the Future* 2, no. 7, 1944.

"Peace—The Business of Every Citizen." *Think*, October 1944, pp. 5-7.

"The Presidential Address." *Science* 100 (1944):366-67.

"Science and Humanism." *Scientific Monthly* 59 (1944):95.

"Social Objectives and the College Curriculum." *Association of American Colleges Bulletin* 30 (1944):216-30.

"Annual Report of the President." *The Johns Hopkins University Circular*, n.s., 1945, no. 7, pp. 1-10.

"Bowman's Talk to Senators." *New York Herald-Tribune*, 9 October 1945.

"The Dumbarton Oaks Proposals." *Association of American Colleges Bulletin* 31 (1945):32-43.

"The Dumbarton Oaks Proposals." *The Johns Hopkins Alumni Magazine* 33 (1945):37–43.

"English Speaking Union." 1 January 1945. JHU

Foreword to *Chung-kuo Ti Li Hsüeh Yen Chiu*, by Chi-yun Chang. *Ta Kung Pao*, Chungking, 16 May 1945. In Chinese.

"Franklin Delano Roosevelt 1882-1945." *Geographical Review* 35 (1945):349-51.

"Freedom in Service." 17 June 1945. JHU

"Land Settlement and Resource Development." *Nature* 155 (1945): 5-10.

"The New Geography." *Journal of Geography* 44 (1945):213-16.

"Pending Legislation for Federal Aid to Science." *Science* 102 (1945):545-48.

"Testimony of Isaiah Bowman, president, Johns Hopkins University." In *Hearings on Science Legislation*, hearings before a subcommittee of the Committee on Military Affairs, Senate. 79th Cong., 1st sess., 1945, pp. 10-24.

"Address at the Unveiling of a Statue of Sidney Lanier at the Hall of Fame, New York City." 3 October 1946. JHU

"Citizen-Scientists." 3 May 1946. JHU

"Contributions of Chemistry and Physics to Medicine." *The Journal-Lancet* 67 (1947):71-73.

"Exploring World Politics. Is an International Society Possible?" *Explorers Journal* 24 (1946–47): p. 6.

"Gilman and His Doctrine." Baltimore *Evening Sun*, 5 November 1946.

"Impact of Geography on National Power." Address presented at The National War College, Washington, D.C., 30 September 1946, Mimeographed.

Is an International Society Possible? American Affairs Pamphlets. New York: National Industrial Conference Board, 1947.

"The Johns Hopkins Program: An Interpretation. History and Interpretation of the Full-time Principle." JHU

"Millionth Map." 15 March 1946. JHU

"The Millionth Map of Hispanic America." *Science* 103 (1946):319-23.

"The Social Composition of Scientific Power." *Metal Progress*, June 1946, pp. 1210-11.

"The Social Composition of Scientific Power." In *Science and Civilization: The Future of Atomic Energy*, pp. 25-44. Pittsburgh: Westinghouse Educational Foundation, 1946.

"The Social Contract of an Educated Man." 20 September 1946. JHU

"The Social Contract of an Educated Man." *Time* 48 (1946):94-95.

"The Social Contract of an Educated Man." *Association of American Colleges Bulletin* 32 (1946):498-505.

"Statement of Dr. Isaiah Bowman." In *National Science Foundation Act*, hearings before a subcommittee of the Committee on Interstate and Foreign Commerce, House of Representatives. 79th Cong., 2nd sess., 1946, pp. 6-15.

"The Strategy of Territorial Decisions." *Foreign Affairs* 24 (1946): 177-94.

Two Worlds — Or One? Baltimore: The Johns Hopkins University (1946).

"An Unbridged Chasm to Cross." *American Affairs*, July 1946, pp. 151-58.

"Your Debt to the Hopkins." Baltimore *Evening Sun*, 11 June 1946; *Hospital Management* 62 (1946):4, 18.

"Annual Report of the President." *The Johns Hopkins University Circular*, n.s., 1947, no. 8, pp. 3-29.

"Discovering South America. Abstracted in "The Ever-New El Dorado," *New York Herald Tribune*, 10 March 1947.

"Discovering Your Place In This Complex World." 22 September 1947. JHU

"A Message From President Bowman: To All Johns Hopkins Alumni." In *First Annual Report*, the Annual Alumni Fund, pp. 2-3.

Baltimore: The Johns Hopkins University, 1947.

"Your Guild." 21 October 1947. JHU

"Annual Report of the President." *The Johns Hopkins University Circular*, n.s., 1948, no. 8, p. 3-25.

"Definition of a Man." December 1948. JHU

"Determination of University Policy." *Association of American Colleges Bulletin* 34 (1948):221-25.

Foreword to *Acclimatization in the Andes*, by Carlos Monge. Baltimore: The Johns Hopkins University Press, 1948.

"The Geographical Situation of the United States in Relation to World Policies." *Geographical Journal* 112 (1948):129-45.

"How Far Can United States Resources Go?" *The Listener*, 8 July 1948, pp. 42-43.

"The Invisible Walls of Our City." *Hood College Bulletin*, series 24, no. 144 (1948):6-10.

"The Limits of Compromise in International Affairs." 13 May 1948. JHU

"A Message From President Bowman: To All Johns Hopkins Alumni." In *Second Annual Report 1948*, The Annual Alumni Fund, pp. 2-3. Baltimore: the Johns Hopkins University, 1948.

"Peruvian Physiography." 1948. JHU

"President Bowman's Address at Farewell Assembly of Students." *The Johns Hopkins News Letter* 53 (1948):1-2.

"Remarks at a Conference of all Section T Associates," *The News*, Applied Physics Laboratory, 3 (1948):1-2.

"Universal Military Training." In *Hearings before the Committee on Armed Services*, Senate. 80th Cong., 2nd Sess., 1948, pp. 268-78.

"Dr. Bowman's Response." *Baltimore* 42 (1949):19-21.

"Geographical Interpretation." *Geographical Review* 39 (1949):355-70.

"Geographical Objectives in the Polar Regions." *Photogrammetric Engineering*, March 1949, pp. 6-12.

"A Response." *The Johns Hopkins Alumni Magazine* 37 (1949):45-50.

"Where the Forces Strive." 8 March 1949. JHU

"Mark Jefferson." *Geographical Review* 40 (1950):134-137.

Foreword to *The Earth's Crust*, by L. Dudley Stamp. London: Harrap, 1951.

"Settlement by the Modern Pioneer." In *Geography in the Twentieth Century*, edited by Griffith Taylor, pp. 248-66. New York: The Philosophical Library, 1951.

Index